Göttinger Wirtschaftsinformatik
Herausgeber: J. Biethahn† · L. M. Kolbe · M. Schumann

Band 113

Maike Greve

Exploring Mobile Health Technology for Development

An Investigation of Design and Action to foster Utility, Scalability, and Sustainability of Interventions in the Global South

CUVILLIER VERLAG

Herausgeber

Prof. Dr. J. Biethahn† Prof. Dr. L. M. Kolbe Prof. Dr. M. Schumann

Georg-August-Universität
Wirtschaftsinformatik
Platz der Göttinger Sieben 5
37073 Göttingen

Bibliografische Information der Deutschen Nationalbibliothek
Die Deutsche Nationalbibliothek verzeichnet diese Publikation in der Deutschen Nationalbibliografie; detaillierte bibliografische Daten sind im Internet über http://dnb.d-nb.de abrufbar.
1. Aufl. - Göttingen : Cuvillier, 2022
Zugl.: Göttingen, Univ., Diss., 2021

1. Auflage, 2022
Gedruckt auf umweltfreundlichem, säurefreiem Papier aus nachhaltiger Forstwirtschaft.

ISBN 978-3-7369-7570-5
eISBN 978-3-7369-6570-6

Exploring Mobile Health Technology for Development

An Investigation of Design and Action to foster Utility, Scalability, and Sustainability of Interventions in the Global South

Dissertation

zur Erlangung des Doktorgrades

der Wirtschaftswissenschaftlichen Fakultät

der Georg-August Universität Göttingen

vorgelegt von

Maike Greve

geboren in Göttingen

Göttingen, 2022

Betreuungsausschuss

Erstbetreuer:	Prof. Dr. Lutz M. Kolbe
Zweitbetreuer:	Prof. Dr. Alfred Benedikt Brendel
Drittbetreuer:	Prof. Dr. Sebastian Vollmer

Acknowledgments

In 2011, I was sitting in the middle of kids at an elementary school in Addis Ababa, Ethiopia. This was the moment I realized how privileged and lucky I could consider myself regarding the life I had lived so far and the education I had received and can receive. This was when I decided never to forget these kids in whatever I will do in my life.

In 2019, I talked to a man in eSwatini who had HIV and diabetes. This was the moment I realized how privileged and lucky I could consider myself regarding the life I had lived so far and the healthcare I had received and can receive if needed. This was when I decided never to forget this man in whatever I will do in my life.

Today, I neither have a photo of the kids in Ethiopia nor the man in eSwatini next to my desk, but one that shows smiling community health workers with a tablet in their hands. Every morning, when starting my laptop, I look at this photo. It reminds me of these people's joy when we told them that we had developed an app for them to support their work routines to enable better healthcare provision and health education.

I do not think that technology such as a tablet with an app is the sole answer and solution by itself. But I am convinced that it is support and a catalyst to tackle development goals and that digital and health equity go hand in hand.

Reflecting on the last three years, I see the parallels between my trips to Ethiopia and eSwatini and the journey to my Ph.D. All being exhilarating experiences that encouraged new world views and increased my curiosity and willingness to explore unfamiliar terrains. The phenomenon of culture shock is common in affecting travelers in unexpected ways. There is no doubt that I experienced one in Ethiopia, and now I am very confident that I also went through the stages of culture shock during my time as a Research Associate. If I learned only one thing in the past years, it would be that a good thinking/research approach needs a specific theoretical foundation. Therefore, building on the stage model of a culture shock (see Figure 1) as a theoretical lens, I would like to acknowledge the people that supported me on my journey to the Ph.D. and for whom I am truly grateful.

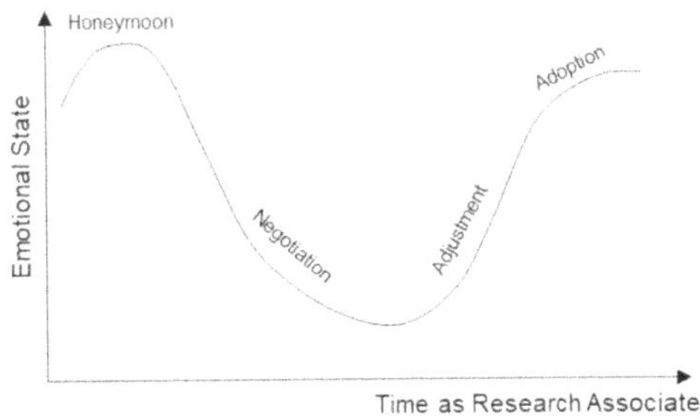

Figure 1: Culture Shock Curve

The Honeymoon Phase: My start at the Chair of Information Management was overwhelmingly positive. I was excited to work with students, euphoric to start the project work, and infatuated with the new research world that was opening up for me. Although everything was new and unfamiliar, I knew that I had made the best decision to stay at the university and that the Information Systems research discipline would be an exciting adventure. At this point, it became clear to me that the foundation of the coming years would be Prof. Lutz Kolbe, Prof. Alfred Benedikt Brendel, and Prof. Sebastian Vollmer. That they would eventually form my dissertation committee was a long way off at that time. Instead, they gave me the confidence to be on the right track and the freedom to pursue my own research interests, knowing that I could count on their support at any time. I would like to acknowledge Bene's support over the past years and hopefully also in the future. Your unconditional enthusiasm for research and this job put the "honey" to my starting phase, and I am very thankful to call you my co-author and mentor.

The Negotiation Phase: I think everyone with a Ph.D. will confirm that the way towards it includes phases marked by frustration and fear. This also happened to me after the initial excitement gradually disappeared and I was confronted with unpleasant situations (e.g., paper rejection) for the first time. These situations make you doubt and negotiate with yourself: Am I good enough for a Ph.D.? Is this the right job for me?

At that point, I could rely (as always) on my private environment. I would like to thank my boyfriend René, who was always at the forefront of these situations. The true honor goes to you for your unconditional patience, support, and love for me and my decision for this job. My family also contributed through their encouragement and pride and the regular joint breakfasts and lunches on Sundays or self-made cake, which brought back my energy when most needed. But the best panacea in such times was a distraction. My friends (especially Leo, Pascal, Hannah, and Erik) and the many hours with you in the basketball cleared my mind and gave me the energy to continue and go back to work with joy on Monday mornings. I would also like to thank you all for your understanding when I had to work late again, had to write a paper on the weekend, had to make a quick phone call to a colleague, or just had to send this one last e-mail. Being surrounded by wonderful people that remind you that life is more than research papers and project proposals let me overcome the negotiation phase.

The Adjustment Phase: After a good year as a research associate, I had the feeling that I was beginning to know all the processes, and a work routine was setting in. I started to find my way around. Of course, I still encountered some difficulties, but I could cope with them more rationally and moderately. If you have played a team sport, you know that success depends largely on the collective and that each individual can only make their contribution. All my colleagues made and still make their contributions to this thesis. Together we wrote papers (Kristin and Simon), traveled the world (Tim, Tine, Tizian, Flo, and Sascha), and discussed "research and the world" over coffee (Christoph, Henrik,

Mathias, Jannes). The topic of digital health especially bonded us (Aycan, Till, Marvin, Morten, Benni), and the motivation to impact people with our work and research became the engine of our work. I am very thankful to work with such a strong and motivated group. The motto of René's basketball team, which has led to many victories, is: "teamwork makes the dream work." I think this motto applies to so much more than basketball.

The Adaptation Phase: Through all these people, I have successfully adapted to the work and feel very comfortable in what I do. The previous phases resulted in a strong sense of belonging. The doors that have been opened to me in the last years and the trust that was and is still given to me, especially by Lutz Kolbe, demonstrate daily that I am doing exactly the right thing and that this journey should not end. As Head of the Digital Health Research Group, I have many exciting things in the pipeline. By planning those, I think of the children in Ethiopia, the sick man in eSwatini, and the proud healthcare workers with tablets who try to help people every day through health education.

Let this journey continue...

Göttingen, January 2022 *Maike Greve*

Table of Contents

List of Figures

List of Tables

List of Abbreviations

ADR	Action Design Research
CHW	Community Health Worker
eHealth	electronic Health
ICT	Information Communication Technology
ICT4D	Information Communication Technology for Development
IS	Information Systems
IT	Information Technology
LMIC	Low and Middle Income Countries
mHealth	Mobile Health
mHealth4D	Mobile Health for Development
NCD	Non-communicable Diseases
PLS-SEM	Partial Least Squares Structural Equation Modeling
SDG	Sustainable Development Goals
WHO	World Health Organization

A. Foundations

The first part of this thesis builds the foundation of the conducted research. It is divided into two sections that introduce the research agenda and elaborate on the research background of this thesis.

In the first section (A.I), the motivation, research gaps, and research questions are described. Furthermore, the structure of the entire thesis is outlined. This is followed by an outline of the thesis' positioning in the IS research domain, the research design of the individual studies, and the overall research space of the conducted research. The section ends by providing an overview of the implications and anticipated contribution of this cumulative thesis.

In the second section (A.II), the advent of mobile technology is introduced. Building on this, the literature is reviewed regarding the role of information systems (IS) in the healthcare sector. Thereby, the role of mobile technology as an enabler in healthcare is addressed. Furthermore, the section provides a background on research that addresses digital technology's role in supporting development in the Global South. In this context, the emphasis is set on the supportive function of mobile technology to address development goals. Lastly, this section synthesizes the previous related background by deriving a pre-understanding of mobile health technology as an asset for development.

I. Introduction

This section introduces the research topic and agenda of this thesis. In the first subsection (I.1), this research motivation and endeavor's relevance are highlighted. This is followed by an analysis of prevailing research gaps and formulating research questions (I.2). Following this, the structure of the thesis is outlined (I.3), and the research positioning, design, and space are discussed (I.4). Lastly, the introduction concludes with anticipating the contribution and implications of this thesis (I.5).

I.1 Motivation

> *"The use and scale-up of digital health solutions can revolutionize how people worldwide achieve higher standards of health, and access services to promote and protect their health and well-being."*
>
> (World Health Organization (WHO), 2020)

From a historical perspective, human health has greatly improved due to advances in technology (e.g., modern sanitation, the advent of penicillin, vaccines, and magnetic resonance imaging) (Lehoux et al., 2016). This implies that research and technology have always been the main drivers of better health. Following this trend, today's digital technology is opening up new opportunities that are transforming the delivery of care, such as instant diabetes testing and telemedicine (Chiasson & Davidson, 2004). Propelled by the global ubiquity of mobile phones, digital technologies have also changed how people manage their health and gain access to healthcare services. For example, mobile devices enable people to (over)optimize their health through constant tracking of personal vital parameters (e.g., pulse) (Sim, 2019). Meanwhile, such technologies are no longer a luxury, as these are widely available and affordable worldwide (Middleton et al., 2014). Therefore, in low-resource settings such as countries in the Global South[1], digital health services address a diversity of persistent weaknesses in health systems by complementing traditional yet often scarce and limited healthcare (Blaya et al., 2010; Braa et al., 2007).

In terms of global health development, the United Nations' 2030 Agenda is one of the most important global agreements. At the core of this agreement are the 17 Sustainable Development Goals (SDGs), which recognize the world's most pressing challenges; one goal (SDG 3) explicitly strives for universal healthcare coverage and strongly emphasizes the need for health equity and "leaving no one behind" (UNDP, 2015). The use of digital

---

[1] The terms "Global South" and "Global North" are used to characterize the socio-economic and political characteristics of countries, where "Global South" refers to low- and middle-income countries (LMIC) and "Global North" refers to all other countries. There is a strong debate about this terminology; however, this thesis selected it for consistency reasons.

technologies can make a significant contribution to achieving the SDGs, especially regarding healthcare provision and services (Asi & Williams, 2018; Lozano et al., 2018). However, a key challenge is to ensure that all people enjoy the benefits of digital health services while confirming that innovation and technology help reduce inequalities in the world (Howard-Grenville et al., 2019; Rothe, 2020).

While the potential of such technology is especially evident regarding healthcare provision and support, the success and impact of various projects that rely on technology to enhance healthcare access are limited (Heeks, 2002; Riggins & Dewan, 2005; Walsham, 2020). The number of projects in the Global South that face implementation complexities is very high. These projects fail to move beyond their initial pilot phase and hence do not reach scale and are able to be sustained. The result is that such projects do not support and impact long-term developmental processes in healthcare. This is why the term "pilotitis" has emerged, which emphasizes the disease-like spread of technology projects that are discontinued after their pilot phase (Bhatia et al., 2020; Greve et al., 2021; Tomlinson et al., 2013).

To practically address this current phenomenon, a consensus statement, the "Principles for Digital Development,"[2] was developed in 2014, which supports practitioners in using digital technologies for development through nine generic guidelines (see section II.3) (Waugaman, 2016). Various global health and development institutions, such as the U.S. Agency for International Development and the Bill and Melinda Gates Foundation, have endorsed the consensus (Digital Development Principles Working Group, 2021). The principles reinforce the importance of effectively designing digital technology to be supportive for development programs. However, widespread confusion remains about how to put these relatively high-level principles into operational practice (Holeman et al., 2018; Waugaman, 2016).

From a research perspective, the complexity of implementing digital technology for healthcare is a common theme and of significant interest to information systems (IS) scholars (Anderson & Agarwal, 2011; Langtao Chen et al., 2019a). Further, the research field of information and communication technologies for development (ICT4D) is driven by the conviction that information and communication technologies (ICTs) foster development and explore how technology improves lives and creates a better world (Sein et al., 2019; Walsham, 2012, 2017). Bridging the complexities of healthcare (e.g., multiple stakeholders and sensitive data) and the complexities of the setting in the Global South (e.g., limited resources, high levels of illiteracy, and technological backwardness

---

[2] Principles for Digital Development, see https://digitalprinciples.org/

(Chaudhuri, 2012)), it is apparent that the intertwined relationship between digital technologies and such complexities presents a field of tension[3]. This is especially evident when fostering technologies as a driver of socio-economic transformation towards achieving development goals such as the SDGs (Chaudhuri, 2012; Sein et al., 2019; Walsham, 2012).

Research and practice particularly point to the potentials of mobile technology. Mobile applications (apps) and other mobile services (e.g. tracking devices) can support and address a variety of the weaknesses of healthcare systems in the Global South, such as the mediation of health information, connection to health advocates, and health self-management or monitoring (Chib et al., 2015; Latif et al., 2017; Motamarri et al., 2014). Nevertheless, it is apparent that previous interventions that aimed at implementing mobile technology are also suffering from the pilotitis phenomenon and are failing at early stages or showing limited success (Krah & de Kruijf, 2016; Schelenz & Pawelec, 2021). Therefore, the path to reaching the SDGs through these mobile health (mHealth) interventions is controversial (Asi & Williams, 2018; Rothe, 2020). Thus, the problem arises of how to design mHealth and how to implement it so that it endures the transformative processes towards development.

This thesis takes a problem-oriented perspective on the phenomenon of mHealth in the Global South, addressing, on the one hand, its design and, on the other hand, the actions that stakeholders need to take to overcome the challenges of long-term implementation and use. By appreciating the intertwining overlay of the research and practice of the topic (Schelenz & Pawelec, 2021), the focus is set on mHealth initiatives, i.e., specific projects or interventions[4], which generate knowledge from a "doing" perspective while solving a specific healthcare development problem and guiding the learnings and best practices of mHealth initiatives towards a general understanding of the challenges that hamper scale-up and sustainability. In this way, this study aims to shed light on the promising but so far limited nature of mHealth for development (mHealth4D) to support the SDGs and link practical implications to research discourse.

I.2 Research Gap and Research Questions

This thesis seeks to address the described challenge emphasized by the SDG 3 agenda of improving healthcare in the Global South through an exploration of mHealth as a supportive asset for development. The overarching objective of this exploration is threefold and encompasses the derivation of an understanding of the status quo of prior research,

[3] As a remark, the phenomenon of mHealth in the Global South is of a multidisciplinary nature. However, this thesis takes the IS research area as the major lens on this topic, where health research as well as development studies only serve to inform the scope.

[4] The terms "intervention," "initiative," and "project" are used synonymously in this thesis.

the actual research in the Global South, and the synthesis of knowledge. Thus, three research questions with subsequent sub-questions are derived and discussed in the following.

First, research on mHealth is one aspect of the broader digital health research agenda (van Dyk, 2014). Overall, digital health is of substantial interest to the IS research community (Langtao Chen et al., 2019a). The research stream is called Health IS and addresses a variety of aspects—from the impact of digitalization on healthcare cost and quality to digital health services such as telemedicine—but it also includes research regarding health data exchange and data privacy (Langtao Chen et al., 2019a; Ostern et al., 2021). Thereby, digital health studies engage at different levels of intervention, such as the micro-level (e.g., acceptance of health apps for patients (Fox & Connolly, 2018) or individual health monitoring via fitness tracker (James et al., 2019)) or the macro-level (e.g., IS in hospitals for patient data sharing (Pouloudi et al., 2016) or healthcare expenditure control (Thompson et al., 2020)). Against this background, IS distinguishes between two paradigms: a) research that investigates the design of such systems and b) research that explores a system's use, management, and impact based on individual and organizational behaviors (Hevner et al., 2004). Both paradigms contribute to the studies in the Health IS stream and understanding the multifaceted nature of digital health, including mHealth.

As a whole, the knowledge base of the research agenda on Health IS research covers a wide range of application domains, forms of technology, and research foci. There is a need to review the existing body of research, synthesize prescriptive knowledge, and identify research gaps within the broader body of digital health literature to reach the overarching object of exploring the specific intervention of mobile technology to support healthcare in the Global South. Following the notion of "zooming in and zooming out" (Gaskin et al., 2014), the goal is to capture the broader scope of available health discourse in IS research and create an orientation map of promising research directions (vom Brocke et al., 2015) before "zooming in" to investigate the practically-motivated trajectory of mHealth in the Global South. To capture the complexity of healthcare systems as digital socio-technical systems (Ostern et al., 2021) and their discourse in research, the first research question of this thesis aims to analyze existing knowledge:

RQ 1: *What is the status quo of IS research on health, and what future research opportunities can be revealed?*

Second, while the adverse enhancements and potential of digital health become evident in research and practice, the complexity of the socio-technical systems of healthcare conceals challenges that limit its outcome and impact. This is especially seen in low-resource environments, such as the countries in the Global South (Heeks, 2014), where, on the one hand, technology has a tremendous potential to address the need to enhance healthcare systems, and, on the other hand, a lack of success and sustainability of digital health projects is common and critiqued in research and practice (Schelenz & Pawelec, 2021). However, mobile technology can especially address shortages through increased availability, reachability, and affordability (Lichtenberg et al., 2019). Therefore, ICT4D research calls upon intervention studies where the theoretical knowledge base can be leveraged to design development initiatives (Sein et al., 2019). Thus, to design mHealth initiatives, there is a need to conduct studies that create knowledge while addressing actual health contexts in the Global South. Thereby, needs-based design and understanding are anticipated, which recognize the user and culture sensitively. This leads to the following research question:

RQ 2: *How can mHealth interventions be designed to address the challenges and conditions of the Global South?*

This research question is deconstructed into two sub-questions that recognize the specific research context. The first sub-question builds upon the design paradigm by conducting an Action Design Research (ADR) intervention study (Sein et al., 2011) to theorize the design knowledge of an mHealth app to be used by community health workers (CHWs). This user group is of special interest since hospitals and doctors are scarce in many LMIC and often centered in cities (Thondoo et al., 2015). Health-related counseling has shifted to lay CHWs promoting health and providing healthcare services to rural areas (Lewin et al., 2005). Overall, governments increasingly see CHWs as a key means of providing access to basic primary healthcare services (Geldsetzer et al., 2017); further, mobile technology provides a tool for empowering them by supporting their tasks of coordinating care and mobilizing communities (Holeman & Kane, 2020; Walsham, 2020; Whidden et al., 2018). However, too many mHealth projects falter due to simplistic assumptions about end-user preferences and activities (Holeman & Kane, 2020); therefore, there is a need for a human-centered design (Cooley, 2000) of such technology-based services (Holeman et al., 2018). The concept calls for hands-on engagement and iterative participatory design approaches that prioritize users' aspirations and experiences. So far, the design research of mHealth projects is so vast and jumbled that practitioners struggle to make use of the scholarly rigor (Holeman & Kane, 2020). Thus, ADR provides a methodological approach to solve real-world problems while gaining prescriptive knowledge, which is generalizable and transferable for both research and practice (Purao et al., 2013). The first sub-question focuses on gaining this knowledge by investigating the use case of non-communicable disease (NCD) prevention, especially diabetes and hypertension, through CHWs in eSwatini:

RQ 2.1: *How can an mHealth app be designed to support decentralized health systems and be usable for community health workers?*

The second sub-question addresses the social perspective by exploring cultural sensitivity and differences through a hypothesis-based experimental investigation on the micro-level. The focus is set on the security risks that arise when using digital technology to capture health data. The sudden introduction of internet-related technology in the Global South leads to increased security vulnerabilities, especially when using mobile technology (Fichman et al., 2011; McLeod & Dolezel, 2018). Data breaches are very common cybersecurity incidents in the health industry, which are particularly problematic because they affect the confidentiality of data (Masuch et al., 2021). While the risks of a data breach and the loss of personal health information are of practical relevance, research on addressing this security challenge in a culturally sensitive way is still limited (Adu et al., 2021).

Even in the Global North, where the use of digital technology in the health sector is built upon a long history of digital development and hence is more mature, data breaches are a daily occurrence (Goel & Shawky, 2009), and precautions to protect personal health information are a high priority, which is addressed, for example, through the General Data Protection Regulation (Angst & Agarwal, 2009; Broy, 2017). In contrast, many countries in the Global South do not build upon an established technology infrastructure and often lack regulated structures to govern data protection (Lewis et al., 2012; Sweetney, 2015). There is an emerging research direction that focuses exclusively on data breach response because the inevitability of these incidents requires business and customer reaction (Choi et al., 2016; Goode et al., 2017; Gwebu et al., 2018). However, this research is commonly focused on developed countries (i.e., the Global North), even though it is known that cultural differences play a key role in user interaction and communication (Dinev et al., 2009; Hui & Au, 2001). This means that current studies lack an in-depth understanding of how impaired customer perceptions of recovery are culturally conditioned (Goode et al., 2017). The second sub-question addresses this gap by conducting a cross-cultural comparative study between a country in the Global North and the Global South by examining people's response to the design of an announcement of a data breach in which personal health information is breached from an mHealth device (e.g., a fitness tracker):

RQ 2.2: *How can the security challenges of mHealth be addressed and dealt with in a culturally sensitive way?*

Third, building upon the knowledge base and investigation of mHealth intervention, the last step remains, which is to derive a general understanding of mHealth initiatives for development. Leveraging such development projects to create knowledge is an opportunity for research that copes with reflection and learning (Sein et al., 2019). One can argue that the research conducted on RQ2 represents microcosms of empirical contestations. However, such is needed to "zoom out" and analyze broader development processes (Sahay et al., 2017). Therefore, the third and last research question builds upon the learning and best practices of various mHealth initiatives to derive a synthesis of mHealth scalability and sustainability, as both are of high (practical) relevance and are rigorously embedded in research (e.g., Braa et al., 2004). However, as the pilotitis phenomenon indicates, there is a need to generate findings so that stakeholders and the general public can benefit from them (Ilavarasan, 2017; Schelenz & Pawelec, 2021). Thus, the last research question aims to address this need:

RQ 3: *How can mHealth interventions reach scalability and sustainability?*

Figure 2 provides an overview of the research questions and their interdependencies, which are described above. The detailed theoretical background to all relevant topics is provided in section A.II.

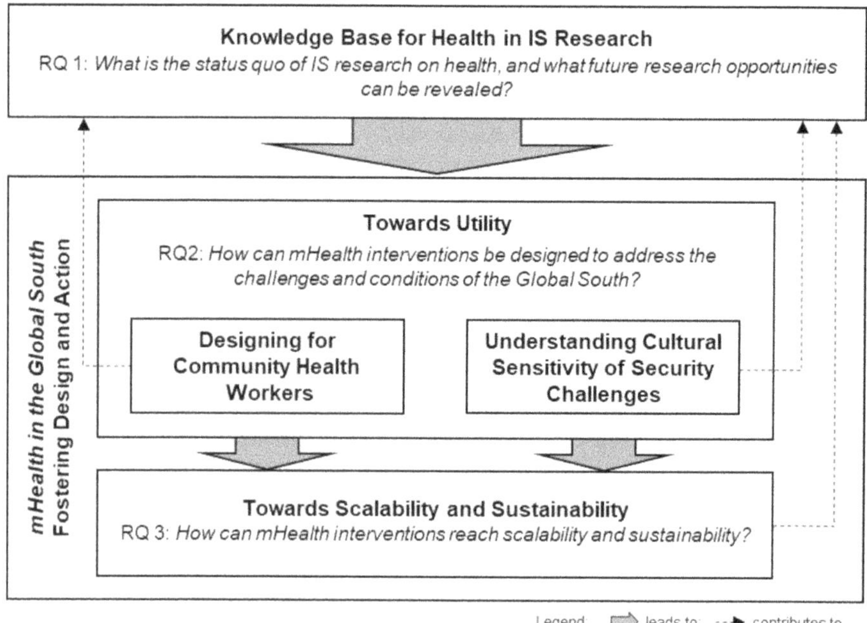

Figure 2: Research Overview

I.3 Structure of Thesis

This cumulative thesis builds around four standalone studies. It is structured in three main parts, as depicted in Figure 3.

Part A provides the foundation of this research by providing an introduction (A.I) and the research background (A.II). The introduction starts with the general motivation of the research (A.I.1.) before deriving the research questions (A.I.2) that seek to be answered in this thesis. This is followed by the structure of the thesis (A.I.3) and the research positioning and design (A.I.4). The introduction ends with a description of the anticipated contributions (A.I.5) of the thesis' research. The background section introduces of the advent of mobile technology (A.II.1) and discusses such in the context of Health IS research (A.II.2) and IS research aiming to support development in the Global South (A.II.3). Lastly, a synthesis of mHealth4D is presented (A.II.4).

Part B encompasses the four studies as the main part of this thesis. The studies provide a facetted view on mHealth in the Global South and address the formulated research questions to contribute to closing the selected research gaps (Table 1). Part C addresses the contribution of this thesis, starting by summarizing and synthesizing the findings of the individual studies included in this thesis (C.I). Building on this, the implications for research and practice are discussed, as well as a recognition of its limitations (C.II). This thesis ends with some concluding remarks (C.III).

Table 1: Overview of Studies Included in this Thesis

No.	Outlet	Status	Ranking[5]	Section	RQ	Main Contribution
1	Proceedings of the 54th Hawaii International Conference on System Sciences (2021)	Published[6]	C	B.I.	1	Overview of the status quo of Health IS research with a focus on social, organizational, and environmental contexts to synthesize existing prescriptive knowledge
2	European Journal of Information Systems[7]	Submitted (under Review)[8]	A	B.II	2	Exploration of the design of an mHealth app for CHW in decentralized healthcare systems.
3	Proceedings of the International Conference on Information Systems (2020)	Published	A	B.II	2	Understanding of the cultural sensitivity on the impact of security challenges of mHealth through a comparison of Bolivia and Germany
4	Information Systems Journal	Submitted (under Review)[9]	A	B.III	3	A process model of reaching scalability and sustainability for mHealth projects in the Global South.

[5] According to VHB-JOURQUAL 3
[6] Invited for Resubmission in the Journal of Information Technology (VHB A)
[7] Previous version published at ECIS 2020 (VHB B)
[8] Previously received valuable feedback in the Revision (2nd round) at the Information Systems Journal (VHB A)
[9] Previously received valuable feedback in the Revision (2nd round) at the European Journal of Information Systems (VHB:A) and invited for Resubmission in the Journal of the Association of Information Systems (VHB A)

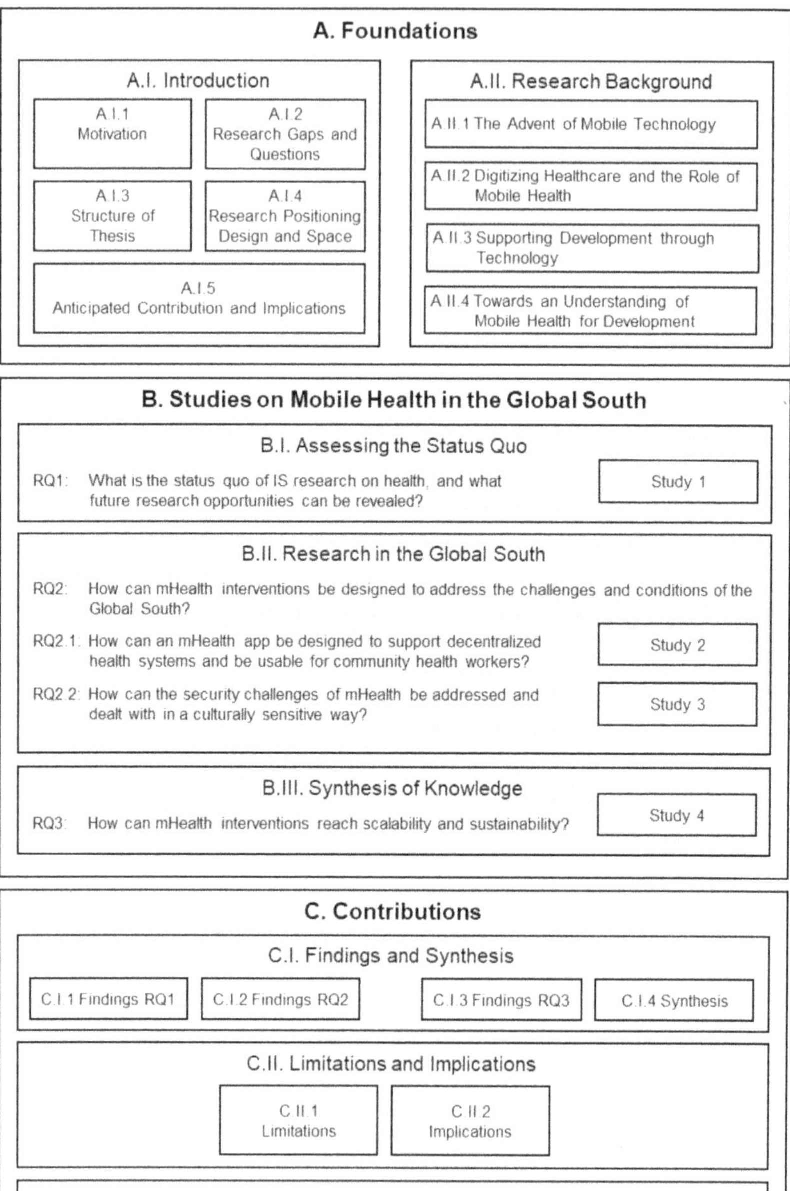

Figure 3: Structure of this Thesis

I.4 Research Positioning, Design, and Space

Generally speaking, "research is a problem-solving or phenomenon-exploring exercise" (Berthon et al., 2002, p.421) that generates knowledge in and through the process of solving such problems and exploring such phenomena. In this general notion, IS research explores "how to understand, interpret, adapt to, and effectively manage" the role of (emerging) technologies as phenomena themselves or in relation to or as supportive tools in problem-solving (Banker & Kauffman, 2004, p.294). The IS discipline has made a considerable effort to provide some structural guidance, such as an overview of research streams (Banker & Kauffman, 2004) and theory types (Gregor, 2006), to position research within the growing body of IS research.

In the following, this thesis' positioning within the IS discipline is discussed (see section I.4.1). Furthermore, the research design of the individual studies of the thesis is analyzed (see section I.4.2). This includes a detailed review of the methodological approach of each study. Based on this, the overall research space of the thesis is elaborated (see section I.4.3).

I.4.1 Research Positioning

An overview of the discussed positioning criteria, which are established and well discussed in the IS discipline, is depicted in Table 2. The individual criteria are briefly explained and further discussed in the context of this thesis and its four independent studies.

Table 2: Overview of Positioning Criteria in the IS Discipline

Epistemology	Positivism	Interpretivism	Critical Realism		*Pragmatism*
Paradigm	Behavior-oriented			*Design-oriented*	
Theory Type	I. Analysis	II. Explanation	III. Prediction	IV. Explanation and Prediction	*V. Design and Action*
Research Stream	Decision Support and Design Science	Value of Information	*Human-Computer Systems Design*	*IS Organization and Strategy*	Economics of IS and IT
Research Method	Case Study	*Conceptual Model*	Mathematical Model	*Literature Analysis*	Survey
	Secondary Data	*Design Science*	*Experimental Research*	Interview	Content Analysis

Note: *Italics* indicate Characteristics of Positioning Criteria that are Mainly Acknowledged in this Thesis

Four main perspectives are differentiated in the IS discipline to classify the epistemological stance of the research (Goldkuhl, 2012; Orlikowski & Baroudi, 1991). These stances shape the research since they concern how the researcher perceives and views the world. Most common in ICT4D research is the positivist approach, which assumes an objective apprehension of the world (often considered for theory testing and prediction), and the interpretive approach, which assumes a subjective socially constructed world (often considered for field studies that examine the interplay of various stakeholders with a social environment, e.g., actor networks) (Walsham & Sahay, 2006). Additionally, there are two other stances, which so far are scarce in ICT4D research (Heeks & Wall, 2018): the critical realistic approach, which combines the two beforementioned stances by assuming a subjective socially constructed reality with objective properties as influencing factors, and the pragmatic approach, which assumes action and change, e.g., through an intervention with artifacts (action) that humans react to in a certain way (change). The choice of stance is highly dependent on the research objectives and the corresponding research design. Therefore, the epistemology is discussed in each study individually. However, the overall manner of this thesis is pragmatism, aiming for constructive knowledge that is useful for action (Goldkuhl, 2012). This is determined by the main objective of this thesis—to conduct research that starts with a (real-world) problem and aims to contribute practical solutions that inform future practice (Ågerfalk, 2010).

The two distinct paradigms that characterize research in the IS discipline (behavior oriented and design oriented) (Arnott & Pervan, 2012; Hevner et al., 2004) have been mentioned before and are a research criterion of the structured literature analysis to derive the knowledge base of health research in the IS discipline provided by Study 1. Overall, this thesis is rooted in the design-oriented paradigm, which seeks to generate knowledge on designing and implementing IS artifacts (Gregor, 2006) to solve relevant problems for society, organizations, and individuals (Hevner, 2007). However, the two paradigms are complementary (Hevner et al., 2004), and especially when exploring phenomena, the behavioral paradigm provides an opportunity to apply kernel theories and test propositions (see Study 3).

As the advent of IS research builds on the controversy between responding to practitioner concerns (relevance) and the methodological rigors required for academic contributions (Benbasat & Zmud, 1999; Gallupe, 2007), Gregor (2006) distinguishes five types of theory to classify the structural nature of "how" the research is conducted. This thesis generally strives for a type V theory, "design and action," which says how to do something by giving explicit prescriptions (e.g., principles). However, to derive this overarching design and action knowledge, the individual studies build upon different theory types. Study 1 derives a type I theory, as it says "what is" by analyzing and describing the current status quo in digital health research. Study 2 is a design-science research, which says "how to do something" and derives prescriptive knowledge for designing an artifact (type V theory), while Study 3 follows a quantitative study design, which provides predictions and has a testable proposition (e.g., hypothesis) and causal explanations (type IV theory). Study 4 derives a type II theory by building on a qualitative research design to explain the phenomenon of pilotitis.

In addition to the structural theory nature, a retrospective analysis of the intellectual growth of the IS discipline by Banker & Kauffman (2004) identified five different research streams that define the "thrust of the theory" (p.282). Among the five streams, this thesis best fits into the stream of IS organization and strategy because it recognizes the holistic analysis at different levels (i.e., the individual level, system level, and organizational level) by conducting research based on field studies, as well as qualitative and quantitative methods. However, since this thesis also includes design-science research, the research stream of human-computer system design blends this thesis by enhancing the ability to design effective technological means that deal with specific problems.

Moreover, as this thesis focuses on a complex socio-technical phenomenon, it contains four distinct studies that, as a whole, explore mobile technology for development using different methodologies. Overall, this thesis conducts a mixed-methods approach (Bhattacherjee, 2012) comprising a literature analysis, design science, experimental research, and conceptual modeling.

I.4.2 Research Design

In the following, the research design of the studies is discussed, including the methodology, data collection, and data analysis (see Table 3).

Table 3: Research Design of Studies

No.	Methodology	Data Collection	Data Analysis
1	Systematic literature review (vom Brocke et al., 2009; Webster & Watson, 2002)	Literature review	Coding
2	Action design research (Sein et al., 2011)	Interviews, focus group discussion, technical meta data	Coding, descriptive statistics
3	Online experiment with 2x2x2 factorial design (Dennis & Valacich, 2001)	Survey	PLS-SEM
4	Conceptual model based on stakeholder analysis (Pouloudi et al., 2016)	Problem-centered expert interviews	Coding, framework derivation

Study 1 employs a meta-perspective on the status quo of health research in IS research by conducting a systematic literature review following the structured data collection and coding of Webster & Watson (2002) and vom Brocke et al. (2009) to synthesize existing knowledge and propose a future research direction to create knowledge. This study serves as a fundamental basis to explore mHealth in the Global South based on the identified research agenda from a phenomenon-driven perspective in the following three studies.

Study 2 conducts design research that recognizes one specific mHealth app for diabetes and hypertension prevention for health workers in eSwatini as an ensemble shaped by organizational context during development, use, and refinement (Sein et al., 2011). The method focuses on the building, intervention, and evaluation of the mHealth app, which reflects the theoretical precursors but emphasizes the user's role and use in context. The evaluation includes qualitative (expert interviews and focus-group discussions) and quantitative (technical metadata analysis) approaches that are analyzed through coding and descriptive statistics.

Study 3 builds upon empirical research (Dennis & Valacich, 2001) to conduct a cross-cultural study that compares individual behavior towards an mHealth device data breach of private health information between Bolivians and Germans. A scenario-based survey is conducted based on a research model and tested using structural equation modeling with the partial least square analysis (PLS-SEM). The cultural differences are explored using the GLOBE culture dimensions (House et al., 2004).

Finally, Study 4 derives a conceptual model by conducting problem-centered expert interviews (Döringer, 2021) for a stakeholder analysis (Pouloudi et al., 2016). This study evaluates the best practices and experiences of mHealth initiatives in the Global South to derive a framework that guides the scalability and sustainability of such mHealth initiatives.

I.4.3 Research Space

Based on an analysis of the thesis' research positioning and the research design of the studies, the research space, including the four-dimensions problem, theory, methods, and context, can be summarized (Berthon et al., 2002). While the framework of research space by Berthon et al. (2002) is intended initially to guide replication research, it further provides a conceptual space for gauging the nature of one particular piece of research. In the following, all four dimensions are described. Each dimension may imply a discussion at different levels. In this case, a discussion at two levels is warranted: one concerning the more general picture, which means an overarching thesis-level analysis, and the other a more specific picture, which means an analysis based on the individual studies. Thus, the specific level of the studies presupposes the general level of the thesis.

The problem dimension addresses *what* is being investigated in this thesis, the overall general phenomenon of which can be described as how to design and implement mHealth in the Global South to support healthcare provision and health supply equity (aimed for by the SDGs). This general problem is split into different research questions (see section I.2). The individual studies address the focused problems, which build upon more specified and focused propositions and research questions.

Second, the theoretical dimension of the thesis supports the exploration of *why* the phenomenon might occur. The overall theoretical positions of this thesis have been defined through an epistemological stance, which serves as the philosophical underpinning for all the studies. However, each study includes a specific theory and level of analysis.

The methodological dimension addresses *how* to generate knowledge about the phenomenon. This thesis follows a mixed-method approach (Bhattacherjee, 2012) to combine practical and scholarly perspectives to gain a deep understanding and knowledge that provides implications for research and practice. Each study consists of an individual data collection and analysis.

The last dimension of the research space considers the context, which concerns the *who, what,* and *where* to describe the content of the phenomenon. The context can be split into the investigative context and interpretive context. As described before, in general, this thesis investigates mHealth in the Global South, which contains investigations that address specific mHealth aspects. Further, the cultural background and county specifics are considered. The interpretive context is dependent on the individual study but acknowledges the contextual interpretation of the data (e.g., authors have different cultural backgrounds than interviewed people) and the referenced body of literature that informs the individual study.

I.5 Anticipated Contribution and Implications

By studying mHealth as an asset for healthcare development in the Global South, the main objective of this thesis is to derive an understanding of how to design, develop and implement such technologies to provide utility for healthcare development demanded by the SDGs. While aiming for design and action, this thesis constitutes a contribution through knowledge and implications for research and practice. This knowledge is synthesized towards a socio-technical view on mHealth (see section C.I.4.2). Thereby this thesis follows the current calls for ICT4D research on "making a better world with ICT" (Sahay et al., 2017; Walsham, 2012) and research which build upon the role that ICT can plan to foster development (Sein et al., 2019). Further, Health IS research calls to address the usability of technology to be implementable in healthcare domain under the consideration of diverse stakeholders (Langtao Chen et al., 2019a) and call for research on the dynamics of using mobile devices for healthcare delivery (Varshney, 2014; Vogel et al., 2013).

To anticipate the contribution of the work, the current state of research must be understood as the commonplace on which to build (Leidner, 2020). In the following section, the research background is eluded with regard to mobile technology (see section II.1), the digitization of healthcare (see section II.2), and technology to foster development (see section II.3). Following the five-point assessment, a contribution extends outwards towards one or more points of the five points to attract the reader's intention and hence make a contribution (Leidner, 2020). In the following, each of these five points is discussed concerning its extension through this thesis. Table 4 summarized this anticipated contribution.

First, this work anticipates a *theoretical contribution* by deriving design knowledge and actionable guidance by analyzing, developing and designing mHealth4D (Gregor, 2006). Generating prescriptive knowledge (Jones & Gregor, 2007) to derive an understanding of utility, scalability, and sustainability ("how could mHealth be implemented and designed in the Global South"), this work builds upon descriptive research (Iivari, 2010) ("how is mHealth in the Global South") through a) assessing the status quo of health research in the IS discipline to identify research opportunities (Study1), b) understanding challenges through hands-on research in countries of the Global South (Study 2 and 3) and c) analyzing mHealth initiatives concerning scalability and sustainability (Study 4). While the individual studies build on mature theories (e.g., Study 3 includes the Justice Theory) the originality of this work lies in the development of design principles (see Study 2) and the derivation of a conceptual framework to guide actions of practitioners (see Study 4).

Second, through a mixed-method approach, this thesis builds upon various rigorous methods, such as a structured literature review (vom Brocke et al., 2009; Webster & Watson, 2002), PLS-SEM (Hair et al., 2014), an ADR (Sein et al., 2011). Building on mature methods limits the *methodological contribution* (Leidner, 2020), however, the combination provides multifaceted and holistic insight into the phenomenon. The selection of methods is rigorously conducted to answer the broader range of research questions needed for an exploration to enable stronger evidence for a conclusion through convergence of findings and increase generalizability of results (Recker, 2021).

Third, this work anticipates a *contribution in framing* by synthesizing the research streams Health IS and ICT4D. By exploring the phenomenon of mobile technology informed through the findings of both research streams, this thesis provide a novel frame. Study 1 provides a superficial framing which tends to provide a fundamental knowledge base of what has been studies in the context of healthcare. This solely relies on the Health IS research stream. The remaining three studies build on this knowledge and synthesize this with ICT4D previous research. By considering both streams together, a captivating and novel frame is given in which to encase this thesis.

Forth, the *contribution in the phenomenon* is provided through the exploration of the emerging phenomenon of mHealth as an asset for development. Motivated by the SDGs and current mHealth initiatives in the Global South the thesis faces a real-world problem of high importance and relevance to the individuals (e.g., people or health workers), organizations (e.g., governments or development agencies), and societies.

Lastly, the *contribution in the composition* is given as the academic style which provides an appropriate communication instance for practitioners and researchers is used to asset the contributions of this work.

Table 4: Five-Point Assessment of Contribution

Type of Contribution	Anticipated Contribution of this Work
Theoretical	- Deriving a granular theoretical understanding that advances step by step through a case study, empirical results, and artifact design. - No overarching theory is considered, but existing theories (e.g., justice theory and stakeholder theory) are useful tools for this phenomenon-based research (Dennis, 2019).
Methodological	- Combining qualitative (e.g., expert interviews), quantitative (e.g., PLS analysis), and design-oriented (e.g., ADR) common and robust methods to derive a deep, multifaceted, and holistic understanding.
Framing	- Mainly building in two research streams: ICT4D and Health IS, but tracing back to the here underlying domains of health research, IS research and development studies. - Synthesizing the past findings by considering these streams together to build a captivating and novel frame that informs and guides this thesis research
Phenomenon	- Building on the mature phenomenon of mobile technology this thesis considers the real-world problem of the phenomenon in the context of healthcare development in the Global South. - These two components enable an emerging phenomenon with challenges facing individuals, organizations and society and hence are of relevance ad importance.
Composition	- Academic style to be apprehensible for practitioners and researchers.

Furthermore, through descriptive and prescriptive knowledge, this thesis provides some notable implications for research and practice that are directed to scholars and practitioners as a consequence of the contribution of this work (Ågerfalk & Karlsson, 2020). The research implications are separated by the two research streams (ICT4D and Health IS) that are underlying in the IS discipline (see sections II.2 and II.3). In both streams, the focus is set on mobile technology.

The challenges of utilizing mobile technology in the healthcare sector is an important field of interest in IS research, especially Health IS. Therefore, this work seeks to anticipate implications for research practices by providing opportunities for theorizing about mobile technology for healthcare and generalizing to theory regarding its impact on healthcare. This implication builds upon three contributions. First, the systematic review of existing health research in the IS discipline aims to organize the existing body of knowledge and provides a research agenda for socio-technical services in healthcare as phenomena at the macro and micro-levels. Informed through this, this thesis intends to explore mHealth as an asset for development in the Global South that considers the local characteristics of the healthcare system, which include a high burden of disease, lack of resources, and institutional capacity (de Carvalho et al., 2021). Hence and second, this thesis derives prescriptive knowledge for designing an mHealth app service to support diabetes and hypertension prevention. This app especially targets lay CHWs as users, as they are commonly present in LMICs to complement the shortages of healthcare systems in the Global South (Olaniran et al., 2017). The work of the CHWs decentralizes healthcare from central clinics and hospitals towards community counseling. The design study anticipated to generate transferable knowledge that is applicable for a class of design problems. Third, this thesis explores the aspects of IT security challenges that are especially evident when handling personal health data (Collins et al., 2011; Kruse et al., 2017) through a cross-cultural comparison that reveals culturally sensitive behavior.

Concerning ICT4D research, this work aims to derive implications to a better understanding of the relationship between ICT and development goals, i.e., as formulated through the SDGs (Sein et al., 2019). Focusing explicitly on goals towards better healthcare and ICT in the form of service via mobile technology, this thesis implies opportunities to explore how to theorize about mobile technology as an asset for healthcare development and how to generalize towards a theory about the long-term impact of mHealth initiatives. The studies presented in this thesis contribute insights through the actual "doing" of a mHealth intervention for CHWs in eSwatini as well as "researching" mHealth interventions through discussing lessons learned with various stakeholders of initiatives in the Global South. Building on this, this works moves towards a synthesized understanding of the processes towards long-term impact of such initiatives through a phased conceptualization of their scalability and sustainability.

In addition, this work anticipates valuable implications for practitioners. Through the multidisciplinary nature of the topic, its high relevance provides implications for various groups of practitioners. First, mHealth designers and developers can take advantage of the introduced artifact, as well as its iterative development process and the way it works. Second, this thesis provides opportunities for development agencies by providing insights on mHealth as an assent for development. Third, health ministries and governments can become informed about the use of mobile technologies for healthcare services and healthcare providers. Table 5 summarizes the anticipated implications for the research and practice of this thesis.

Table 5: Summary of Anticipated Implications

Audience		Anticipated Implications through Thesis' Contributions
Implications for Research	*Health IS Research*	Opportunities for theorizing about mobile technology as an asset for healthcare and generalizing design and action knowledge regarding its context-specific utility through: - an overview of the status quo of IS research on health, including a micro and macro-level analysis based on theoretical grounding and derivation of specific gaps and avenues for future research - prescriptive knowledge of the design of a mobile app for NCD prevention in decentralized healthcare systems - insights on the handling of security challenges of personal health data - contextualizing mHealth projects and theorizing their process towards scalability and sustainability from a stakeholder perspective
	ICT4D Research	Opportunities for theorizing about mobile technology for healthcare development and generalizing design and action knowledge about mHealth initiatives long-term sustainability in the Global South : - gaining insights and deriving generalizable knowledge through "doing" an ICT4D intervention to address a particular development problem - leveraging mHealth projects to create knowledge through "researching" ICT4D interventions - a synthesized understanding of the long-term perspective on mHealth initiative through theorizing scalability and sustainability
Implications for Practice	*mHealth Designer/ Developer (IS Focus)*	Opportunities for taking advantage of new mHealth *artifacts* to be deployed in the Global South through: - actionable design principles - insights on cultural-dependent behavior and interpretation - design implications through the consideration of long-term perspective (scale-up and sustainability)
	Developmental Agencies (Development Focus)	Opportunities for getting informed about mHealth as an assent for development and hence for *empirically informed change* through: - insights on the involvement of stakeholders through a participatory design process and co-creation - improved understanding of cultural differences and its challenges of international cooperation - Best practices and lessons learned regarding the long-term operation and impact from existing mHealth initiatives
	Health Ministries/ Governments (Health Focus)	Opportunities for getting informed about mobile technology to provide healthcare services and hence for *empirically informed change* through: - insights on the need of considering the user perspective through participatory and iterative design processes for mHealth design - awareness of challenges and risks that mHealth initiatives include that may impact the long-term health outcome - an improved understanding of the stakeholder network and the role and tasks of individual stakeholders in mHealth initiatives

II. Research Background

IS research has a long-lasting history that evolves around the interplay of individuals and technology (Briggs et al., 2010). Among this technology emerges the role of mobile technology (see Figure 4). This is also recognized in specific contexts, such as in numerous studies in health (health IS research), as well as the use of ICT for development (ICT4D research). Both research streams inform this thesis (see Figure 4, light-gray shaded areas). Building on this, a distinct sub-stream in Health IS research emerged, namely mHealth research. This research stream focuses explicitly on mobile-device advances in healthcare. Conversely, ICT4D research does not incorporate this distinction. The interplay of Health IS and ICT4D considers the use of mobile technology in the healthcare context with the objective to support development in the Global South. Following the abbreviations of the research streams, this intersection is referred to as mHealth4D in this thesis (see Figure 4, dark-gray shaded area).

The research background of this thesis presents the related research streams as the fundamentals and grounding for the whole thesis while trying to minimize redundancies with the studies in Part B wherever possible.

In section II.1, the advent of mobile technology is discussed, including devices, services, and users. This is extended in a review of Health IS (section II.2) and ICT4D research (section II.3) with a specific emphasis towards its research scope in themes, concepts, and practical relevance rather than specific studies, which are reviewed in the specific background section of the individual studies in Part B. Finally, the background section is synthesized towards a pre-understanding of mobile technologies that can be particularly exploited in healthcare as assets for development (section II.4).

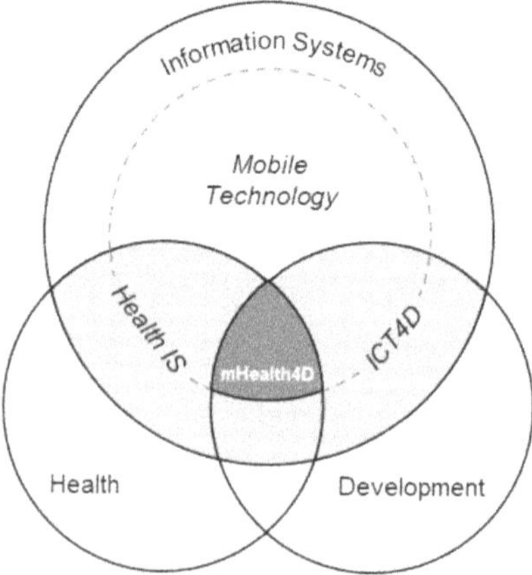

Figure 4: Interplay of Research Streams which Inform this Thesis

II.1 The Advent of Mobile Technology

In the early 2000s, IS research focused on the novelty of mobile technologies (e.g., Van Der Heijden & Junglas (2006); Varshney (2003)). While IT structures were already established in companies at that time, the rapid spread of mobile devices (i.e., smartphones and tablets) resulted in a shift in focus (Heeks, 2012). This widespread uptake of mobile devices opened markets to new services (e.g., digital bookings for transportation, such as Uber) (Dery & MacCormick, 2012) and influenced individuals' expectations as to how they engage in personal and work activities in their daily lives (e.g., permanent accessibility via email and communication apps, such as WhatsApp) (Majchrzak et al., 2016). To discuss this advent of portability and independence of location of IS from a research perspective, Middleton et al. (2014) suggest three distinct key areas: the evolution of mobile devices, the development of mobile services, and the roles of mobile users; reflecting on the relevance regarding their contextualization in Health IS and ICT4D research, those three areas (device, service, user) are reviewed in the following.

(1) **Mobile devices:** The mobile phone changed the technology era from stationary to mobile. While their functionality was initially limited to telephone calls, their scope and services rapidly expanded to text messaging, image sending, and access to the web. Today, smartphones bundle various functionalities in a customer-friendly and easier-to-use manner. This results in multifunctional tools that are an indispensable part of everyday life. But while the smartphone is the most widely spread mobile device, tablet computers and smart gadgets such as fitness trackers extend the scope of the devices and complement their functionality.

In most countries in the Global North, active mobile-broadband subscription rates have reached over 100% per capita (see Figure 4), meaning that individuals often subscribe to more than one mobile device (Dery & MacCormick, 2012). In contrast, the number of active mobile users in developing regions (Global South) is only half that of the Global North. However, the spread is increasing and has already reached more than 60% per capita. It is quite common to share a device in a family or community, especially in rural areas of countries in the Global South (Aker & Mbiti, 2010; S. Lee et al., 2017). Therefore, the actional number of users is even higher than the number of smartphone owners.

On the research agenda of IS, Riemer & Johnston (2014) emphasize that the technology itself is dissolving its research center. As such, the focus is shifting towards services that offer value to individuals, organizations, and society as a whole and rely on technology as equipment.

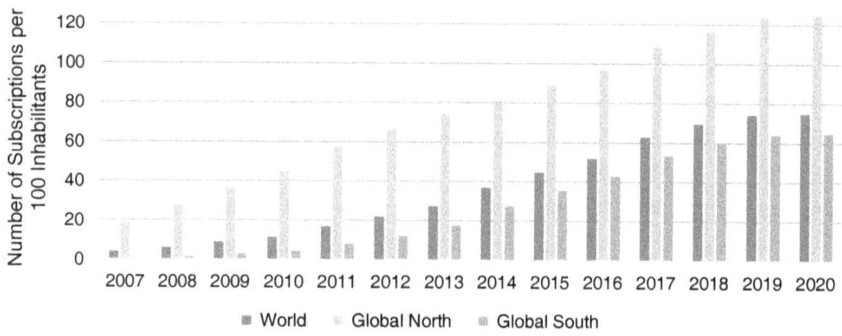

Data Source: International Telecommunication Union (2020)

Figure 5: Region-Wise Active Mobile-Broadband Subscriptions

(2) Mobile services: With the wide spread of mobile technologies, society is becoming increasingly connected. This provides a potential for new services that leverage mobile and ubiquitous technologies. Universal access to the Internet has enabled a multitude of commercial IT services that had been only possible in analog if at all. Meanwhile, "mobile by default" has become the norm, with digital offerings often functioning cross-platform and mobile access being a standard for all new systems.

In particular, the market for smartphone apps demonstrates the scale and scope of the "mobile as default" upswing (Basole & Karla, 2011). The oversupply makes success difficult, as users readily switch to the next service. Recent studies show that mobile service development (e.g., in the form of smartphone apps) is very costly, and despite the success of a few, the majority of services are not as successful as expected or fail (Jobe, 2013). For example, only 1% of all mobile apps have been downloaded more than one million times, and one in four mobile apps is never used again after being downloaded (Hoehle & Venkatesh, 2015). In such a competitive and dynamic environment, the issues of user-centricity and usability become particularly relevant (Cooley, 2000; Nickerson et al., 2009).

This problematic trajectory is combated by IS research through a focus on acceptance (e.g., Wu and Wang (2005)) usability (e.g., Hoehle and Venkatesh (2015)), and design (e.g., Spohrer et al. (2021)). This includes research on the design of such services to meet the needs of individuals and society (e.g., design-science research (Hevner et al., 2004; Peffers et al., 2007; Sein et al., 2011)), as well as conceptual work that classifies prior offerings and addresses the human–computer interaction in such services (e.g., Nickerson et al. (2013)). While both approaches recognize specific application contexts and address new, innovative technological advances, such as sensor technology, they emphasize the need to design and develop with and for the user (e.g., using human/user-centered design methods (Bannon, 2011; Gasson, 2003)).

(3) Mobile users: Through mobile devices and the ever-increasing availability of diverse services, the user is empowered. Thus, we can speak of user-enabling IT, which enriches people's lives with new, individual behaviors through its services. By extending access to information and services beyond the home and office space, ubiquitous mobile services provide a powerful platform to reach a broad consumer and market base, both for private and professional purposes. This results in a spectrum of services and functions that offer added value to individuals, organizations, and society.

However, users and their demands are as diverse as the services offered (Gasson, 2003). In this context, the individual mobile user has multiple roles. For example, the role of the user varies between the individual as a private person or the individual as an employee (Kupfer et al., 2018). Thus, the multiple contexts that enable the use of mobile technology can be differentiated according to the respective role of the mobile user (private and professional). These roles also change usage demands, e.g., for the individual as an entertainment seeker or the individual as a professional (Middleton et al., 2014). Figure 6 shows the two distinct roles, which illustrates that both roles are highly dependent on the surrounding contexts of influence and thus cannot be considered in isolation, as they are inseparable and interwoven in context. Furthermore, previous research has shown that individuals tend to merge their different roles in the case of mobile technology (Duxbury et al., 2014; Scheepers et al., 2006), although these roles could be analytically disaggregated.

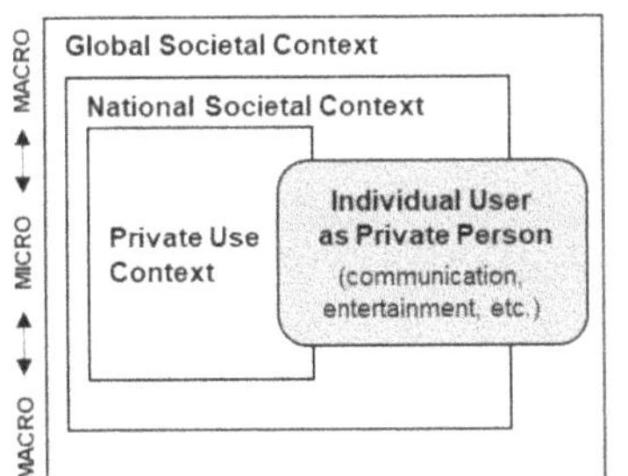

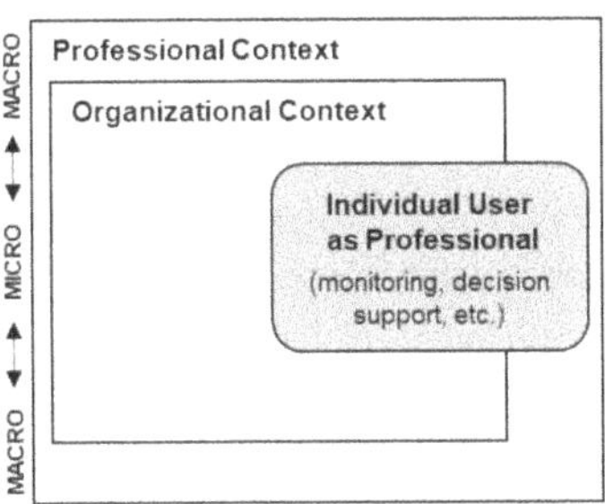

Adopted from Middleton et al. (2014)

Figure 6: Contexts of Mobile Technology Use

Overall, mobile technology offers the advantage of widespread, multipurpose functionalities, and user empowering that effectively enhances the digital transformation (Agarwal et al., 2010; Majchrzak et al., 2016). The advent of mobile devices can be seen worldwide, as also in developing regions the majority of people have begun to engage in ICT, especially through the rapid expansion of ownership and use of mobile phones. This makes the technology ubiquitous for almost everyone in the world, both in private and professional life (Walsham, 2012).

II.2 Digitizing Healthcare and the Role of mHealth

The research regarding the digital transformation of the healthcare sector is interdisciplinary and located at the intersection of the macro-level including societies and organizations (e.g., healthcare providers such as hospitals), and the micro-level including individuals (e.g., healthcare recipients such as patients) (Baird et al., 2018). The term digital health has been established as a flagship for some form of IT or systems used in the health context, such as data management IS in healthcare facilities or digital tools to support individual disease management (Meskó et al., 2017). The phenomenon-driven investigation of digital health has established one of the main subdisciplines in IS research (often referred to as Health IS), which provides insights into the thematic trajectory and how the health context contributes to and advances IS theory formation and practice (Baird et al., 2018; Chiasson & Davidson, 2004; Davidson et al., 2018; Hailemariam et al., 2010; Romanow et al., 2012).

Increasing prominence and growth can be observed through the number of publications in the IS discipline that address healthcare as the context or phenomenon itself (Langtao Chen et al., 2019a). This is largely due to socioeconomic and technological developments within the healthcare sector that have created new opportunities and a demand for research (Davidson et al., 2018). For example, digital tools including software and infrastructure have been touted as important components for reducing healthcare costs and improving healthcare quality, access, and outcomes (Agarwal et al., 2010; Bashshur et al., 2011). Further, it is recognized that digitalization in the health sector depicts a long-term solution to the problems and challenges of demographic change (Lozano et al., 2018), intergenerational equity (George et al., 2018), and skills shortages (Ditsa & Ojo, 2011).

Conceptual subcategories have become established in the field of digital health that differentiate mainly by the form of technology (Otto et al., 2018). eHealth, as an acronym for "electronic health," is an umbrella term for all digital technologies and applications used for patient care, such as electronic health records or hospital information systems (Kelley et al., 2011). The term is most often used in the context of patient behavior and the professional healthcare provider (Kelley et al., 2011; Kenny & Connolly, 2015; Sommer et al., 2018). In contrast, the *mHealth* subcategory refers specifically to mobile communication and information services provided by devices such as smartphones, tablets, and smartwatches for health-related purposes (Liwei Chen et al., 2019; Källander et al., 2013). Nacinovich (2011) emphasizes the overall potential of mHealth as a health communication tool, healthcare delivery tool, and dissemination tool for health information.

Focusing on mHealth, it becomes evident that such tools can strengthen existing medical care through a wireless infrastructure that provides users with healthcare access, reducing temporal and spatial constraints compared to traditional forms of healthcare access

(Fei Liu et al., 2018; Yang & Varshney, 2016). While some mHealth services aim for everyday support of patients by, for example, monitoring medication intake or emergency response systems, others focus on disease surveillance and control, such as chronic diseases like diabetes (Mechael, 2008). Due to its manifold application areas, the importance of mHealth technology is constantly growing (Xinying Liu & Varshney, 2020; Rowland et al., 2020). Further, the actual number of mHealth services is also steadily increasing. Current studies have identified more than 350,000 health-related smartphone apps that are available for customers with more than 90,000 new apps introduced in 2020 (IQVIA Institute, 2021). The practical strength of mHealth lies in the fact that the decentralized distribution of technology reaches many people with a minimum amount of effort and thus enables easy access to a multitude of services and knowledge for individuals (Baird et al., 2018). Therefore, mHealth technology has the potential to act as a catalyst in the provision of health knowledge and basic healthcare, which is particularly helpful in regions that lack sufficient healthcare provision and supply (Latif et al., 2017; Motamarri et al., 2014). Further, mHealth can provide benefits in the context of public health crises, such as the COVID-19 pandemic. When patients were temporarily separated from face-to-face interactions with physicians, healthcare shifted to telemedicine, enabling remote or virtual visits. This further pushed the market and relevance of mHealth (Giansanti, 2021; IQVIA Institute, 2021).

As mHealth can be seen as a novel, dynamic, interdisciplinary, and expanding field that generates innovations in short cycles and is part of a changing environment, it is becoming of interest for research, as it is slowly gaining traction in high-ranking IS journals (e.g., Fox & Connolly (2018); Spohrer et al. (2021)). Varshney (2014) has synthesized the research on mHealth by identifying four categories as key components.The central mHealth technology contains a specific healthcare-related *mobile service* (see section II.1 (2)). Often this service is provided via smartphone apps, but SMS reminders and fitness-tracker interfaces are also application forms. Given the rapidly growing mHealth market, one research topic is to classify the different practice instantiations of mHealth services, thereby enabling generalization of knowledge, identification of patterns in mHealth conceptualization, and aligning practice with theory (Greve, Diederich, et al., 2020; Olla & Shimskey, 2015; Plachkinova et al., 2015).

Further, the effectiveness and evaluation of the individual mHealth services are of research interest. Thereby, clinical studies, design-science approaches, and research-building on theoretical models and user requirements can derive design knowledge and medical impact (Yang & Varshney, 2016). Driven by the universality and rapid expansion of mHealth, it is important to consider the privacy and security of the sensitive personal health data that are collected or transferred in many services (Martínez-Pérez et al., 2015). This security challenge results in regulatory restrictions. However, incidents of information security breaches of mHealth gadgets are rising sharply, which are observed almost daily (J. Liu & Sun, 2016; McLeod & Dolezel, 2018). This results in the need to understand the complex global problem of security challenges to guide mHealth developers (Martínez-Pérez et al., 2015) and investigate the consequences of such (e.g., what to do after a breach) (Masuch et al., 2021).

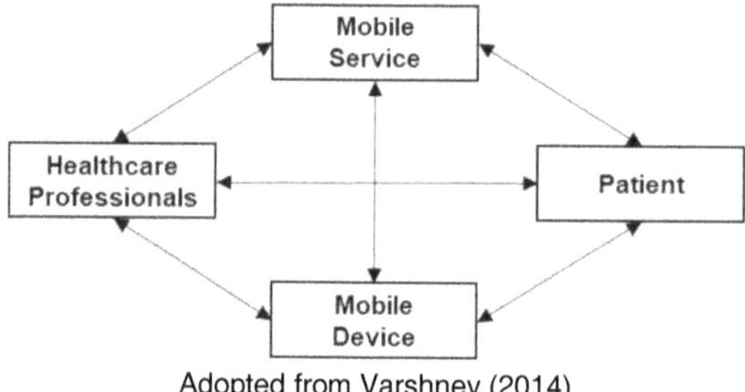

Adopted from Varshney (2014)

Figure 7: mHealth Components and their Interplay

In the healthcare context, the role of the mobile user (see section II.1(3)) contains two distinct groups of people. On the one hand, the *patient* plays a critical role, as mHealth has the objective to assist the patient in some sense. This assistance can be direct, meaning the patient is the user (Sherer, 2014); this is the case of so-called patient-facing mHealth (e.g., DIGAs—mHealth apps for prescription in the German healthcare system (IQVIA Institute, 2021; TWT Digital Health, 2020)). Alternatively, mHealth can indirectly assist patients by providing a supportive tool for *healthcare professionals* (Gagnon et al., 2016) (e.g., healthcare workers (Early et al., 2019) or physicians (Sezgin et al., 2018)). Further, mHealth can provide interactive communicative tools between patients and healthcare professionals, such as for telemedicine (direct communication, e.g., via chat) and patient data exchange (indirect communication) (Varshney, 2014). From a research perspective, the heterogeneity of both user groups is of interest, as technical affinity and experience (Zhang & Li, 2004) impact the interaction with the device and service and hence needs to be considered for the design. In this regard, the users' interaction, acceptance, and usage are of interest as an outcome. Long-term and continuous use are desired to improve users' health behaviors and health outcomes (Al-Ramahi et al., 2016).

Lastly, the various forms of *mobile devices* (see section II.10) offer high potentials for the healthcare domain. The mobile devices include portable systems (e.g., smartphones or smart watches), implanted systems (e.g., sensors or RFID), and environmentally embedded systems (e.g., smart hospital care (Varshney, 2014)). However, they differ in complexity, reliability, security requirements, and infrastructure. Some of these devices are highly innovative and offer numerous potentials for healthcare. Further, the COVID-19 pandemic emphasized technological requirements and privacy standards for tracing apps (which belong also to the group of mHealth services). Research in this regard investigated users' privacy concerns (Fortagne et al., 2021) and mass acceptance (Trang et al., 2020).

II.3 Supporting Development Through Technology

Countries in the Global South are heterogeneous in many aspects, such as culture and political regime. Heeks (2017) outlines some typical features of context that separate countries in the Global South from those of the Global North. This includes uncertainty (e.g., volatile markets and unstable political regimes), resource constraints (e.g., skills shortage and limited infrastructure), inequality (e.g., among material resources and power distances), institutional differences (e.g., cultural norms and values), and localism (e.g., seeking advice). Addressing the specifics of the Global South, there is a need for specific research that explicitly fosters the use of digital technology as assets for development. In research and practice, the term ICT4D is manifested to explore and apply the role and use of digital technology ("entities that process or communicate digital data" (Heeks, 2017, p.10)) driven by geographic and agenda-specific development ("particular progressive changes (e.g., SDGs) in countries of the Global South" (Heeks, 2017, p.11)).

Following the definition of ICT4D, the goal is to support agenda-specific development. While there is a long history of development paradigms, the most recent agenda of international development is unified in the SDGs of the United Nations. Hence, the 17 goals provide a practical-driven problematization for ICT4D research. Therefore, a diverse range of studies is conducted on digital technology for economic opportunities (e.g., Hatakka et al., 2020), capacity building (e.g., Heeks & Ospina, 2019), or agricultural enhancement (e.g., Vaidya & Myers, 2020). The overarching research field is motivated by problems observed in the Global South. However, a theoretical contribution is desired as a lens to understand digital technology and the development in this context, as well as describe mechanisms that enable the transformative process of reaching development outcomes (Sein et al., 2019).

Nevertheless, the underlying assumption that digital technology can support development is critically assessed in research. Walsham (2012) confronts research with the provocative question, "are we making a better world with ICT?" (p.87). This critique is further supported by high project-failure rates, which are reported by practice (WHO, 2011, 2019). The causes of failure include pilot interventions that are unable to reach scale and sustainability (Braa et al., 2004; Greve et al., 2021; Sanner et al., 2012); individual projects "reinventing the wheel" rather than considering shared services, platforms, or existing infrastructure (Waugaman, 2016); and not meeting the needs of users and inaccessibility of data for decision making (Mechael et al., 2010; Stroetmann, 2018).

To derive some practical guidelines, the Principles for Digital Development were derived as a consensus. They emphasize to "design with the user", "understand the existing ecosystem", "design for scale", "build for sustainability", "be data-driven", "use open standards, open data, open-source, and open innovation", "reuse and improve", "address privacy & security," and "be collaborative" (Digital Development Principles Working Group,

2021). Many development agencies have promised to follow these guidelines and endorse them in their projects. However, the high-level and abstract nature of the principles presents a lack of clarity on how to put them into practice (Waugaman, 2016).

Reviewing ICT4D research in regards to mHealth, it is apparent that the health domain is one specific application context of projects, which receives attention in global development through the SDG 3 "good health and well-being" (Howard-Grenville et al., 2019; Rothe, 2020). On a global level, the introduction of digitalization and particularly the integration of mHealth into existing healthcare systems aim to contribute to long-term solutions to the problems of demographic change (Lozano et al., 2018), generational equity (George et al., 2018), and a shortage of skilled workers (Ditsa & Ojo, 2011).

As generally observed for ICT4D projects, mHealth interventions in the Global South also cope with numerous challenges. Latif et al. (2017) summarize three global challenges that hinder the growth of mHealth in the Global South: insufficient health literacy, cultural barriers, and a lack of infrastructure. By tackling those challenges, the focus is shifted towards human-centric design, improvement of health education, and strategic planning (Latif et al., 2017). Hence, the local context and regional conditions, as well as the available resources, are taken into account to pave the way towards efficient management, scale, dissemination, and sustainability of mHealth implementations (Venkatesh, Bala, et al., 2016). Further, WHO (2021) reports that the COVID-19 pandemic is threatening health systems' hard-won health and development gains in achieving the SDGs.

In this context, the role of mHealth increases in importance. An analysis of the key components of mobile technology (see section II.1) is also considered in the existing research on mHealth4D. Heeks (2020) argues that advances in technology and the use of devices (see section II.10) can be used as an indicator of stages in ICT4D research. Since the mid/late 2000s, mobile phones have been the primary devices (Heeks, 2012). However, the technology has evolved and shifted towards "digital," underscoring the broad nature, widespread use, and everyday utility of the mobile technology that is now commonplace in the Global South. It can be summarized that in the Global South, mobile phones are well-rooted, smartphones and internet use are still nascent but growing rapidly, and sensors and gadgets are still in their early stages (Heeks, 2020). Reviewing existing literature on mHealth4D, the targeted users (see section II.10) can also be differentiated as patients and healthcare professionals. However, among the professionals are CHWs. These are lay health workers who are closely embedded in the community by visiting people at home to counsel and provide general health information. Governments increasingly see CHWs as a key means of providing access to care to basic primary healthcare services (Geldsetzer et al., 2017), and many mHealth initiatives specifically target this group (e.g., (Early et al., 2019; Lemay et al., 2012).

Further, the literature identifies how and through what services (see section II.1(2)) mHealth can improve health situations in the Global South. Latif et al. (2017) identify that mHealth solutions, such as apps or SMS messaging services, can target health education and awareness. For example, regarding NCDs, an awareness of specific risk factors supports disease management and testing in a cost-effective and very efficient way. This educational service can also be applied in the context of CHW training and knowledge provision. In addition, services such as remote monitoring (e.g., telemedicine), epidemic outbreak tracking (e.g., tracing apps and warning systems), and clinical decision support based on mobile sensors (e.g., fitness trackers) are of interest to support health systems via mHealth in the Global South.

II.4 Towards an Understanding of mHealth4D

Drawing on the research background described in the previous sections, this section relates the three research areas and their themes to synthesize them towards an understanding and identification of the research agenda for mHealth4D design and action. Table 6 synthesizes the knowledge and provides an overview of the status quo in literature. The advent of mobile technology in the combined contexts of health and development, with the objective of being a supportive tool for healthcare development in the Global South, represents a highly relevant asset for practice (e.g., emphasized by the SDGs) but also an interesting phenomenon for research, where design and action guidance are grounded in existing theory and investigations.

While mHealth is becoming increasingly popular due to its numerous applications in the healthcare sector, the use of mobile technology does pose some specifics compared to its application in other industries. These specifics are discussed in the literature and cope with challenges of consideration (see Table 30 in A.III.1.7.1). In light of the studies included in this thesis, the following three aspects are of particular relevance. First, mHealth essentially targets two specific user groups: patients and healthcare professionals; however, its design must be targeted to the needs of the user group and its characteristics. Second, user interaction plays an essential role, as desired health outcomes (e.g., behavioral changes) can often only be achieved through long-term and continuous use. Third, security challenges arise from the integral aspect of sensitive health data, which often forms the basis of mHealth services.

Due to the wide dissemination of smartphones and their functionalities, mHealth apps are highly accessible and can directly provide a multitude of services and knowledge for individuals (Baird et al., 2018), which is especially valuable in countries with limited healthcare supply (e.g., countries of the Global South). However, the Global South environment adds further barriers and challenges to the discussed specifics of the healthcare domain. These include limited infrastructure (e.g., limited power supply and mobile data), the proliferation of outdated devices, and low trust and experience in technology on the part of users. While existing literature points out the multitude of challenges in the use of mHealth in the Global South, the potentials (e.g., achieving health equity by overcoming geographical, temporal, structural, and organizational barriers to the supply and uptake of healthcare services (Latif et al., 2017; Martínez-Pérez et al., 2013; Motamarri et al., 2014)) are promising, so that research is urgently requested to contribute to addressing mHealth as a design and implementation issue. It is imperative to examine the role of mobile technology concerning diverse forms of exclusion, marginalization, and vulnerabilities, as well as investigate the design and actions needed to support healthcare coverage and supply in the uneven landscape of development. Various aspects already motivating the literature play an essential role in this respect.

First, the targeted design of mobile technology for the user group is becoming even more relevant than before. It is emphasized that mHealth solutions are particularly suitable for the CHW user group (Early et al., 2019). Targeting CHWs can catalyze the delivery of health knowledge and basic healthcare (Tariq & Akter, 2011). CHWs represent a user group that is positioned centrally between patients (as they are part of the community) and healthcare professionals (they are tasked with providing health education but have no/little training) (Koh & Naing, 2006). In addition, personal characteristics such as illiteracy and limited technical experience (Mechael, 2009) result in unique design requirements, so that mHealth solutions from the Global North are intangible in the Global South.

Second, mHealth cannot be designed according to a "one size fits all" approach, as demonstrated by the heterogeneity of users and the need for user-centered design. The fact that design preferences differ across cultures should also be considered (Reinecke & Bernstein, 2013). A common criticism is that ICT4D projects show little awareness of cultural differences, local conditions, and power relations. An understanding of the local and cultural positioning of users (e.g., following Hofstede (2001) or Globe (2020)) enables an awareness of the subtle interactions of technology and culture (Schelenz & Pawelec, 2021). It has long been recognized in IS research that cultural differences can hinder the successful use of IT and its adoption by users (Leidner & Kayworth, 2006).

In addition, the influence of culture is also significantly reflected in ethical perceptions regarding confidentiality, anonymity, data protection, and privacy (Traxler, 2012). In this context, cross-cultural studies are particularly suitable for investigations in which a social exchange takes place, such as the interactions between mHealth providers and users, as the values of the two parties involved are each influenced by their cultural background (Mattila & Patterson, 2004b).

Table 6: Synthesis of Knowledge – Contextualizing Mobile Technology

Research Stream	*Mobile Component*		
	Devices	**Services**	**Users**
Mobile Technology			
IS	- Bundles of multipurpose features of several services into a single integrated device (e.g., smartphone, tablet) (Middleton et al., 2014) - Changing nature of technology devices towards equipment (Riemer & Johnston, 2014) - The increasing importance of design and development (Hevner et al., 2004; Iivari, 2017)	- Providing value for individuals, organizations, and societies (Bruns & Jacob, 2014) - Strong demand for mobile services (Middleton et al., 2014) and ubiquitous computing (Balasubraman et al., 2002) - Mobile by default (Basole & Karla, 2011) - Competitive and dynamic markets cause high failure rates (Hoehle & Venkatesh, 2015)	- Empowerment of users (Middleton et al., 2014) - Multiple and even overlapping roles of the individual user (e.g., private or professional) (Kupfer et al., 2018) - Highly dependent on contexts which results in changing demands (Gasson, 2003)
mHealth Technology			
Health IS	- Portable systems (e.g., fitness tracker), implanted systems (e.g., sensors), and most commonly, environmentally embedded systems (e.g., smartphone apps) (Varshney, 2014) - Aim to strengthen existing medical care (Yang & Varshney, 2016) - Provide users with healthcare access by reducing temporal and spatial constraints (Fei Liu et al., 2018)	- Numerous possibilities for services (e.g., monitoring medication intake or emergency response systems, diseases surveillance, patient-doctor communication, and information supply (Varshney, 2014)) - The healthcare support is manifold, which results in the need for conceptualization (Olla & Shimskey, 2015) - The effectiveness and evaluation of individual services need to be investigated. Especially long-term usage of interest for behavioral change (Spohrer et al., 2021) - Demand for security of personal health data (Martínez-Pérez et al., 2015)	- Two distinct groups of users: patients (Sherer, 2014a) and healthcare professionals (Gagnon et al., 2016) - Fostering interaction between user groups, such as telemedicine (Peters et al., 2015) - The heterogeneity of users groups (e.g., patients) impacts the design i.e., impact of individual privacy concerns and technical experience (Asaddok & Ghazali, 2017)
mHealth4D Technology			
ICT4D	- Mobile technology shift from specialist tools towards everyday utility (Heeks, 2012) - Internet via mobile data is still limed, but fast-growing (however, expensive) (Heeks, 2020) - Sensors and Gadgets are slowly emerging (Heeks, 2020)	- Services aiming to reach rural areas and people with limited access to healthcare provision (Mahmud et al., 2010) - Various services (e.g., education and awareness, CHW training (Latif et al., 2017)) - High failure rates of projects at pilot level, not reaching scale and sustainability (Greve et al., 2021; Leon et al., 2012)	- Besides patients and healthcare professionals, such as physicians and nurses, CHWs are a targeted user group (Eze et al., 2020) - Need for human-centered design (e.g., illiteracy and limited technical affinity of users) (Holeman & Kane, 2020) and cultural and contextual understanding (e.g., distrust due to political control) (Asi & Williams, 2018; Leon et al., 2012)

Third, as a consequence of the previous points and other obstacles[10], it can be observed in practice that many mHealth initiatives are short-term and do not achieve their desired outcomes (Bhatia et al., 2020). The need for scaling and sustainability is twofold. First, the mHealth service content is usually designed for long-term interaction and continuous use to achieve the desired individual health improvement (Spohrer et al., 2021). Second, in terms of health development, projects should take into account the broader socio-political context to reach many people and support the local health system in the long term (Braa et al., 2004; Sanner et al., 2012). Another problem here is the alleged gap between practitioners and researchers, as the former rarely leverage academic findings and therefore do not benefit sufficiently from advances in research (Best & Dialogue, 2010). Conversely, researchers are criticized for not being engaged enough in local realities and should focus more on the impact on the ground (Walsham, 2017). The fact that mHealth projects are chaotic and prone to failure is acknowledged by researchers and practitioners (Krah & de Kruijf, 2016). However, when it comes to publicizing such shortcomings and failures or acknowledging, investigating, and resolving problems, the research community is reticent and sometimes conceals unpleasant realities (Schelenz & Pawelec, 2021).

As a whole, while much is known about mobile technology from individual research areas (health and health IS; development and ICT4D), their dyadic relationship is, to date, not well understood, and previous research emphasizes the need for further research due to the high complexity. This is further highlighted by the practical relevance and experienced problems in the field. Nevertheless, prior work in the areas outlined above provides valuable ground and has informed the work in this thesis. In this notion, three key aspects have been identified in this synthesis, of which the investigation can contribute to the overall understanding of the phenomenon mHealth4D. While the first and the second aspects aim for an investigation towards an understanding of the utility of mHealth as an asset for development, the latter emphasizes the need for considering the scalability and sustainability of mHealtth4D initiatives to reach their full potential. Overall, utility, scalability, and sustainability need to be addressed through new artifacts (for design research) as well as interventions (for action research).

[10] See Study 4, section 1.7.1 for an overview of the barriers of mHealth in the Global South.

B. Studies on mHealth in the Global South

As explained in detail in Part A, this cumulative thesis aims to provide an exploration of mobile technology as an asset for health agenda-driven development in the Global South. To achieve this goal, three research questions were derived and will be answered in the four studies included in sections I, II and III of Part B.

The first section, B.I, contains Study 1 and offers a systematic overview of prior IS research on healthcare. In doing so, it answers RQ 1, regarding future research opportunities on digital health in the IS discipline.

Subsequently, B.II, containing Studies 2 and 3, provides an in-depth view on research regarding mHealth conducted in the Global South. The studies include two different contexts: the design process of an mHealth app for CHWs to support NCD prevention and the consequences of designing the interaction with mHealth user after a security incident. This section thus answers RQ 2, concerning the actual utility of mHealth by addressing how to design mHealth interventions to address the challenges and conditions of the Global South.

Finally, the third section (B.III), containing Study 4, provides an overarching analysis of mHealth initiatives in the Global South by analyzing the challenges faces as well as the role of stakeholders in helping to reach scale and sustain in the long-term. Thus, it provides answers to RQ 3 concerning the scalability and sustainability of initiatives to overcome project failure at pilot stage.

The studies included were adapted to a small degree where required to correct minor errors or careless mistakes and to ensure a consistent layout.

I. Assessing the Status Quo

As this thesis explores mobile technology to support healthcare provision and coverage in the Global South, it focuses, first. on the implementation of health interventions that are built upon mobile technology (i.e., the design of intervention, e.g., user-centered design and cultural perception) and, second, on the scalability and sustainability of such interventions. However, the topic of digital health intervention builds on a long-lasting tradition in the IS discipline. The existing knowledge base of the research agenda on Health IS reflects the multifaced nature and complexity of healthcare systems and digital tools as assets. There is a need to review the existing body of research, synthesize prescriptive knowledge, and identify research gaps of the broader body of digital health literature.

To address this need, Study 1 employs a meta-perspective in drawing on existing health-related research in the top IS journals. Building on the Belief-Action and Outcome Framework (Melville, 2010) existing studies are structured and analyzed at micro and macro-level engagement. By doing so, the broader scope of available health discourse in IS research is captured, to create an orientation map of promising research directions (vom Brocke et al., 2015) which informs the later studies of mHealth interventions in the Global South.

1. Study 1: Framing Research Questions Intersecting IS and Health

Table 7: Fact Sheet of Study 1

Title	Framing Research Questions Intersecting Information Systems and Health: A New Research Perspective at Micro- and Macro-Level
Authors	Maike Greve[a], Morten Gantner[a], Christine Harnischmacher[a], Alfred Benedikt Brendel[b], Lutz M. Kolbe[a] [a]Chair of Information Management, University of Goettingen, Humboldtallee 3, 37073 Göttingen [b]Chair of Business Information Systems, esp. Intelligent Systems and Services, TU Dresden, Helmholtzstraße 10, 01069 Dresden
Outlet	Published in the Proceedings of the 54th Hawaii International Conference on System Sciences (2021) (VHB C) Invited for Resubmission in the Journal of Information Technology (VHB A)
Abstract	Digital health is an established research area in information systems (IS) research. The domain involves individual human behavior, the broader social, healthcare providers, and other organizations. The rapid spread and use of health technologies have opened up considerable opportunities for research to evaluate and test existing theories. To generate an overview of the status quo, we apply the belief-action-outcome (BAO) framework as a lens to understand how current research has addressed the various aspects of digital health. Overall, we analyzed 46 studies from well-regarded IS outlets. Therefore, we aim at providing a comprehensive review and synthesis of the literature. Our results indicate a focus on behavioral research and action formation, but also a void regarding design-oriented studies, as well as multi-level studies. In summary, this study develops a research agenda for digital health, which includes six research questions that address research focus, health phenomena, at the macro- and micro-level.

1.1 Introduction

The increasing digitalization of our society promises various benefits for private and professional life (Hansen & Baroody, 2020). The healthcare sector in specific has been benefiting from improvements through digital technology and related innovations (Gastaldi & Corso, 2012; Romanow, Cho, et al., 2018; Singhal et al., 2018). For example, the European commission's report on the impact of an interoperable electronic health record system concludes that even if its implementation takes a long time (six to eleven years), the benefits are manifold and substantial (e.g., improved compliance with clinical guidelines and better patient safety and reduced clinical risk, such as technical mistakes due to information availability) (European Commission, 2009; Shaw & Stahl, 2011). However, the benefits of digital health concepts also come with challenges, rendering research in the domain of digital health-relevant is important (Baird et al., 2018). Against this background, IS research can play a key role in investigating the design of such systems as well as in exploring phenomena related to their use, management, and impact (Hansen & Baroody, 2020; Pinsonneault et al., 2017).

Accordingly, this paper has two main objectives. Firstly, we want to demonstrate the potential of the belief-action-outcome (BAO) framework of Melville (2010) to structure and guide digital health research. The extensive framework includes variables at the macro- and micro-level connecting social and organizational context with belief, action, and outcome formation. It links beliefs, actions, and outcomes of individual, organizational, and societal actors and is therefore well suited to analyze the impact of digital health. The system gives an extensive way to deal with analyzing the role of IS in empowering and changing feasible practices

Secondly, by applying the BAO framework to analyze current literature on digital health in IS research, we aim to identify research directions and to uncover research gaps to guide researchers to fill these gaps (Melville, 2010). Given the connections laid out in the BAO structure, we build up a concept matrix that enables us to methodically orchestrate and integrate prior research, identify research foci (vom Brocke et al., 2009; Webster & Watson, 2002), and formulate directions for future research.

In order to achieve our objectives, the paper proceeds as follows. We begin by summarizing the current directions and research areas of digital health. Subsequently, we are conceptualizing the gap the BAO framework fills within our understanding of how IS impact healthcare. Next, we present the conceptual bases on which BAO was developed and the BAO framework itself. Following, we conceptualize how the framework can be adapted to fit the new context of digital health. We demonstrate the framework's value by applying it to recent research on health in the top-ranked IS journals. Based on our analysis, we elicit future research directions and questions.

1.2 Health in Information System Research

The research area of health in information system research is interdisciplinary and located at an intersection between societies, organizations, and consumers (Baird et al., 2018). In general, the term "digital health" refers to some form of information technology or systems, which is applied in the context of health, such as in health institutions or for health management (Meskó et al., 2017). The term digital health has many definitions in scientific practice and can generally be described as the use of information and communication technologies to monitor and improve patient health and well-being (Iyawa et al., 2016). Sub-categories of digital health are eHealth and mHealth. They particularly describe the form of technology use in health concepts. eHealth is an umbrella term for all digital technologies and applications used for patient care, such as electronic health records or hospital information systems (Kelley et al., 2011). In contrast, the term mHealth is derived from 'mobile' and addresses mobile devices, such as smartphones, tablets, or smartwatches, for health-related purposes (Liwei Chen et al., 2019).

Overall, digital health research can be seen as an advancement of IS theory and practice (Baird et al., 2018). Previous research has provided insights into the thematic progress of this research stream. Current literature reviews aim to provide an overview of the previous research by addressing digital health often with specific foci. The review articles reveal that the authors limit themselves to the study of IS specific clinical pictures, such as mental disorders (Wahle & Kowatsch, 2014) or the use in certain geographical regions, such as countries of the Global South (Cohen et al., 2015). Besides, particular challenges, such as data protection concerns and privacy connected with certain applications are examined (Koffi et al., 2018). Those current literature reviews that are not limited to specific niches but consider digital health as a broader field of research show limitations in the search terms used or the journals considered. In the methodical approaches of the existing literature reviews, either search terms were used to investigate eHealth (E. V. Wilson et al., 2014) or mHealth (Koffi et al., 2018), but not both components together, which limits the overall research agenda. For example, the study of. Koffi et al. (2018) limits the investigation area to mHealth in combination with privacy. This approach categorically excludes papers referring to terms, such as eHealth or digital health and makes the consideration of privacy a necessary prerequisite. This seems to be insufficient, especially against the background of the manifold ways of defining digital health. In addition to the aforementioned content restrictions, all literature reviews known to us are limited in the selection of the journals examined. For example, Cohen et al. (2015) or Hur et al. (2019) search in various databases including Google Scholar, which does not consider the quality of outlet publication. Our research did not identify any literature review that exclusively analyzes the contributions of the high quality IS journals, such as the AIS basket of eight and could, therefore, derive insights relevant for the future IS research agenda.

1.3 The Belief-Action-Outcome Framework Intervention Research

The BAO framework by Melville (2010) provides a conceptual setting for "the development and adoption of information systems for environmental sustainability" (p.15) and the improvement of a promote understanding of context-related key issues. Hereby, the framework provides a structure that gives a far-reaching way to deal with IS research on this topic by understanding human conduct as an interaction of affecting elements at the macro- and micro-level. Figure 8 visualizes the interplay of dimensions, where the vertical dimensions (macro- and micro-level) of the framework interact recursively with the horizontal dimension (belief, action, outcome).

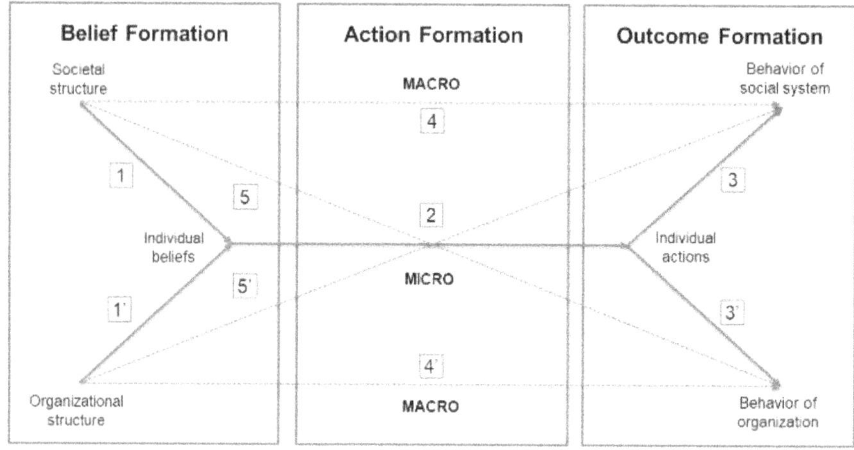

Adopted by Melville (2010)

Figure 8: Belief-Action-Outcome framework

The framework was originally developed and applied for the context of environmental sustainability (Tan & Vasa, 2011). However, we argue that the general nature of the framework enables the application in other contexts. The advantages of the BAO framework can be found especially in its ability to demonstrate the importance of information systems in changing environments, such as sustainability or health.

An essential aspect of the model is the distinction between the micro- and macro-levels, which considers the mediation and linkage of the individual with societal and organizational structure and the social system and organizations' behavior. The micro-level touches on individual beliefs and actions and the macro-level reflects social and organizational structures and their ecological and economic outcomes. The social structure refers to social and natural systems and includes individual and entrepreneurial actors (Melville, 2010). Accordingly, the framework encompasses human behavior and the broader social and organizational contexts at the macro- and micro-levels. It considers social and organizational behaviors resulting from belief formation, action occurrence, and outcome evaluation. In digital health research, the vertical dimensions of the framework are distinguished between the societal, organizational, and individual perspectives. Research on a societal level addresses society's influence on health (e.g., cultural or institutional structures or national campaigns). At the organizational level, research focuses on the influence of organizations on health. This contains digital health suppliers, such as mHealth operators and healthcare providers, including hospitals. The research in this area concerns, for example, management strategies, organizational culture and structure, and disease management. On the individual level, research focuses on the individual's health attitudes, including patients with a specific disease and generally people operating with (e.g., online health platforms).

The framework's horizontal dimension differentiates between the level of belief formation, action occurrence, and outcome assessment. Subsequently, the three dimensions are addressed in further detail and regarding the health context.

Belief – Belief formation is described by Melville (2010) as "psychic states (beliefs, desires, attitudes, opportunities, etc.) about the natural environment" (p.4). As we substitute the context, beliefs address the micro-level focus on the individual psychic state based on norms and values towards the health ecosystem. Individual belief formation about health is based on personal values, norms, and beliefs. As the health ecosystem conditions directly influence personally high valued subjects, such as personal health, the health of family and peers, and individuals' beliefs that they can take measures to mitigate these conditions, beliefs are found encouraging pro-health behavior (Steg et al., 2005). On the macro-level, belief formation within the societal and organizational structure is assessed. Individual beliefs are influenced by a variety of societal and organizational factors (Melville, 2010). Normative patterns on the micro-level are thus influenced by societal factors (macro-micro: link 1), such as political discourse and family life, that form the belief about the state of the health ecosystem (Lülfs & Hahn, 2013) as well as organizational structure (macro-micro: link 1'), representing how organizations allocate and coordinate labor, and use IS that create transparency regarding health aspects (Mintzberg, 1989).

Action - The phase during which individual beliefs are converted into concrete actions is the action formation stage. On the micro-level (micro-micro: link 2), health-related actions, for instance, include the usage of mobile health applications (Fox & Connolly, 2018), telemedicine systems (Hur et al., 2019), or interacting through online health communities (Hansen et al., 2019). On the macro-level, the BAO framework suggests that on the one hand, organizational structures influence the behavior of societies and organizations (macro-macro: link 4' and link 5') and on the other hand, societal structures directly influence health-related actions of societies and organizations (macro-macro: link 4 and link 5). Within the framework, an organization is defined as a group of homogenous agents, abstaining from individual human behavior (Melville, 2010). On the macro-level, actions can include, for instance, the use of digital patient records (Lin et al., 2019), the reduction of healthcare spending through IS use (Adjerid et al., 2018), or the creation of social value (Goh et al., 2016).

Outcome –The effects of combined individual health actions on social (micro-macro: link 3) and organizational (micro-macro: link 3') behaviors are reflected in the outcome assessment. On the societal level, health outcomes refer to all influences on society and the entire health ecosystem, such as social health disparities, healthcare costs, and waste (Melville, 2010). On the organizational level, organizational performance (e.g., reducing costs or increasing productivity) is the basis for outcome assessment, thus combining the importance of health outcomes and economic performance to transform the health ecosystem.

1.4 Research Approach

To review existing work on health in IS research, we conducted a systematic literature review process based on the approaches of Webster & Watson (2002), vom Brocke et al. (2009), and Brendel et al. (2020).

Table 8: Research Approach Phases

	Phase 1: Gather Literature	**Phase 2:** Code Literature	**Phase 3:** Analyse Literature
Input	Published journal articles	Literature database	Coded literature database
Method	Literature search	Coding	Analysis
Steps	Conduct search and filter literature	Define dimensions + code literature	Interpret coded literature
Results	Literature database	Coded literature database	Derive research questions

Our research approach is threefold (see Table 8). Firstly, the digital health publications from IS outlets are gathered. Secondly, the relevant literature is analyzed by coding along the dimensions of the BAO framework. Thirdly, the coded database is analyzed and discussed to identify research gaps and opportunities.

1.4.1 Phase 1: Gather Literature

During the first phase, we gathered literature to develop a digital health literature database in high-quality IS research. The publications include all studies that deal with physical or mental health, focus on health-related artifacts, such as electronic health records, or set the primary focus on the healthcare context. We excluded all kinds of meta-analysis, literature reviews, or research framework publications to focus on empirical research with practical contributions. Furthermore, we limited our database to publications from the AIS basket of eight to ensure that our sample includes publications with high-level impact and rigor (Levy & Ellis, 2006). For the search, we applied the following search query:

(health) OR (mhealth*) OR (m-health*) OR (ehealth*) OR (e-health*)*

The literature search was conducted in May 2020 via the databases Taylor and Francis (EJIS), ScienceDirect (JSIS), SAGE (JIT), and EbscoHost (others). All articles were filtered via a two-step process. The articles were selected by title, keywords, and abstract. Afterward, they were reviewed regarding their fit for the research database, following the previously defined criteria (i.e., empirical research in digital health). We gathered a total of 47 publications to form our research database. The results of the literature search are documented in Table 9.

Table 9: Overall Literature Search Results

Journals	Total	Abstract / Title	Final
ISR	33	20	6
MISQ	41	35	16
JMIS	23	14	5
JAIS	28	18	8
JIT	55	9	2
ISJ	23	16	6
JSIS	45	4	0
EJIS	81	10	3
	Total	**116**	**46**

1.4.2 Phase 2: Code Literature

To generate insight into the selected database, we structured the literature along with the different levels and stages of the BAO framework to construct a concept matrix. Three authors coded the literature independently and discussed the results to reach a common understanding. All publications from the database were selected to fit at least one characteristic of each dimension.

1.4.3 Phase 3: Analyze Literature

To analyze the coded literature, we conducted a table for each level of the BAO dimension. We synthesized and interpreted the results of the identified studies. This phase is essential for a literature review to identify directions for future research by formulating research questions (Webster & Watson, 2002). Since the micro- and macro-levels show the most distinct differences in the literature database, the results are presented for these levels.

1.5 Results

We identified 46 relevant papers that we further analyzed according to the attributes and links of the BAO framework through the literature review. Our review finds a significant differentiation between micro-level studies (18 studies), that include the micro-micro action link 2 and the micro-macro outcome links 3 and 3' and macro-level studies (28 studies) that include macro-micro links 1 and 1' as well as the macro-macro links 4, 5, 4' and 5'. Furthermore, most studies examine the action formation (40 studies, 17 on micro-level and 23 on macro-level), while fewer but equivalent studies focus on belief formation (30 studies, 4 on micro-level and 26 on macro-level) and outcome assessment (30 studies, 9 on micro-level and 21 on macro-level). Additionally, we unambiguously assigned the studies by research focus, differentiating between design studies (19 studies, 5 on micro-level and 14 on macro-level) and behavior studies (27 studies, 13 on micro-level and 14 on macro-level).In the following, we provide a more in-depth evaluation of the studies, separated by micro-level studies (Table 10) and macro-level studies (Table 11)

1.5.1 Micro-level Studies

Based on Table 10, we note that most micro-level studies address the individual level in combination with the influence of either the society level (four studies) or the organizational level (nine studies). However, four studies are restricted to the individual level. Regarding the formation level, the appropriation of studies is focused on the action formation (17 studies), while outcome assessment (nine studies) and belief formation (four studies) are seldomly addressed. Concerning the research focus, most studies consider behavioral aspects (13 studies), while only five studies address the design.

Some studies focused on action formation and the role of the individual. Such research promotes the design of online systems to enhance user engagement (Hansen et al., 2019; H. Hao et al., 2018), or analyzes the behavior of users, such as information use behavior of people with disabilities (Liang et al., 2017), communication in virtual health communities (Kordzadeh & Warren, 2017), or disease management behavior (Son et al., 2020). However, several studies combine such individual action with the belief formation encouraged by organizations. Online health communities and online health platform interventions thereby offer such research possibilities by user engagement and activity (Hur et al., 2019; Yan & Tan, 2017; X. Zhang et al., 2019). Similarly, Venkatesh, Bala, et al. (2016) address eHealth kiosks in India to raise individual awareness of infant care and change individual behavior.

While the beforementioned studies use an organizational study to form beliefs, our sample does not include a single study in which society aims to form individual health beliefs. Furthermore, action formation is also often combined with the outcome assessment. For example, van Laere & Aggestam (2016) investigate the so-called champion user's behavior in health IS and its impact on collective social interaction. Bao et al. (Bao et al., 2020) investigate the engagement of people with chronic diseases in digital patient portals and its influence on the frequency of hospital and emergency visits, readmission risk, and length of stay. While these two studies are examples of how individual behavior and action influence an organizational outcome, Venkatesh et al. (Venkatesh et al., 2020) develop a two-stage model that shows the impact of individual behavior on the village and hence the society in the context of eHealth kiosk. The societal outcome is also assessed by X. Liu et al. (2020), who derive contribution to public health practices based on individual engagement with health content in social media platforms.

Table 10: Concept Matrix - Micro-Level Studies

Paper	Outlet	Focus		Formation			Level			BAO Link
		Design	Behavior	Belief	Action	Outcome	Society	Organization	Individual	
(Hur et al., 2019)	EJIS		X	X	X			X	X	1'+2
(van Laere & Aggestam, 2016)	EJIS		X		X	X		X	X	2+3'
(X. Zhang et al., 2019)	EJIS		X	X	X			X	X	1'+2
(James et al., 2019)	ISJ		X		X	X		X	X	2+3'
(Hansen et al., 2019)	ISJ	X			X				X	2
(Bernardi & Exworthy, 2020)	ISJ		X		X	X		X	X	2+3'
(H. Hao et al., 2018)	ISR	X			X				X	2
(Khurana et al., 2019)	ISR		X		X	X	X		X	2+3
(Kordzadeh & Warren, 2017)	JAIS		X		X				X	2
(Liang et al., 2017)	JAIS		X		X				X	2
(Yan & Tan, 2017)	JMIS		X	X	X			X	X	1'+2
(Baird et al., 2017)	JMIS	X			X	X		X	X	2+3'
(Venkatesh, Rai, et al., 2016)	MISQ		X	X	X			X	X	1'+2
(K. Y. Huang et al., 2019)	MISQ		X		X	X	X		X	2+3
(Xiao Liu et al., 2020)	MISQ	X			X	X	X		X	2+3
(Son et al., 2020)	MISQ	X			X				X	2
(Bao et al., 2020)	MISQ		X		X	X		X	X	2+3'
(Venkatesh et al., 2020)	MISQ		X		X	X	X		X	2+3
Total (n=18)		**5**	**13**	**4**	**18**	**9**	**4**	**9**	**18**	

Overall, it is notable that studies on the micro-level show considerably limited interplay with the society level, while the interaction with specific organizations is well researched. Lastly, studies on the micro-level are limited in design focus. However, this is an important aspect, as the few existing studies emphasize.

1.5.2 Macro-level Studies

When looking at the distribution displayed in Table 11, we note an even distribution of studies regarding the focus on either design (14 studies) or behavior (14 studies). For the dimensions of formation, a similar even distribution is observed. Twenty-six studies consider belief formation, 23 studies address action formation and 21 studies on outcome assessment. Regarding the influence on either society or organizations, we note that most studies focus on organizational influence (20 studies), while only 14 studies assess influences on a societal level. Overall, nine studies connect to the micro-level. Seven studies connect the organizational and individual levels, while only two studies address the interplay of societal and micro-level.

In the context of aligning digital health and organizational structure, most studies consider the design aspects that form outcomes in the behavior of organizations. Overall, eight studies can be allotted to research that assesses the design focus on outcome formation in an organizational context. Three different lines of focus can be identified in this research. Firstly, some studies examine general conditions and challenges in the implementation process of IS in the health context, such as withholding of information and differing stakeholder interests (Pouloudi et al., 2016; Yaraghi et al., 2019). Subsequently, the second research focus pinpoints tangible scopes of the application of IS systems in the context of health (Lin et al., 2017), (Baird et al., 2017). Lin et al. (2019) use the data generated through electronic health records to derive health risk assessments for patients that can consider multiple possible adverse health events. Finally, the third line of research discloses the general effects of IS's implementation in the health context. Pinsonneault et al.(2017) examine the direct and indirect effects of health information technology on the quality of care as a central dimension of the entire health sector.

Research that can be allotted to the parameters "behavior," "outcome," and "organization," commonly focus on the effects of the usage of electronic health records. The effects that are assessed in this context are rather diverse. While Ayabakan et al. (2017)point out that waste can be reduced by avoiding the necessity of duplicate testing, Romanow, Rai, et al. (2018) evaluate how computerized order entry can benefit patient care teams in their coordination of patient care and to inform patients about their care. They find that the use of computerized order entry leads ultimately to improved patient satisfaction. Baird et al. (2017) evaluated electronic health record assimilation in 10 small physician practices in a similar vein.

Within the macro-level, the research aligning digital health and societal structure is primarily focused on the influence on the social system's behavior. Langtao Chen, Baird, and Straub (2019b) and Goh et al. (2016), conduct research regarding the effects of online health communities. While Langtao Chen et al. (2019b) emphasize the effect of online communities in the provision of social support, Goh et al. (2016) find that online communities create social value by overcoming rural-urban health disparities. Contrary to these studies, Thompson et al. (2020) focus their research on the economic effects through IT use in healthcare besides patient health outcomes and find that healthcare costs can be reduced through the use of IT in the context of chronic disease management. Bernardi, Sarker, and Sahay (2019) took a different viewpoint and uncovered the need for disruption of dysfunctional health information system routines embedded in institutions or deinstitutionalization for health IS to unfold their full potential in improving citizens' health in low and middle-income countries.

Table 11: Concept Matrix - Macro-Level Studies

		Focus		Formation			Level			
Paper	**Outlet**	Design	Behavior	Belief	Action	Outcome	Society	Organization	Individual	**BAO Link**
(Fox & Connolly, 2018)	ISJ	X		X				X		1'
(Mettler, 2018)	ISJ	X			X			X		4'
(Murungi et al., 2019)	ISJ		X		X			X		4'
(Demirezen et al., 2016)	ISR		X	X	X	X		X	X	3'+4'
(Adjerid et al., 2018)	ISR	X		X	X	X	X	X		4+5
(Lin et al., 2019)	ISR	X		X	X	X	X	X		4'+5'
(Hansen & Baroody, 2020)	ISR		X	X	X	X	X	X		4'+5'
(Pouloudi et al., 2016)	JAIS	X		X	X	X		X		4'
(Bernardi, 2017)	JAIS		X	X	X	X	X	X		4+5
(Dadgar & Joshi, 2018)	JAIS	X		X				X	X	1'
(Liwei Chen et al., 2019)	JAIS		X	X			X		X	1
(Dissanayake et al., 2019)	JAIS	X		X				X	X	1'
(Yaraghi et al., 2019)	JAIS	X		X				X	X	1'
(Findikoglu & Watson-Manheim, 2016)	JIT	X		X	X	X	X			5
(Klecun et al., 2019)	JIT	X		X	X	X	X	X		4+5
(Pinsonneault et al., 2017)	JMIS	X		X	X	X		X		4'
(Langtao Chen et al., 2019b)	JMIS		X	X	X	X	X			4
(Saifee et al., 2019)	JMIS		X	X	X	X		X		4'
(Goh et al., 2016)	MISQ		X	X	X	X	X			4
(Ganju et al., 2016)	MISQ		X	X	X	X	X			4
(Lin et al., 2017)	MISQ	X		X	X	X		X	X	4
(Ayabakan et al., 2017)	MISQ		X	X	X	X		X		4'
(Romanow, Rai, et al., 2018)	MISQ		X	X	X	X		X	X	3'+4'
(Bernardi et al., 2019)	MISQ	X		X	X	X	X			4
(Essén & Värlander, 2019)	MISQ		X	X	X	X	X	X		5'
(W. Zhang & Ram, 2020)	MISQ	X		X	X	X	X		X	3+4
(Q. Ben Liu et al., 2020)	MISQ		X	X	X	X		X	X	3'+4'
(Thompson et al., 2020)	MISQ		X	X	X	X	X			4
Total (n=28)		**14**	**14**	**26**	**23**	**21**	**14**	**20**	**9**	

Additional research at the macro-level focuses on outcomes at the organizational as well as the societal level. Research in this area is primarily concerned with the implementation of electronic health records. While Adjerid et al. (2018) argue that health records reduce medical care spending and frictions in information sharing, Klecun et al. (2019) pinpoint that forcing the introduction of such in a top-down approach thus exercising institutional pressure on medical professionals will yield negative outcomes rendering the benefits. In line with the research of Klecun et al. (2019), Findikoglu & Watson-Manheim (2016) find that the goal alignment between governments and medical professionals is critical for the success of electronic health records enabled transformations of healthcare services. Their research is focused on the link between societal beliefs and organizational outcomes. They conclude that healthcare goals on a societal level need to be linked to the system usage on an individual level to contribute to these goals; otherwise, they will lead to unintended negative health outcomes. This can only be done through the organizational context in which societal goals are embedded.

In contrast to the research above, Liwei Chen et al. (2019) research the influence of societal belief regarding health on the individuals' beliefs as they focus on uncovering what channels individuals prefer in the context of mHealth use to deduce insights for the design of m-health offers. Notably, most studies on the societal level take a country-specific perspective, as health ecosystems tend to differ strongly due to varying economic and political backgrounds.

1.6 Directions for Future Research

Our study aims at examining the current focus of health in IS research. In our literature review, we identified 46 relevant papers that were analyzed using the BAO framework. Our review reveals a lack of studies that analyze the interdependencies of the micro- and macro-level and design of health IS. In the following, we propose directions for future research based on our findings.

All studies analyzed addressed the outcome level only in combination with some links on the action level. It is noticeable that the papers mostly analyzed some form of action (e.g., champion behavior and its impact on the organization (van Laere & Aggestam, 2016)). However, we could not identify a single study that solely focused on the outcomes. For example, this could be addressed by an examination of various outcome types, such as social phenomena that drive adoption of health IS, or impact on society of mHealth applications in place. The publications of, Hansen and Baroody (2020), Klecun et al. (2019), and Adjerid et al. (2018) for example, cover all formation stages but leave out the consideration of the role of the individual. Therefore, we call future research to work on outcome investigations that isolate BAO link 3 and 3'. To summarize, we propose the following research question:

RQ 1: How can organizational and societal outcomes result from the use of health IS?

Our results have identified the organizational level as the dominant focus also in combination with the micro-level. In total, nine studies at the micro-level and 20 studies at the macro-level address the organizational level. However, it is noticeable that only a few studies examine the organizational level by setting the research focus on an IS design. Notably, at the interaction with the micro-level, there is a lack of studies. This raises the question of why the design focus is underrepresented in this context. Research in this area could examine specific design elements in mHealth apps, such as gamification features like rewards on the individual health course. Therefore, design studies are needed that address the design of an organization's health IS and analyze how this design influences the individual.

RQ 2: What design approaches are effective for developing health IS that influence individual beliefs and actions?

When looking at the societal perspective, research is commonly showing the positive impact of IS on health outcomes, especially in low- and middle-income countries. Moreover, researchers agree upon the necessity to align institutional and organizational goals (Klecun et al., 2019). However, research addressing the necessary structures to overcome such obstacles is lacking. For instance, the involvement of medical professionals in government institutions or possible direct communication channels between political decisionmakers and medical professionals is not addressed in research yet. Thus, we propose the following research question:

RQ 3: What institutional structures foster the adoption of digital health systems at the organizational level?

On the micro-level, we only identified four studies addressing belief formation. In comparison, we identified 26 studies on the macro-level. Our results indicate a need for further research in the field of belief formation, which also addresses the individual action formation at the micro-level. Until now, belief formation has solely focused on organizational and societal levels, largely ignoring the impact on the individual. However, such research is important because the macro perspective can influence individual action through belief formation. For example, Fox and Connolly (2018) have shown how mHealth applications can reduce costs for the healthcare system on the one hand and encourage patients to take a proactive approach on the other. Likewise, Dadgar and Joshi (2018) investigate how the design of digital health applications influences the self-management of diabetes patients.

RQ 4: Which opportunities and solutions can digital health offer to influence belief formation that affects individual action formation positively?

In our research, we were not able to identify any multi-level studies that investigated micro-level and macro-level in the categories of belief formation, action, and outcome assessment. As the considered studies do not address this complex interplay at full range, we encourage future research to employ more research in this area to address the complexity of information systems in healthcare entirely is not fully covered. If this research gap is not closed in the future, IS research will not meet its aspirations for interdisciplinarity.

RQ 5: How do multi-level interactions between macro- and micro-levels impact belief formation, action formation, and outcome assessment?

Our research reveals that the influence of institutional, societal, and organizational structures on individual health-related beliefs is strongly underrepresented in current research and should thus receive more attention, as beliefs are a powerful instrument in the process of long-term sustainable changes. Thus, we propose the following research question:

RQ 6: How do societal, institutional, and organizational structures influence individual actors' health-related behaviors and usage of digital health systems?

1.7 Concluding Remarks

The goal of this study was to analyze the current health agenda in IS research. Our study extended previous literature reviews in the health context by applying a structural framework to the research body of high raked studies. Furthermore, we contribute to research by showing that the BAO framework can be a relevant lens to shape and conduct digital health research. Lastly, our study is not free of limitations. Our results are limited to the selected outlets' scopes and keywords that we included in the search string. Future research should elaborate on our future research directions and research questions, and also apply for a broader scope of health research in IS conferences, other journals, and in interdisciplinary research outlets.

II. Research in the Global South

The previous section assessed the existing knowledge on health intervention research in the IS discipline and derives directions for future research. One of the resulting directions pinpoints the need of conducting design studies at the micro-level. Especially, the design science paradigm enhances the creation and evaluation of IT artifacts (e.g., mobile apps) by respecting technology proactively (Hevner, 2007). The research interest is on creating or changing artifacts to improve existing solutions to problems or perhaps providing new solutions to problems (Recker, 2021). Furthermore, the behavioral science research paradigm considers technology reactively, by explaining and predicting phenomena related to the use of such technologies (Arnott & Pervan, 2012). However, Hevner et al. (2004) argue to apply both paradigms.

Therefore, Study 2 is an ADR study that focuses on the design of one specific mHealth intervention with the objective of improving diabetes and hypertension prevalence in eSwatini. By building on empirical methods (e.g., interview, focus groups, meta-data analysis) the utility of the app is demonstrated and design principles provide the prescriptive knowledge of the instantiation of the broader problem domain of NCD prevention in decentralized healthcare systems (Gregor et al., 2020; Sein et al., 2011).

In contrast, Study 3 follows the quantitative research approach, which investigates the culturally sensitive perception of security challenges of mHealth. The study takes the mHealth technology as "given". Based on the reactive role of technology, the study explains people's response to the design of the announcement of a data breach in which personal health information is breached from an mHealth device (e.g., a fitness tracker). It is a cross-cultural comparative study that investigated German and Bolivian user responses based on cultural dimensions.

1. Study 2: Fostering NCD Prevention in The Global South

Table 12: Fact Sheet of Study 2

Title	Fostering Non-Communicable Disease Prevention in The Global South: An Action Design Research Project of a Mobile Health Intervention in eSwatini
Authors	Alfred-Benedikt Brendel[a], Maike Greve[b], Sascha Lichtenberg[a], Lutz M. Kolbe[b] [a]Chair of Business Information Systems, esp. Intelligent Systems and Services, TU Dresden, Helmholtzstraße 10, 01069 Dresden [b]Chair of Information Management, University of Goettingen, Humboldtallee 3, 37073 Göttingen
Outlet	Under Review in the European Journal of Information Systems (VHB A) Previous version published at ECIS 2020 (VHB B) Previously received valuable feedback in the Revision (2nd round) at the Information Systems Journal (VHB A)
Abstract	Typically, low- and middle-income countries, such as eSwatini, employ community health workers (CHWs) to provide primary healthcare education at the community level. Shifting healthcare-related tasks to CHWs as a solution to substitute for weak healthcare infrastructure raises specific issues that arise from the CHWs' lack of experience and limited access to education. For instance, providing non-communicable disease (NCD) diagnosis care requires medical equipment and long-term surveillance, whereas NCD prevalence can be offered through individualized recommendations based on simple health measures and frequent monitory and, thus, with some support, are suitable for the scope of activities of CHWs. This study addresses the implementation of a mobile application as a supportive tool for CHWs in their daily NCD prevention education and counseling in eSwatini. Through an action design research approach, the application is iteratively developed based on the evaluations with healthcare experts, policymakers (e.g., the Ministry of Health), and CHWs. This study provides insights on the design of a mobile health intervention that supports the health counseling by the CHWs. This paper further provides generalized knowledge on how to design applications in other instances of NCD care in the Global South with decentralized healthcare systems via the inductively developed set of three design principles
Keywords	Mobile Health, Non-Communicable Diseases, Decentralized Healthcare, Low-and Middle-Income Countries, Action Design Research

1.1 Introduction

The sustainable development goal (SDG) of the United Nations regarding "Good health and Well-being," addresses the detailed target to reduce premature mortality from non-communicable diseases (NCDs) through prevention and treatment (UN, 2015). Prevention and risk reduction strategies of NCDs are dependent on non-modifiable factors, such as age, gender, ethnicity, and genetics, but are also highly dependent on people's lifestyles (Peiris et al., 2014), which includes modifiable factors, such as smoking and alcohol intake, as well as lack of exercise and unhealthy diets (Bukelo et al., 2015).

Since the SDGs are intended to secure sustainable development at the economic, social as well as environmental levels worldwide and thus designate real contemporary problems, they are a solid guide for problem-oriented research that aims to take responsibility and strive for a better world, by addressing such problems with their studies (Howard-Grenville et al., 2019). In the context of NCD prevention, most prominently, digital interventions including information communication technology (ICT) have shown the potential to promote behavior change by tailored health education (Briscoe & Aboud, 2012). Although these digitally enabled solutions have been introduced in industrialized countries, low- and middle-income countries (LMIC) have yet to be engaged to the same extent (WHO, 2011).

In many LMICs, the healthcare system is "decentralized," meaning that many primary health services are shifted from the few scarce hospitals and doctors to smaller healthcare facilities, such as clinics. Due to a severe lack of physicians and nurses in such clinics, health-related counseling has shifted to community health workers (CHWs). Such counseling includes education about key infectious disease prevention and hygiene standards. Overall, governments increasingly see CHWs as a key means of providing access to care to basic primary healthcare services (Geldsetzer et al., 2017). However, the CHW cadre generally lacks knowledge of NCD risk factors and prevention, even though the number of people affected by NCDs is rising (Bukelo et al., 2015).

Hence, decentralized healthcare in the Global South requires support to overcome the burden of NCDs. Against this background, the following research questions are proposed in this paper: *How can an ICT be designed to support NCD prevention in decentralized healthcare in the Global South?*

To answer these questions, we followed an iterative action design research (ADR) approach (Sein et al., 2011), enabling us to solve a relevant generalizable problem during the research project. Subsequently, we derived a solution for the health system in eSwatini[11] and contribute to the country's desire for health equity by providing NCD prevention at the community level. Specifically, we developed mobile health (mHealth) application (app) that supports the counseling process of the CHWs by, for instance, providing personalized information material based on the client's data and additionally reduces the variability in the quality of care between health workers. Thereby, CHWs address the prevention of NCDs through their individualized support and counseling. In the end, 18 CHWs tested the app for 2 months, using the app for overall 1500 hours and providing digitized NCD prevention counseling to 793 citizens of eSwatini.

During the research project, we actively supported and included the perspective of CHWs, clients, health organizations, and policymakers (e.g., Ministry of Health). Our ADR project also contributed to research by systematically formulating prescriptive knowledge on how such solutions should be designed to be effective and efficient (Haj-Bolouri et al., 2018; Iivari, 2015). In this regard, our study provides design principles (DPs) (Gregor et al., 2020; Iivari, 2015) for the problem of decentralized NCD prevention in the Global South. We provided evidence for researchers in the field of mHealth and ICT for development (ICT4D) on the use of mHealth apps to support decentralized healthcare and how CHWs and clients will react to the changes in their care procedures. In summary, this research approach provides a blueprint for the development of ICT tools to strengthen primary care for NCDs in LMICs and, thus, makes a research contribution by demonstrating how a novel artifact, where the sphere of influence is not just the hardware-software bundle but also all actors and the authentic environment surrounding its use (Purao et al., 2013), helps to make the world a better place concerning one particular target of the SDGs.

1.2 Background

In recent years, NCDs have shown an increasing impact on the health status of the population worldwide, with disproportionately high rates in the Global South (Islam et al., 2014). The World Health Assembly has adopted a range of global targets in the prevention and treatment of NCDs (WHO (World Health Organization), 2013). One possible solution lies in the advent of mobile apps, which are expected to spread worldwide (Fei Liu et al., 2018), making the technology ubiquitous for almost everyone in the world, both in private and professional life (Walsham, 2012). Even in low-income regions of the world, people have begun to engage in ICT, primarily through the rapid expansion of ownership and the use of mobile phones and tablets (Latif et al., 2017). This potential should mainly be exploited in such a vital area as healthcare (Braa et al., 2007). To provide a baseline

[11] The Kingdom of eSwatini is a landlocked country in South Africa. It is formerly known as Swaziland, as it was officially renamed in 2018. eSwatini means „Land of the Swazis" in the local language „siSwati". The lower-case „e" is a locative prefix that expresses something like "in" or "at" in many South African languages. The main root of a word is what gets capitalized, even if it's not the first letter.

for our research project, the following sections offer a brief introduction to the decentralized healthcare in countries of the Global South, particularly regarding NCDs, before introducing the ICT4D research discipline and mHealth research for development.

1.2.1 Decentralized Healthcare in the Global South

In the last 40 years, several LMICs started to decentralize their healthcare system (Cobos Muñoz et al., 2017; Senkubuge et al., 2014). Especially in rural areas, there is a significant shortage of physicians and nurses that decentralization aims to compensate for by shifting tasks from hospitals and physician-led facilities to CHWs (Singh & Sachs, 2013). The CHWs perform diverse health-related delivery functions, although not having a formal professional or paraprofessional tertiary education but usually short job-related training (Lewin et al., 2005). The goal is to increase the overall population's access to essential health services (World Health Organization, 2006). Research shows that decentralization strengthens the healthcare system in the developing world, generates more resources for health, and increases access to healthcare services which results in overall equity in health provision (Cobos Muñoz et al., 2017; Kruk et al., 2010).

In the context of LMICs, for instance, most African health systems have evolved to focus on the treatment of acute and infectious diseases rather than NCDs (Gale, 2006; Whiting et al., 2003). Therefore, CHWs are generally first trained on such diseases, for instance for the successful dispersion of HIV treatments (De Neve et al., 2017; Geldsetzer et al., 2017). As a result, the need for treatment and prevention of NCDs is often unmet. For example, most sub-Saharan health systems fail to identify the majority of diabetes patients because only a third of all people with diabetes recalled their diabetes diagnoses, and only one-third reported having received treatment (Manne-Goehler et al., 2016). However, NCDs are the cause of death for over 41 million people a year, which corresponds to 71% of all deaths globally (WHO, 2018). LMICs, in particular, show a high premature death rate (between 30 and 69 years) due to NCDs (Islam et al., 2014). Despite the general approaches for decentralization, service delivery for NCDs mostly concentrates on hospitals in large cities, and health systems in sub-Saharan Africa are rarely able to deliver the continuous service required to identify and treat patients adequately (Rabkin et al., 2012; Whiting et al., 2003). Given the unusually low density of hospitals (Ouma et al., 2018), hypertension and diabetes care are practically inaccessible for African people. It is desired to extend the prevention and treatment of NCDs via CHWs (Gale, 2006).

1.2.2 The ICT4D Research Agenda

In research and practice, the term ICT4D is used to explore and apply the role and use of ICT in improving the well-being of nations (Ganju et al., 2016). The World Bank reported that between 1997 and 2007, more than 37 billion US dollars were invested in ICT4D projects worldwide (World Bank. 2012). Nevertheless, the sustainable use of such technologies is often not achieved (Chipidza & Leidner, 2017). This is attributed to a lack of understanding of the various underlying perspectives and contextual differences (Avgerou 2008). The use of ICT is also critically questioned in research. Walsham (2012) raised the provocative question: "Are we creating a better world with ICT?" His call seeks for research that explores the use and implementation of technologies that can effectively contribute to the improvement of the individual life, community life, and the world as a fundamental vision of making our world a little better (Díaz Andrade et al., 2019).

The fields of application for such research are diverse and range from the study of ICT for economic opportunities (e.g., Hatakka et al., 2020), to capacity building (e.g., Heeks & Ospina, 2019), or agricultural enhancement (e.g., Vaidya & Myers, 2020). A concrete application context of ICT4D projects is the health sector, which receives special needs and attention in the context of development through the SDG (Howard-Grenville et al., 2019; Rothe, 2020). On a global level, the introduction of digitization and particularly the integration of ICT in healthcare systems aims, for example, to reduce costs and outages, seamlessly integrate customer data, and enable more efficient and effective healthcare (Gastaldi & Corso, 2012). The purpose is to contribute to long-term solutions to the problems of demographic change (Lozano et al., 2018), generational equity (George et al., 2018), and the shortage of skilled workers (Ditsa & Ojo, 2011). In the development context, however, implementation presents many challenges due to the complex interaction of various actors in the healthcare sector, so that an ICT solution cannot be viewed in isolation but must be integrated into the overall healthcare system (Peiris et al., 2014).

ICT4D research deals with precisely these problems. Hence, the local context and regional conditions, as well as the available resources, must be taken into account to effectively manage, scale, disseminate, and sustainably support the implementation and use of health-related ICT (Venkatesh, Bala, et al., 2016). Latif et al. (2017) summarize this as three global challenges that hinder the growth of health-related ICT in countries of the Global South: insufficient health literacy, cultural barriers, and lack of infrastructure. To address these challenges, the focus should be on human-centric design, improved health education, and strategic planning (Latif et al., 2017).

1.2.3 Mobile Health for Development

Research has shown that, in particular, mHealth supports the reach for health equity by overcoming geographical, temporal, structural, and organizational barriers to the supply and uptake of healthcare services (Latif et al., 2017; Martínez-Pérez et al., 2013; Motamarri et al., 2014). It is emphasized the development of such digital solutions is particularly suitable for the CHW user group (Early et al., 2019). In general, mHealth can strengthen the existing medical care through wireless infrastructure and reduce temporal, structural, and spatial constraints (Fei Liu et al., 2018; Yang & Varshney, 2016). Due to the wide dissemination of smartphones and their functionalities, mHealth apps are highly accessible and can directly provide a multitude of services and knowledge for individuals (Baird et al., 2018). For instance, previous research has shown that the usage of mobile technologies improves health education, health behaviors, and patients' adherence to treatments (Burton et al., 2007; Fjeldsoe et al., 2009; Lim et al., 2008).

An opportunity to improve the mentioned issues related to the target group of CHWs and NCD prevention is the ongoing dissemination of new mHealth technologies (Braa et al., 2007). Previous research has provided insight into various aspects of ICTs and their contribution to broader access to healthcare services (Hailemariam et al., 2010). One prominent example is the mHealth tool for CHWs to enhance communication with doctors via text messaging that is applied in Malawi. The intervention saved working time and net costs, as well as doubled the capacity of the tuberculosis treatment (Mahmud et al., 2010). Additionally, it catalyzes the provision of health knowledge and basic healthcare, which is particularly helpful in the context of countries with large rural areas (Tariq & Akter, 2011). However, specific challenges also arise for mHealth in the development context. Some of these issues can be transferred to the design of mHealth. Praveen et al. (2014) describe a specific mHealth tool for cardiovascular disease treatment in India. They determine that the design has to be optimized and tailored to its users. In their case, these optimizations entailed a simplification of the user interface, correct language font installation, and increased emphasis on the use of color for communicating risk to the patients. Lastly, Holeman & Barrett (2017) allude to the metaphor of imbrication and bacterial "back talk" to illustrate the entanglement of ICT development and context in ICT4D projects. Their mHealth study results in six overlapping activities through which designers may guide the emergence of socio-material practices, including implementation of a prototype, experience of practice breakdowns, and ongoing performance of new practices. Thus, current research provides a rich background for the development of mHealth apps to support CHWs in preventing NCDs but lacks specific knowledge on how the app should be designed to reach high effectiveness, efficiency, and impact.

1.3 Guiding Research Framework

Because research emphasizes the relevance of tailoring the design of the ICT to context and target user group (Holeman & Barrett, 2017; Peiris et al., 2014; Praveen et al., 2014), we guide the development of an ICT for NCD prevention in LMIC upon a guiding framework to structure our thinking and the development and evaluation process (Gregor & Hevner, 2013). This guiding framework is considered a fundamental part of our project's knowledge base (Hevner et al., 2004). Explicitly, we draw on the information systems (IS) success model of DeLone and McLean (1992, 2003), which has its origin in the structured consolidation of past contributions on system impact and success in IS research. The model aims to capture the critical influences on the success of IS in practice and the interrelationships between them. It thereby explains the process from quality-driven components to actual use and, further, to the overall net benefits of the system (DeLone & McLean, 2003). Besides, the model has already shown its potential in the context of health IS, being successfully applied several times (Hossain, 2016; Liang & Xue, 2013). Overall, the IS success model provides us with a guiding framework to structure the design process and evaluate the developed ICT tool, focusing our research project on factors influencing usage, satisfaction, and net benefits.

The IS success model includes three quality components that specifically address the system, the information, and the service. A system's design needs to address information, system, and service quality to be effective and efficient. In the context of evaluation, the operationalization of these three quality components includes a wide range of measurements, which highly depend on the object of investigation. *Information quality* refers mainly to the degree to which individuals believe that the obtained information through the IS is of high quality (Liang et al., 2017). In the context of an NCD prevention mHealth tool for CHW in LMIC, measures, such as usability of the app's content, personalization of prevention content of clients health condition, and accuracy of health information are relevant in the association of information quality (DeLone & McLean, 2003; Liang et al., 2017; Motamarri et al., 2014; San Nicolas-Rocca et al., 2014). The *system quality* incorporates the information system aspects, such as system accessibility, and usability (DeLone & McLean, 2003; San Nicolas-Rocca et al., 2014). In the context of LMIC and a target group with limited technical experience, usability has to be specifically tailored to the user ability. Lastly, *service quality* addresses aspects, such as responsiveness and assurance (Jiang et al., 2002). In the context of service quality, the infrastructure of LMIC has to be considered where CHWs require a portable tool with stable functionality, particularly in rural areas.

All of the quality characteristics affect the actual use, intention to use the system, and user satisfaction with the system (DeLone & McLean, 2003). Resulting from the use, certain net benefits are achieved that additionally influence user satisfaction and further affect the use of the system. The *net benefits* correspond to the overall impact of the mHealth intervention. It captures the balance of the positive and negative effects of the information system on users, organizations, economies, and even society (DeLone & McLean, 2003). In the health context of NCD prevention in LMIC, aspects, such as an increase of health education and care of clients, standardized educational work of CHWs, and the general support of the health system imply a successful intervention (Liang et al., 2017). Table 13 provides an overview of the assessment criteria along the dimensions of the IS success model (DeLone & McLean, 2002, 2003).

Table 13: Assessment Criteria

Guided by the IS Success Model (DeLone & McLean, 2002, 2003)

IS Success Model	Construct	Source
System Quality	Accessibility Usability	(Liang et al., 2017) (San Nicolas-Rocca et al., 2014)
Information Quality	Ease of Understanding Accuracy Personalization	(San Nicolas-Rocca et al., 2014) (Motamarri et al., 2014) (San Nicolas-Rocca et al., 2014)
Service Quality	Assurance Responsiveness	(DeLone & McLean, 2003) (DeLone & McLean, 2003)
Use	Navigation Patterns Time on Pages in App	(Liang et al., 2017) (Motamarri et al., 2014)
User Satisfaction	Perceived Ease of Use Perceived Usefulness	(Davis, 1989) (Davis, 1989)
Net Benefits	Number of Client Treatments (Work efficiency) Counselling Time (Time efficiency) Perceived Quality of Care	(Yusof et al., 2006) (Yusof et al., 2006) (Buntin et al., 2011)

1.4 NCD Prevention in Decentralized Healthcare: The Case of eSwatini

The country of eSwatini has a particularly high prevalence of NCDs, especially diabetes and hypertension, compared to other countries in sub-Sahara Africa. A quarter of Swazis, aged 15–69 years, have hypertension, and almost one fifth is living with diabetes or pre-diabetes (WHO, 2019). The growing number of NCD patients is exceeding the capacity of the health system in eSwatini. Similar to many other countries in sub-Saharan Africa, eSwatini provides service delivery for NCDs through physician-led teams in hospitals. This provision further intensifies the situation because the country has a particularly low density of hospitals—only 6.1% of its inhabitants reside within two hours of travel time to the nearest hospital (Ouma et al., 2018)—which makes hypertension and diabetes care practically inaccessible for most Swazis. However, the government is eager to address this topic. They developed the National NCDs Policy to address the issue and reduce premature death due to NCDs after the third United Nations high-level meeting on NCDs in 2018. Its key component is to strengthen the primary healthcare system with the expansion and professionalization of the CHW program.

The government supports over 5000 CHWs nationwide, forming the major backbone of the community level of health service delivery in eSwatini. The so-called Rural Health Motivators (RHM) Program[12] is a community-based healthcare volunteer program to fa-

[12] The RHM program was established in 1976 by the Ministry of Health. To ensure participation and ownership of the community, RHMs are chosen by traditional community leaders and trained by the Ministry of Health. RHMs are active in all of the 59 Tinkhundla (districts) of eSwatini, ensuring full penetration of service delivery in all communities including traditionally under-served and hard to reach areas. The RHM Program is directly managed by the Eswatini Government through the Ministry of Health and funded entirely from domestic resources. RHMs are a non-salaried and non-specialist cadre. 53% of RHMs are over the age of 55, and 94% are female.

cilitate the extension of health promotion services to the communities through interpersonal communication. The current service package focuses on primary health promotion messaging for sexual and reproductive health, nutrition, and child health.

However, caring for or preventing NCDs exceeds the current level of care that the RHMs provide. The experience of successful large-scale antiretroviral treatment, which is now mostly provided by nurses through public-sector, primary care clinics, has encouraged the Swazi Ministry of Health to consider primary care-based approaches for diabetes and hypertension screening, diagnosis, treatment, and care. A recent feasibility pilot in the Lubombo region of eSwatini (Sharp et al., 2020) has further strengthened the commitment of the Swazi Ministry of Health to establish primary care- and community-based approaches to decentralize NCD (particularly diabetes and hypertension) care nationwide. Whereas the clinics need to be equipped with NCD medication, and the nurses must be trained for NCD treatment, there is a high potential of including the RHMs into the scaling of the NCD prevention. Therefore, the government desired to have an ICT developed for a high-performing and sustainable approach to supporting NCD counseling of the RHMs at the clients' homes, serving as a blueprint project for other countries.

Some research papers have investigated the country's health system related to the research context. For example, medical studies on the risk assessment study of HIV (Berner-Rodoreda et al., 2020), risk assessment of cardiovascular diseases (Palma et al., 2018), technology-centered studies on the ICT policy of the country (Metfula & Chigona, 2014), and a pilot study on using no-cost mobile phone reminders for HIV testing (Kliner et al., 2013).

1.5 Research Approach

Our research follows the ADR framework of Sein et al. (2011) (see Figure 9), which focuses on the building, intervention, and evaluation of an artifact, resulting in the attempt to generalize the gathered knowledge inductively (see Figure 10). It explicitly recognizes the emergence of artifacts at the intersection of technology and local practices, addressing practical impact and contribution to research. In this context, we follow the definition of an artifact by Lee et al. (2015) that emphasizes the interplay of a technology artifact (e.g., a mobile app), information artifact (e.g., NCD prevention information), and social artifact (e.g., a relationship between the health worker and client) to form an IS artifact. Following Iivari (2017), this notion of the IS artifact is valuable for action research-oriented design science research (e.g., ADR).

Research following the ADR methodology is considered to be a genre of design science research (DSR) that focuses on designing practice-inspired artifacts (Peffers et al., 2018) by combining the two established research paradigms of DSR (Hevner et al., 2004) and action research (Davison et al., 2004; Mansell, 1991). By aiming for practical problem-solving and theoretical reflection of the design problem, the approach is viable for studying the design of sociotechnical systems in the healthcare sector (e.g., Mettler, 2018; Sherer, 2014). Generally, the approach is applied to develop artifacts that solve "wicked" problems (i.e., problems without a final formulation and associated with conflicting perspectives), ultimately making it uncertain whether a solution can even be found (R. W. Gregory & Muntermann, 2014; Hevner et al., 2004). The notion of an ensemble artifact considers the IT artifact not merely as a technical tool, but as a dynamic ensemble that carries traces of the organizational and social domain, inscribes by all parties involved in its design and use (Purao et al., 2013).

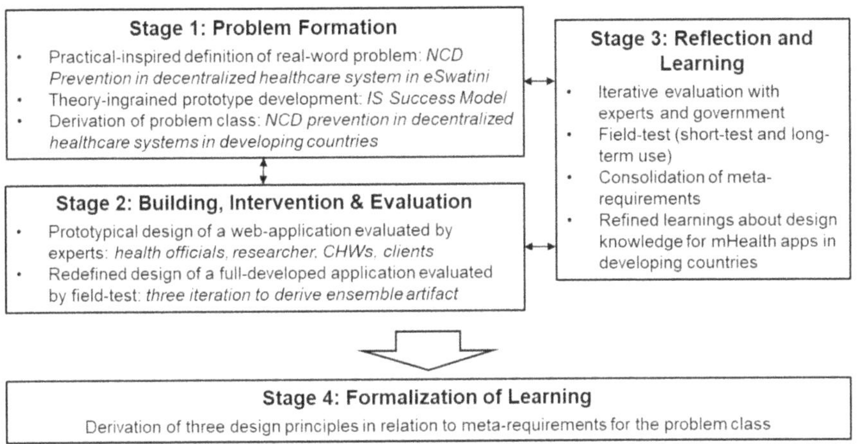

Figure 9: Applied Research Process

1.5.1 Stage 1: Problem Formulation

In the problem formulation, we defined the practice-inspired problem as a basis for the formulation of a research opportunity. Furthermore, relevant knowledge bases are consulted regarding available technologies, preset research results, and existing theories, which can be leveraged in the development and evaluation process to design a theory-ingrained artifact (Hevner et al., 2004; Sein et al., 2011).

Tackling the research opportunity of supporting NCD prevention through ICT for CHWs in LMICs, we addressed the research literature and consolidated interdisciplinary experts. Furthermore, the literature underlines the importance of multidisciplinary research as well as governmental support to ensure the sustainability of the project (Holeman et al., 2018; Tariq & Akter, 2011; Whidden et al., 2018). The country of eSwatini was selected to consider a specific use case that allows us to derive transferable knowledge, which can serve as a blueprint for other instances. The research team consists of a project consortium funded by the European Commission (Horizon 2020), with each partner having a specific role and work responsibility, where all strive for a situational implementation that specifically addresses the situation and needs of the specific situation in a country.

With the focus of designing an mHealth intervention, the IS success model (DeLone & McLean, 2002, 2003) was selected as a guiding framework (see Section 3) for the development of a theory-engrained artifact (Sein et al., 2011). This approach copes with the interacting nature of design and evaluation of the ADR method, where the quality measures and net benefits of the artifact are considered in every development phase.

1.5.2 Stage 2: Building, Intervention & Evaluation

In the building, intervention, and evaluation stage (Sein et al., 2011), we build the mHealth app, apply it to intervene in the health system in eSwatini, and continually evaluate the design of the app and the effects of the intervention. In total, we followed a three-stage iterative process that includes the initial development and repeated adjustment of the app's design. The process is visualized in Figure 10. A description of selected interview partners can be found in the Appendix A. Further methodological details are depicted in Appendix B.

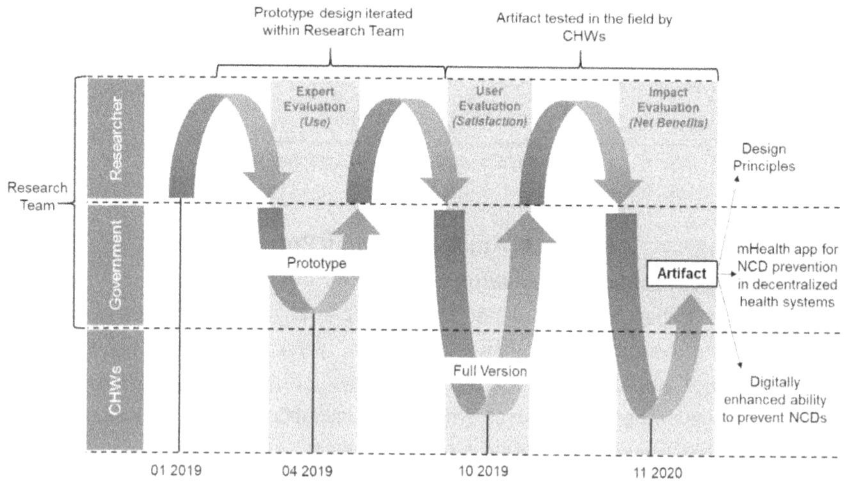

Figure 10: Building, Intervention, and Evaluation of mHealth App

During the first iteration, the prototype is developed and "formatively" evaluated. The assessment focused on evaluating potential app usage. The aim was to generate insight into user interface navigation patterns, usage time, and other related aspects. We received formal feedback through qualitative online feedback and written unstructured feedback via mail by local and research partners and conducted group discussions with research associates (see Appendix B). The second iteration addresses the evaluation results of the first iteration. Close collaboration between the implementing partners, government, and the developing team helped to guide the process along. The revised app was evaluated by a field test to determine actual usage and assess user satisfaction (see Appendix B). In the third iteration, we summarized the results of the field evaluation and made minor adjustments to the app design over three months. After the revision, the app was rolled out in the field and was used by 18 CHWs in their daily work routine for two months. The final evaluation of the long-term use and realized net benefits of the intervention was conducted via analyzing logged data and qualitative interviews (see Appendix B).

1.5.3 Stage 3: Reflection and Learning

Sein et al. (2011) emphasize that conscious and constant reflection on the problem and the evolving artifact are necessary to generate knowledge and learning. Thus, during the iterative process of stage 2, we continuously reflected on our work and inductively derived lessons learned and best practices. Furthermore, we iteratively formalized and revised a set of meta-requirements (MRs) that summarize the gained understanding of the problem.

1.5.4 Stage 4: Formalization of Learning

In the final stage, the acquired knowledge regarding the artifact design was further formalized and generalized. We followed an inductive theorizing approach (R. W. Gregory & Muntermann, 2014; Iivari, 2015) to derive DPs (Gregor et al., 2020), encapsulating the actionable and prescriptive knowledge of how to design an mHealth app for decentralized healthcare systems of LMICs. To be specific, after each iteration, the following two steps were completed. First, we formulated (first iteration) or reviewed (second and third iteration) previously formulated DPs, evaluating the need for refinement based on the newly gathered insights and match to the MRs. Second, if refinement was deemed necessary, we iteratively adapted the DPs accordingly to the newly gathered insights until all new knowledge was incorporated. As a result, we were able to generalize three DPs that gathered the specific insights into the problem instance of healthcare in eSwatini to apply to the problem class of NCD prevention in decentralized healthcare in LMICs.

1.6 Results of the ADR Process of Designing an mHealth App

1.6.1 Defining the Research Opportunity

Developing an ICT to support NCD prevention in decentralized healthcare in the Global South can be considered a wicked problem because it has yet to be addressed by research and promises the support of the healthcare infrastructure. Some characteristics of the wickedness include i) generally, LMICs suffer from the burden of NCDs (Atun et al., 2018); ii) CHWs are not trained to diagnose NCDs and cannot easily be trained due to a deficiency of education and medical equipment; iii) CHWs lack technical experience, and some are illiterate (Lewin et al., 2005). Hence, a research problem is given that demands repeated interventions in local structures to gain a deep understanding of the artifact-context relationship (Sein et al., 2011), which is required to develop a socio-technical design agenda for the general requirement of NCD care in decentralized health systems in the Global South. Overall, there is a general problem class of preventing NCDs in countries of the Global South that have a decentralized health system.

We assembled a research team that is both interested in the specific practical solution for eSwatini (including local government and organizations) but also aims to generate transferable knowledge and learning (local and international multidisciplinary research partners). As Figure 11 shows, the research teams existed of a local task force that worked in-country, including the health workers, an implanting organization, the government representatives, as well as local research who closely collaborated with the government and the implementing organization. To expand the multidisciplinary team, international research submissions are among them. While the authors as IS researchers design the artifact, the other disciplines focus on health outcomes, as well as medical and health content for NCD prevention.

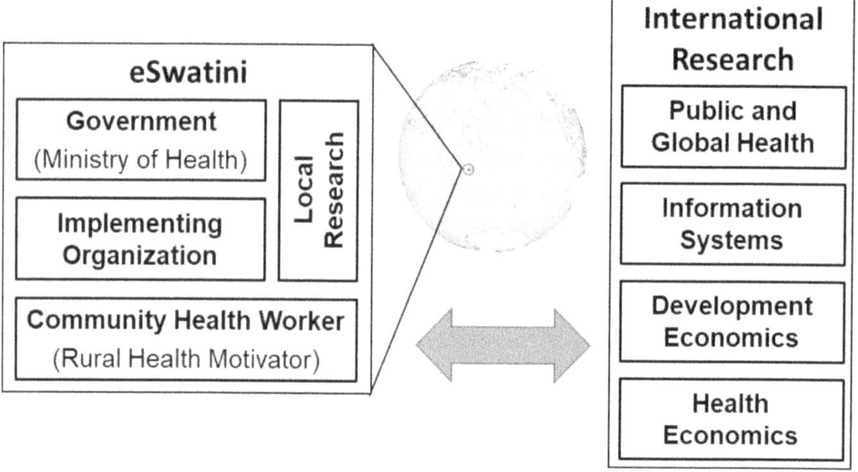

Figure 11: Research Team

We discussed the contextual background regarding the country, the health system within the country, and the general NCD health status in the area with all involved partners (e.g., government from eSwatini, research partners of public health). All partners expect an ICT tool in the form of a mobile app to be an effective and efficient solution because it provides a place and time-independent access to necessary NCD prevention-related functions (e.g., accessing risk factors and levels) and information (e.g., on preventive measures, such as healthy eating) (Holeman et al., 2018; Tariq & Akter, 2011; Whidden et al., 2018), which is what CHWs need during their routine visits to clients at their respective homes.

In close collaboration with the Ministry of Health of eSwatini and external governance committees composed of local and global stakeholders, we (IS researchers) jointly collected the initial requirements to develop a prototype for the situated problem of designing an mHealth app to be used by the governmental-deployed CHWs.

1.6.2 Designing the mHealth App

In the following, we will summarize the results of each research iteration.

1.6.2.1 First Iteration

The research team followed the current and common conventions on app development and used a hybrid app development framework that utilizes web developing functionalities and standards and enables device and operating system independence. This decision was made based on an initial assessment that the mobile infrastructure of CHWs will be heterogeneous (including various devices and operating systems as well as versions of operating systems).

The selection, structure, and implementation of the app functions were guided by the quality components of the IS success model. Content-wise, the research team decided to focus on four major functions: First, a setup of a client profile including demographics and medical information. Second, a personalized NCD risk calculation for the client based on the entered information. Third, a schedule function where the RHM could set appointments for the next house visit with the client. Fourth, the integration of a navigation tool that showed the way to the next client on a map.

In the context of information quality, personalization was addressed to provide a tailored-counseling process based on the client's health data. Concerning system quality, the usability and adaptability for users were considered essential to ensure that CHWs could easily use the app, ensuring continuous usage. Because many of the CHWs have little experience with mobile devices and apps, the specific emphasis lies on the usability and accessibility of the graphical user interface. Regarding service quality, for the prototype, no specific requirements were identified at this stage. The screenshots in Figure 12 show the prototype's design. The app was tested by experts and evaluated with a focus on its potential usage by CHWs.

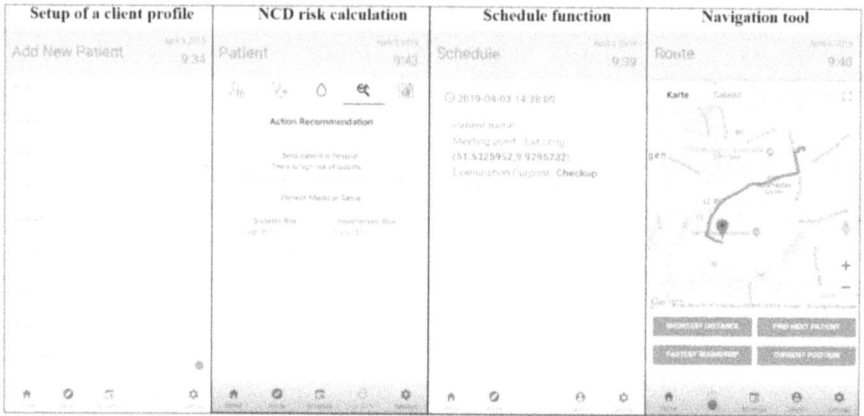

Figure 12: Screenshots of the Prototype (First Iteration)

Regarding the functionality, the evaluation posed the removal of the route planning and the adding of a medical history and informational videos. The problematic aspects of the route planning are: (1) rural areas that do not have many "mapped" roads; (2) the CHWs are not used to maps, and (3) navigation takes battery and internet capacity:

> *"The health worker probably knows the fastest way, and sometimes this is not on a road because they are closed due to heavy rain or anything" (Expert 7)*
>
> *"I'm not sure if the map functionality will work well for rural. Map literacy is an important aspect." (Expert 11)*
>
> *"The route planning only works with an internet connection." (Expert 13)*

The partners from medical research suggested adding a medical history, as the risk calculation should always be based on the most recent data. This statement was also emphasized by others, as a medical history would provide time-series health data of the client that could indicate behavioral changes.

> *"It would be a great motivation if people could track the data " (Expert 1)*

Furthermore, the function presenting videos regarding NCD prevention was added. Culturally appropriate videos that explained the risks of NCDs regarding gender were developed for the specific context and included in the app so that the CHWs can show the clients. The idea of including videos went along with the suggestions by partners to add further information material:

> *"It would be great to add some pictures to show the client about the risks of NCDs [...] this way, the client will better remember." (Expert 2)*

A minor concern that was pointed out several times by the experts was the need for an email address for the sign-up and login of the CHWs. The government representative confirmed that a username or ID would be better because it cannot be expected that the CHWs have an email address.

"It's likely that a health worker does not have an email address. Would it be possible to limit the login to name& password?" (Expert 6)

Regarding the design of the app, experts noted that the usability should be "simplified" and be provided in English and the local language—siSwati. Further feedback concerned the low literacy rates among the target user group:

> *"We should discuss ways to make the app more intuitive. And also how we could adapt it for RHMs with low literacy (which symbols could be used where, which text can be substituted by symbols etc.)." (Expert 4)*

Thus, wherever possible, icons were used instead of text to make the app more accessible for the CHWs. Nevertheless, when considering the choice of icons, local partners from eSwatini mentioned that the icons are "too abstract". One example was the pin as an icon for "location", which was misleading because many people are not familiar with the idea of a pin on a map. Furthermore, Expert 8 suggested inserting buttons on the landing page that guided to the main pages of the app rather than using the small tab bar at the bottom of each page.

"We should discuss how we could adapt the app for health workers with low literacy. Easy symbols could be used and text can be substituted by symbols." (Expert 9)

Lastly, we discussed with the in-country partners and the government of eSwatini that the data generated by the app should not be stored online or on a server out of the country for data security reasons but be stored on a server owned by the government.

1.6.2.2 Second Iteration

Based on the results of the evaluation, the initial requirements were revised and adjusted. Similarly, the functions and interfaces of the app were improved. This included a medical history, an information tab with information material and videos to enhance information quality. A button to switch language was added and icons were used instead of text, wherever possible. Furthermore, the icons were selected to be interpretable in the local context. The cultural awareness also had to be accounted for the security requirement (replacing email by username for login). Additionally, three main buttons on the landing page (home tab) were added for a simplified navigating of the app. Regarding the service quality, the partners required a local in-country solution, where data is only stored within the country. Therefore, the changes caused a substantial redesign of the backend, switching over from a externally hosted cloud service to a self-managed local server structure. Figure 13 shows the screenshots of the fully re-designed app version.

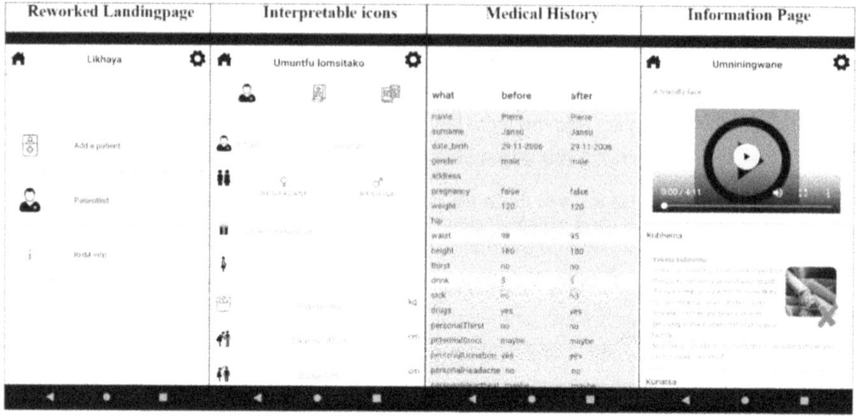

Figure 13: Screenshots of the App (Second Iteration)

This version was tested by the RHMs. The authors observed the behavior and their intuitive usage of the app. The user satisfaction assessment drove the evaluation.

Overall, RHMs, as well as clients, reacted positively regarding the implemented app. The RHMs emphasized how proud they are that the government appreciates their work and equips them with such a technological tool for their daily work. The clients highlighted the benefits they received through the app.

> *"The people [clients] were also happy that we use a tablet. They were all welcoming to the new technology." (RHM 2)*

Concerning the app functionality, the creation of a client data record and the verification of these data at each home visit is a significant help to the RHMs.

> *"Having the tool, it sort of gave me a guide on the sort of questions to ask and like comparing it to the past, where we used to come in to emphasize going to the clinic." (RHM3)*

Furthermore, the personalized risk calculation for each client individually was recognized as a helpful tool that supports the suggestion to visit a clinic in case of high risk.

> *"[The app is] something that will help them [the clients]. Because sometimes they are lazy to go to the clinic." (RHM1)*

Several people emphasized that through the app, the issue of NCDs and the high number of people suffering from NCDs in eSwatini is taken more seriously by the government. Hence, the mHealth app supports NCD care and prevalence.

> *"Or when we [RHMs] even asked about the NCDs, they are happy to express themselves. Not all the time to hear about HIV/AIDS and other things" (RHM2)*

Even though the RHMs seemed excited about using the tablets, we observed that some struggled to use the app and the technology intuitively. However, by showing and training them, they seemed eager to learn how to use the app. This idea was also supported by the two RHMs who used the tablet for a more-extended period:

> *"The more I was doing or using the tablet: I ended up mastering it." (RHM 5)*

To simplify the use for the RHMs further, the app was further automated and simplified to enhance intuitive usability.

1.6.2.3 Third iteration

Based on the evaluation in the second iteration, the app was further refined. The functionalities did not need any further refinement, whereas the interface design was enhanced to further suit the RHMs' capabilities. This enhancement included enlarging buttons (e.g., on the landing page). A validation for each field in the input tab for the client data was added. This adjustment included the provision of corresponding feedback. Hence, the user is able to correct the inserted information directly if a field is not filled out properly. To ensure completeness, all information fields are required to be completed. Additionally, the format of the inserted data is validated. Only when all fields are filled in completely and in the required formats can the data set be entered into the database to prevent incomplete data sets. An automated flow along the counseling process was enhanced. Hence, the CHW is guided through the app. For example, after inserting the client data, the app automatically moves to the personal risk calculation with filtered prevention information tailored to the client's status. Thereby, the hardware back button was disabled to avoid unexpected system behavior on the user side due to the fact that some RHMs accidentally had returned to a previous page while inserting patient information (see Figure 14).

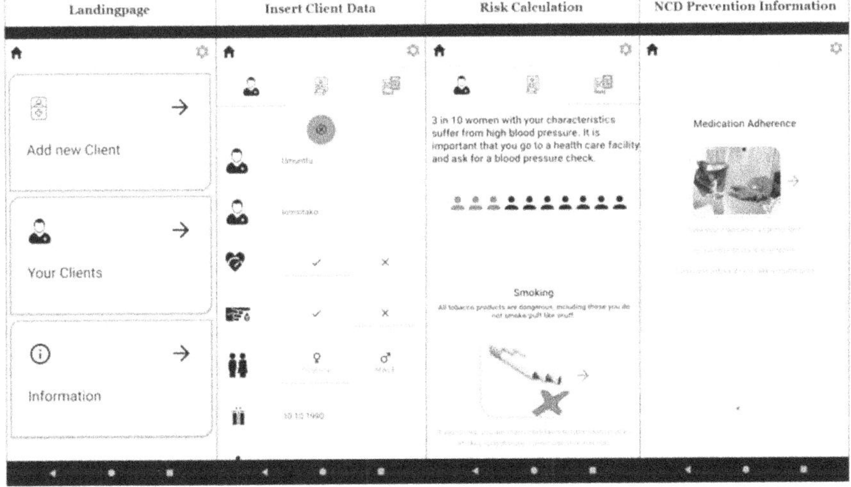

Figure 14: Screenshots of the App (Third Iteration)

This version was used for two months by 18 RHMs for client counseling. During this field pilot, 793 clients were counseled with the app as a supportive tool and received the automated NCD risk assessment and personal prevention information. On average, an RHM added 44.06 client profiles (SD=23.42) during the 8 weeks, resulting in an average of counseling 2.48 (SD=1.30) clients per working day. We assessed the technical metadata to generate insights into the user behavior and interaction with the app. On average, an RHM interacted with the app during the entire pilot 828.17 times (SD=243.34). As an interaction, the access of a new page is counted (e.g., moving from the client profile to the risk calculation).

The RHMs spend on average 3:46 h per working day with the app, resulting in an average 10:30 min per client. As expected, the RHMs spent the most time on the page where the client health data must be added and the page with the prevention information.

Overall, the field test including biweekly monitoring sessions showed that the design of the app is appropriate to be used by the RHMs and that an app is a supportive tool for their working routines that helps them provide NCD-specific counseling and, in the long term, decreases the risk of NCDs for the population. All RHMs stated that they and the clients are happy to use a technical supportive tool to support NCD prevention and even mentioned that they would encourage to expand the app for further diseases than hypertension and diabetes. Based on this result, it is planned to roll out the app for the entire RHM program in the country to enhance NCD prevention at full scale.

> *"It makes working with clients easier. The clients focus when you are talking to them, since it shows pictures that are relevant to the disease and food that clients should avoid. The videos in the App makes teaching clients easy because they excite them." (RHM 9)*
>
> *"The App made teaching easier, enabled users to finish work faster because there is no need to write anything, and everything is kept in one place." (RHM 8)*
>
> *"All RHMs should be taught to use the App." (RHM 6)*

1.6.2.4 The Final Ensemble Artifact

The final artifact emerged through a three-step iterative process from the interaction between design, use, and ongoing refinement. The previous described iterations have demonstrated the embeddedness of the artifact and its role a contextual carries and the design of ensemble artifact which includes manifold components, including hardware, software, devices, routines, procedures and policies (Purao et al., 2013). The ADR method emphasizes that its outputs include design knowledge (see Section 6.3), as well as the IT artifact with its tool properties (Purao et al., 2013). The resulting IT artifact is a mobile app that is specified to the contextual needs of NCD prevention in decentralized healthcare systems in LMIC countries. The architectural structure of the app is shown in Figure 15 and the interfaces are presented in Figure 14. The frontend contains the different pages of the app in the ordered workflow. The backend contains the database with the CHW information for the authorization as well as a database for the client information. Further components are the risk calculation and the educational material needed for the NCD prevention counseling. All frontend and backend components are only saved on the device itself. The only exception is the possible asynchronous uploading of the client database for external backup on a governmental server, when a stable internet connection is available, either via a mobile connection or plugin the mobile device into a desktop computer.

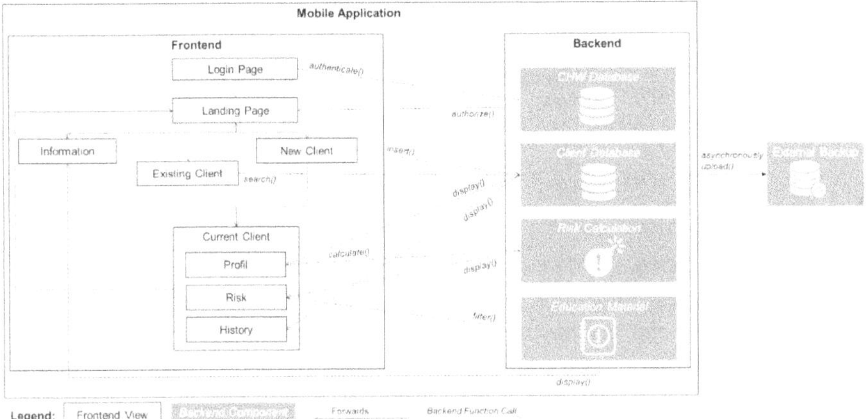

Figure 15: The Architectural Framework of the App

1.6.3 Generalizing the Design

In the following section, we elaborate on the MRs and DPs that result from continuous reflections and learning during the previous stages.

During the iterative design process, we saw that icons caused misunderstanding due to the different cultural backgrounds of the development team and the users. Therefore, the ICT needs to address local customs (such as commonly used icons) (MR1) to ensure non-misleading usability. The artifact addresses lay health personnel as a target user group. Because they usually come from rural areas and have completed little formal education, they have limited digital technical experience, and some are unable to read or write. However, the app must be usable by them (MR2). Due to the limited technical experience, the CHW struggled with the complexity of options while using the app. Hence, the ICT is required to support their workflow (MR3). The field observations have shown that the overall aim is to increase the awareness of NCD care of the client; therefore, the ICT needs to directly engage the clients (MR4) and provide a personalized risk calculation based on their health data (MR5), which relies on the most current data (MR6). To fulfill the requirements of the government and maintain trust in the system, the ICT is required to follow the restriction with regard to data privacy and security as the personal data is collected (MR7). Lastly, the work of the CHWs is as efficient because they do home visits and, therefore, reach the people in the communities independent of whether they visit a clinic or not; therefore, the ICT has to be portable (MR8). The set of eight MR is summarized in Table 14.

Table 14: Overview of Meta-Requirements

	ID	Meta-Requirement	Description
System Quality	MR1	Localization	The ICT has to provide functionalities adjusted to local understanding.
	MR2	Inclusiveness	The ICT has to be usable by illiterate and digitally inexperienced users.
	MR3	Workflow	The ICT has to support the CHWs' workflow.
Information Quality	MR4	Engagement	The ICT has to engage clients to convey health-related information directly.
	MR5	Health Assessment	The ICT has to support CHW in the task of assessing personal client risk for certain NCDs.
	MR6	Up-to-Date	The ICT has to keep the health-related information of clients up-to-date.
	MR7	Data Protection	The ICT has to follow local data privacy policies and secure database.
Service Quality	MR8	Portability	The ICT has to be easily portable to support CHW visiting clients.

Based on the MRs and how they were addressed by the implemented app, we inductively developed three DPs for the problem class of decentralized NCD care in the Global South, encapsulating prescriptive knowledge on how such a supportive ICT should be designed. Following the autonomy of a DP (Gregor et al., 2020), we inductively derived three DPs based on our findings.

The first DP (see Table 15) is the principle of content presentation. It summarizes the collected information regarding the process of presenting and designing the content in a manner that is comprehensible for the CHWs so that they clearly understand how to counsel their clients. On the one hand, the CHWs have to understand the functional content in the app (e.g., the information on the landing page, the profile to enter the client information, the client profile); on the other hand, the CHWs have to clearly understand the NCD prevention content (e.g., behavioral recommendations and risk calculation) that the app provides to support the individual counseling. Accessible and engaging health education is a cornerstone of health behavior change, which is needed in most cases to prevent NCDs. Specifically, we derived four mechanisms for this DP. First, the design should be based on icons that supplement text content. For instance, the three buttons on the landing page contain the written description as well as a representative icon. This way, the requirement of inclusiveness (MR2) is addressed because illiterate users can navigate the ICT by means of symbolic language. Second, all semiotics (e.g., icons, symbols, images, and videos) should be culturally appropriate to the context of the user to be interpretable and comprehensible for that user. This area addresses the requirement of localization (MR1) and is essential to ensure that the content is accessible, engaging, and relevant to the needs, wants, and experiences of the target user (Adam et al., 2019). Third, to address the requirement of engagement (MR4), visual material including images and videos is needed to communicate the prevention content in an engaging manner to the client. For example, the prevention information includes several images for each category of advice. By showing the images to the clients while the CHW talks about it, the comprehension can improve and affect the target behavior (particularly for people with low literacy skills) (Houts et al., 2006). Fourth, the prevention information has to be signaled through simple actionable statements. We included green checkmarks and red crosses at each prevention information to indicate the effect on NCD prevention. Thereby, the CHW can break this information down to signal statements, such as “do not smoke”, “do sport activities”.

Table 15: First Design Principle

DP1: Principle of Content Presentation	
Summary	The content of the ICT has to be presented in a way that ensures that all CHWs clearly understand how to counsel their clients appropriately.
Aim, Implementer, and Users	For healthcare officials to achieve a clear communication design that is understandable for CHWs and clients.
Context	CHWs have different educational backgrounds (e.g., some are (semi)-illiterate). The counseling process of CHWs is interactive communication between the client and the CHW. For NCD prevention counseling the clients have to understand what behavioral actions are in favor and what is increasing the risk of NCDs. Culture and context are important when interpreting content.
Mechanism	M1.1 – Use icons to supplement text content. M1.2. – Identify cultural-appropriate semiotics M1.3 – Visualize content via videos and images to convey health-relevant information to clients M1.4 – Reduce actionable information to a signal statement (Do this…; Don't do that…)
Rationale	M1.1 – Some CHWs have limited reading skills and hence graphical interfaces with icons and images support their comprehension process (Parmar et al., 2009). M1.2 – Interpretation of symbols and icons is highly culturally dependent. Eurocentric symbols can be misunderstood by people with other cultural backgrounds (e.g., Shinar et al. (2003)) M1.3 – The CHWs have material to show the client during the counseling process. Communicating health information through pictures and videos is an effective way to enhance attention (Adam et al., 2019; Houts et al., 2006) M1.4 – Signal statements simplify the information that the CHW has to communicate with the client.

The second DP (see Table 16) is the principle of workflow automation. The aim of consistent, long-term oriented, and comparable NCD prevention for all clients through CHWs is addressed through a support mechanism along the workflow and via automated diagnostics. This means, firstly, that the existing workflow of the CHWs of regularly visiting the clients at their compounds and taking the time to talk to all interested family members as well as providing individual counseling has to remain. Secondly, the automated diagnostic function means that the IS provides a form of health assessment (e.g., a risk calculation based on client data). This function supports the counseling by an individual client-specific assessment. We derived five mechanisms for this DP. First, the IS only functions as a supportive tool that works along the existing workflow. This point is essential to address MR3 and ensure acceptance and integration of the IS. Second, the navigation is strongly guided from one function to the next one and provides standardized support that is intuitively usable. By strongly guiding the CHWs, it is avoided that the users accidentally make mistakes, such as deleting a client profile or not saving or entering health information. This change learns from V1 where a deletion button existed, which caused major problems because often the entire profile was deleted when a minor mistake, such as a typo, was made. Therefore, the deletion function was removed, and only editing is possible.

Table 16: Second Design Principle

DP 2: Principle of Workflow Automation	
Summary	The workflow of CHW-client counseling has to be supported by the ICT and automated diagnostic support has to be provided to achieve consistent, long-term oriented, and comparable NCD prevention for all clients through CHWs.
Aim, Implementer, and Users	For healthcare officials to achieve consistent, long-term-oriented, and comparable NCD prevention through CHWs for clients.
Context	Long-established concept of CHW work routines (Lewin et al., 2005; Singh & Sachs, 2013). The CHWs consult clients about health education and ask about individual health behavior. CHWs usually lack any technical experience and have a limited technical affinity (Chib et al., 2015)
Mechanism	M2.1 – Provide functions and information along the existing CHW workflow M2.2 – After the successful execution of a function, the next function follows along with the workflow logic. M2.3 – Offer automated diagnostic functions based on easy to gather inputs M2.4 – Require CHWs to execute diagnostic functions during every client visit. M2.5 – Automatically record clients health history based on inputs for diagnostic functions
Rationale	M2.1 – The IS needs to support the workflow instead of changing or optimizing it. The existing workflow is a long-term established concept that works very effectively in LMICs and is accepted by all stakeholders (e.g., government, clients, CHWs) M2.2 – This automation reduces inconsistencies and avoids interruptions or cancellations of the counseling. M2.3 – The CHWs can rely on automated diagnostics and do not need disease-specific training. NCDs often do not show symptoms and hence the automated diagnostic supports the trustworthiness of the diagnoses. Furthermore, comparable NCD prevention is guaranteed among CHWs. M2.4 – Some NCD risk factors are modifiable and hence behavioral changes can affect the risk (Bukelo et al., 2015). M2.5. – This enables long-term oriented counseling, where behavioral changes of clients are reported.

Third, the main functionality for successful NCD counseling is the diagnostic function that calculates the individual NCD risk on the most current health data. On the one hand, this function facilitates the work of the CHW because he/she knows exactly which NCD prevention information needs to be discussed with the client. On the other hand, it is an evidence-based assessment that is independent of the knowledge of the CHW and is, therefore, taken seriously by the client. This mechanism is based on requirement MR5 and is an important factor in the assessment of the NCD prevention information. Fourth, because the CHWs routinely visit their clients, the diagnostic function requires updated health data at each visit (MR6). This results in the fifth mechanism that includes the tracking of health data through a client's health history that automatically indicates behavioral changes and resulting risk changes of the client. This mechanism enables long-term oriented NCD prevention.

The third DP (see Table 17) is the principle of mobile counseling. It summarizes the mechanisms to allow flexible, place-independent, and data-secured counseling of clients. This includes the need for mobility for the CHWs to counsel their clients at their homes, as well as the requirement for tailoring the ICT to the employment of the individual CHW. For the DP, we derived five mechanisms. First, the app must be secured by a login because it contains the personal health data of the clients; this approach ensures the mechanism of data protection (MR7). Because the CHWs typically do not have a mail address, the login has to be conducted by an ID and a password. In our case, this is provided by the government to ensure the uniqueness to provide access in case the CHW forgets their login data. Second, through their personal login, the CHWs are only able to access their own clients. This approach further secures the client data and works sufficiently because CHWs have a solid client base; hence, there is no need to share the data between CHWs. Third, to provide a flexible and place-independent solution, the IS tool needs to be developed for mobile devices that can be carried by the CHWs during their home visits. This addresses the requirement of portability (MR8). Fourth, because CHWs visit their clients at home, the functionality has to be workplace independent. Because mobile internet access is often restricted in LMICs, particularly in rural areas, the functions may not rely on it. Hence, all data and functions should locally work and be stored on the device. Fifth, if healthcare officials would like to connect to the client data and for security reasons (e.g., device damage), there should be a possibility for an asynchrony backup of the data. For example, the backup can be possible when the device is connected to Wi-Fi (e.g., when the CHW visits a clinic to report their duties).

Table 17: Third Design Principle

DP 3: Principle of Mobile Counselling	
Summary	The ICT must be mobile for home visits and tailored to the employment of the individual CHW, in order to allow flexible, location-independent, and data-secured counseling.
Aim, Implementer, and Users	For healthcare officials to allow flexible, place-independent, and data-secured counseling of clients by CHWs.
Context	CHWs visit their clients at their home compounds. One CHW is responsible for all people in a geographical area. There is no short-term replacement if a CHW cannot visit their clients. There is no country-wide mobile internet connection and mobile data is very expensive.
Mechanism	M3.1 – Require user login via personal ID and password M3.2 – Only grant access to client data for which CHW is responsible. M3.3 – Develop the IS tool for mobile devices. M3.4 – Store all data and execute all functions on the device M3.5 – Provide a function to asynchronously back up data.
Rationale	M3.1 – The client health data has to be secured and should only be accessible for the CHW. The CHWs usually do not have an email address, hence the CHWs employer (e.g., government) provides unique IDs and passwords for the CHWs to access the ICT. M3.2 – As the CHWs have a solid client base, there is no exchange of client data between CHWs. M3.3 – The CHWs walk long distances and visit their clients at home. They have to carry the device and have to be able to use it place-independent. M3.4 – The ICT has to function everywhere and can therefore not rely on mobile internet. M3.5 – To secure that the data is not completely lost in case of device damage, the client database should have the option of being backed up once in a while. The healthcare officials should take responsibility for secured storage (e.g., cloud, server)

1.7 Discussion

The presented research process contributes to various domains. Before going into detail, we argue that when assessing the contribution within the DSR knowledge contribution framework (Gregor & Hevner, 2013), the problem of mHealth for NCD prevention in decentralized healthcare is somewhat novel and still "wicked". The problem of shifting healthcare-related tasks to CHWs brings a new set of challenges (such as low experience with ICT, cultural differences in understanding symbolic language), which had yet to be systematically identified and investigated. Furthermore, current health systems need support to address the burden of NCDs. Therefore, the SDGs and the WHO address this issue with a call for action. Thus, problem domain maturity, as well as solution maturity, can be seen as low. Subsequently, the developed mHealth approach can be categorized as a novel solution and improvement because it supports the decentralized healthcare system by designing a tool for CHWs.

Additionally, the developed perceptive knowledge on artifact design is situated on two different levels of abstraction. First, the presented mHealth app addresses the practical situation in eSwatini. Second, we provide a blueprint and design principals for NCD prevention in decentralized health systems in countries of the Global South. Following the action design research strategy (Sein et al., 2011), we inform the creation and evaluation of the artifact development. We thereby build upon the IS success model (DeLone &

McLean, 2002, 2003) to structure the process and its evaluation of developing an mHealth tool. The IS Success model enables us to design with regard to use, satisfaction and net benefits on the health system in the country. We finalize our design process by providing generalizations of our reflections and learning to derive knowledge for a more abstract problem class (Iivari, 2015). Overall, we contribute to DSR by providing an instantiated artifact as well as a nascent design theory in form of DPs (Gregor & Hevner, 2013).

1.7.1 Theoretical Implications

Regarding the theoretical implications of our study, our research contributes to the following domains: First, this work contributes to the mHealth literature. Due to the novelty and multidisciplinary of the topic, research is still in its early stages and on the rise (Solanas et al., 2014; Varshney, 2014). Applying mHealth solutions in the Global South further brings new challenges and strives towards a new research area of improving local health systems, services, and equity (Chib et al., 2015; Latif et al., 2017; Motamarri et al., 2014). NCD care in LMIC, in particular, struggles with limited access to care, low detection rates, and poor disease management (Bukelo et al., 2015; Islam et al., 2014). Against this background, our study is amongst the first to address such a challenge holistically. By doing so, we provide several insights into the design of such an app, the behavior of CHWs as well as clients, and the effect on the overall quality of healthcare in a decentralized system. Most prominently, our study showcases how such an mHealth app can function as an important catalyst for digitally enhanced technology solutions in healthcare.

Second, this study contributes to the research area of ICT4D. Whereas NCD prevention can be considered as the application context, our study generally addresses the use of ICT for development. Following the call for "making a better world with ICTs" (Walsham, 2012, 2017), our study finds a practical solution that connects ICT use with development goals. We offer valuable lessons by examining the influence of, and interactions among, a wide range of institutional actors including multidisciplinary researchers, government, and international organizations. Our study further focuses on a relatively marginalized group, the CHWs, within the Global South and the potential role of ICTs to support their development. We acknowledge the need for research on institutional and organizational change (in our case, task-shifting) to understand the potential of digital technology in various structural forms of development.

Lastly, by the selection of the ADR methodology, this study contributes to DSR and especially ADR (Sein et al., 2011). We propose to use a new technological tool, with hard-to-foresee consequences, which is therefore particularly suited to design and action- research approaches (Walsham, 2012). In particular, ADR enables researchers to iteratively redesign the artifact by considering theory and practice simultaneously. It further allows continuous evaluation in the real world and, therefore, considering organizational conditions and user feedback. This process is guided by the IS success model (DeLone

& McLean, 2002, 2003) to, on the one hand, develop a theory-ingrained artifact (Sein et al., 2011) and, on the other hand, structure the evaluation procedure to amplify long-term use. Thus, our research project not only provides knowledge on the actual solution design but also on the design process. Specifically, our study provides a showcase on how ADR can be applied to develop artifacts in similar settings.

1.7.2 Practical Implications

In addition to the theoretical implications, this paper holds practical implications. First, this study contributes, in particular, to enhancing NCD care in eSwatini. The developed app is intended to remain a lasting and reliable tool for CHWs to care for clients. Thus, the net benefits and generated impact on the quality of care are lasting.

Second, our study results contribute to enhanced, effective, efficient, equitable, and sustainable health systems to reduce inequalities and increase health equity and additional societal benefits in the long term. The practical use of our mHealth tool results in better management of CHWs. It enables them to standardize their work routines and, therefore, guarantees treatment standards. The CHWs are more satisfied with their job, and public recognition increases, contributing to reduced attrition. In the long term, this approach could affect labor-market outcomes, including higher productivity and labor force participation. Thereby, we achieve an immediate benefit for people and CHWs, as well as beneficiaries of public health programs, regional administrators, and politicians.

Lastly, our study provides evidence and guidance for policymaker decisions around the globe. eSwatini is among the first to aim for a national scale-up of task-shifting of care for NCDs. Our results indicate that countries with a similarly structured decentralized healthcare system should consider developing an mHealth app based on our provided design. Extending from the formulated MRs and DPs, local differences should be considered, leading to slight changes in the design. Nonetheless, that such an app will provide significant utility remains highly likely.

1.7.3 Limitations and Future Research

Despite the iterative structure of the ADR project and the various evaluation cycles, some limitations remain, which provide the foundation for multiple future research endeavors. First, this study developed an artifact with a three-stage approach, beginning with a prototype that was evaluated by experts, followed by a first field test by a few CHWs, and finally rolled out for 25 RHMs belonging to one clinic. In the future, the goal is to derive a national scale-up. Therefore, future research can engage the long-term use, user satisfaction, and realized impact of the artifact. Thereby, further design changes could be necessary, which provides further ground to understand the problem and artifact design for this type of problem.

Second, following a DSR approach entails a generalization problem. The case of eSwatini is used as an instance to gather knowledge regarding the nature of the problem and also to develop and test solutions. However, any generated knowledge might be biased by the focus on the instance of healthcare in eSwatini. Therefore, future research should attempt to understand how the developed knowledge transfers to other countries and healthcare systems, adding or changing our understanding of MRs and DPs.

Third, this study formalizes practice-oriented DPs during the design process based on the MR discovered during the development and evaluation of the artifact. These DPs, which are identified and refined through the reflection and learning phase, capture the knowledge gained throughout the process of building the artifact for the case of eSwatini. Despite best efforts to ensure that the developed DPs directly address the formulated MRs, further evaluation via different methods might lead to an even deeper understanding of their relation. For instance, conducting laboratory experiments on the relation of a selection of DPs and MRs could lead to further refrainment. To give a specific example, the relation of country-specific icon selection (DP1 and DP2) and usability and accessibility (MR1 and MR2) could be investigated in such a research setting.

Lastly, connecting artifact design and design theories to extend theories constitutes a challenging endeavor. In general, DSR studies are expected to address challenges of substantial relevance and importance, develop highly novel artifacts, building upon a strong connection to theory, and provide contributions to theory (Baskerville et al., 2018). However, it has been agreed upon that tradeoffs have to be made and that DSR contributions exist in the spectrum from artifact instantiation to highly generalized and theory-engrained design theory (Gregor & Hevner, 2013; Sein et al., 2011). Because of the wickedness and complexity of the addressed problem, ranging from challenges regarding computer-human interaction to data security, we conducted an inductive research process (Iivari, 2015). Thus, we see significant value for future research to engage in dividing the addressed problem into sub-problems, each addressable by following a specialist kernel theory. Subsequently, the artifact design for each of the sub-problems can be improved, shifting the nascent design theory towards a well-developed one (Gregor & Hevner, 2013). Against this background, we wish to highlight two areas for future research. First, the diabetes and hypertension prevention information for clients was provided in the form of videos. However, understanding the design of the communication means (e.g., text, infographic, video, chatbot) in order to facilitate understanding and compliance in clients could be a valuable addition to the developed application. Specifically, we see two kernel-theories as valuable bases for future DSR: (1) cognitive fit theory (Vessey, 1991) and (2) media richness theory (Daft & Lengel, 1986). Secondly, we would like to highlight the problem of graphical interface design. Research has shown that cultures play a key role in the individual's preferences for user interface designs (Reinecke & Bernstein, 2013). In our study, we designed interfaces that heavily rely on icons, enabling illiterate users to understand them. Against this background, we propose that the understanding of icons can also be highly dependent on personal dispositions (e.g., culture, technology affinity). Thus, research-based on strong kernel theories, such as visual assumption theory (R. L. Gregory, 1970), could help to develop design principles for an interface in the context of mHealth in the Global South and beyond.

1.8 Conclusion

This study addressed the questions of how an mHealth app for NCD prevention in a decentralized healthcare system should be designed. To investigate the answers to these questions, we developed such an app for the healthcare system of eSwatini. To not only provide a context-specific solution for eSwatini, we also derived MRs and DPs. They address the design of such apps in similar contexts (e.g., other countries). Thus, our research project contributes not only to practice but also to theory.

Regarding the theoretical implications, our research contributes to ICT4D and mHealth research by, on the one hand, addressing the design of a digital tool for CHWs as a target user group and, on the other hand, focusing on the design of a health support system that addresses NCD care and prevention. We demonstrate how the ADR methodology can be applied to address relevant problems and how to derive design knowledge in close collaboration with local organizations, multidisciplinary research, and governmental partners.

Regarding our contribution to practice, our research provides the actual implementation of mHealth tool to support CHWs counseling of NCDs and improve healthcare standards that are designed to scale-up to the national level. The results of our evaluation, specifically from our field test, confirm that RHMs are satisfied with the app and are better guided through NCD counseling. The proposed app can serve as a "blueprint", adaptable to fit other countries' healthcare delivery. Against this background, one of our main practical contributions is to provide evidence and guidance for decision makers and policymakers in countries with a similar setup decentralized healthcare system. Our results implicate that adapting and implementing the proposed design of such an mHealth app can be highly beneficial and should, therefore, be considered.

To conclude our study, we would like to call researchers and practitioners alike to apply, implement, evaluate, and refine the proposed MRs and DPs, advancing the provided prescriptive knowledge to a state of standard means for the support of NCD care in decentralized healthcare systems.

1.9 Appendix

1.9.1 Interview Partner – Qualitative Analysis

Evaluation of the first iteration: formal feedback through an online feedback survey by 6 experts (Expert 1 – Expert 6), written unstructured feedback via mail from three local implementing organizations (incl. Expert 7 – Expert 9), two focus group discussions (incl.

Expert 10 – Expert 14). Evaluation of the second iteration: field test (RHM 1 and RHM 2), group discussion with 16 RHMs (incl. RHM 3- 5), interview with 60 clients (incl. Client 1- Client 3). Evaluation of the third iteration: field test with 18 RHMs (incl. RHM 6-9) and two local experts (Expert 14 and 15). Table 18 provides the description of a selection of interview partners.

Table 18: Description of Selected Interview Partner

ID	Age	Gender	Position	Expertise Area	Year of Work Experience	Phase of Engagement
Expert 1	37	m	Postdoctoral Researcher	Medical / Global Health Research	7	First Iteration
Expert 2	32	m	Postdoctoral Researcher	Global Health	6	First Iteration
Expert 3	28	f	Research Associate	Development Economics	3	First Iteration
Expert 4	55	f	Professor	Sociology	> 15	First Iteration
Expert 5	30	f	Research Associate	Nursing Science	4	First Iteration
Expert 6	32	m	Postdoctoral Researcher	Global Health	5	First Iteration
Expert 7	31	m	Senior clinical Associate at local Health Organization	Public Health	6	First Iteration
Expert 8	38	f	Director of local Health Organization	Public Health	8	First Iteration
Expert 9	28	f	Coordinator at local Health Organization	Public Health	4	First Iteration
Expert 10	31	f	Assistant Professor	Global Health		First Iteration
Expert 11	39	m	Professor	Development Economics	>15	First Iteration
Expert 12	53	m	Professor	Information systems	> 15	First Iteration
Expert 13	28	m	Postdoctoral Researcher	Information systems	5	First Iteration
RHM 1	38	f	Health Worker	-	8	Second Iteration
RHM 2	39	m	Health Worker	-	9	Second Iteration
RHM 3	43	f	Health Worker	-	11	Second Iteration
RHM 4	41	f	Health Worker	-	8	Second Iteration
RHM 5	45	f	Health Worker	-	9	Second Iteration
Client 1	39	m	Farmer	-	-	Second Iteration
Client 2	43	m	Farmer	-	-	Second Iteration
Client 3	62	f	Housewife	-	-	Second Iteration
RHM 6	51	f	Health Worker	-	>15	Third Iteration
RHM 7	33	f	Health Worker	-	4	Third Iteration
RHM 8	46	f	Health Worker	-	12	Third Iteration
RHM 9	41	f	Health Worker	-	6	Third Iteration
Expert 14	33	f	Coordinator at local Health Organization	Public Health	6	Third Iteration
Expert 15	29	f	Coordinator at local Health Organization	Public Health	3	Third Iteration

1.9.2 Method – Building, Intervention Evaluation Stage

Table 19: Description of Methodological Details of Stage 2

	Building	**Intervention**	**Evaluation**
First Iteration	*Light-weight intervention:*	*In a limited context:*	*Experts Evaluation:*
	Prototype	Prototype was tested by multidisciplinary partners	We asked experts to evaluate the extent, nature, quality, and appropriateness of the system use (DeLone & McLean, 2002). All experts were asked to feel into the role of a health worker and use the app accordingly. The aim was to generate insight into user interface navigation patterns, usage time, and other related aspects. Formal feedback: A qualitative online feedback survey via Google forms was answered by Expert 1-6. Written unstructured feedback: Three implementing organizations in eSwatini that work in development and diabetes care provided feedback via mail. Focus Group discussions:´ The prototype was presented in two focus group discussions (Mayring, 2002) with ten members of a development economics research group (including Expert 10, Expert 11 and seven Ph.D. students) and eight members of an information system research group (including Expert 12, Expert 13, and six Ph.D. students). Lastly, group discussions provided informal feedback during monthly calls (all partners) and weekly calls (government and practical partners) throughout the development process.
Second Iteration	*More mature version:*	*In a wider setting:*	*User Evaluation:*
	Full Version	Field Test with RHMs	For the field test, two of the authors traveled to eSwatini to evaluate the app in the field in October 2019. The app was field-tested with 16 CHWs and was thereafter evaluated. Two CHWs tested the app for a total of 10 days and counseled over 60 clients using the app. The evaluation provided insights into real-user behavior, as well as user satisfaction as a measure of the CHWs opinion. In-depth interviews We conducted the interviews with both CHWs (RHM 1 and RHM 2) separately after the first day and after a total of 10 days. Focus Group discussions: We discussed with the participating members about the app use and received feedback and answered questions. Observations: We accompanied two individuals in their work routines and observed how they used the app. During the field visit, we also interviewed 30 clients after they had received counseling by CHWs.

	Ensemble version with contributions:	*In actual use setting:*	*Impact Evaluation:*
Third Iteration	Final Artifact	Roll out with RHMs for 2 months	The final app was rolled out in a pilot. 18 RHMs used the app in the field for their working routines over a period of 2 months. The pilot was monitored by two experts from the local implementing organization (Expert 14 and Expert 15). At the beginning the RHMs were introduced to the app at a kick-off meeting. Formal Feedback at Kick-off: A printed quantitative evaluation form was conducted after the kick-off session to ensure the quality of training and the readiness for own use during counselling. Furthermore, the technical affinity and experience with apps was assessed. Monitoring during pilot: During the pilot the expert checked on the RHMs biweekly to discuss, for example, technical issues. Focus Group discussions after pilot: At the end of the pilot, the two experts conducted focus group discussions with all participating RHMs. This allowed the participants to agree or disagree with each other so that it provided an insight into how the group thinks about the app, and the variation that exists among the participants in terms of beliefs and their experiences and practices of their counseling routines Analysis of logged meta-data: The app tracked meta-data, such as time used, number of clients, navigation through app etc. during the use. This information was analyzed at an aggregated level.

2. Study 3: Overcoming Digital Challenges

Table 20: Fact Sheet of Study 3

Title	Overcoming Digital Challenges: A Cross-Cultural Experimental Investigation of Recovering from Data Breaches
Authors	Maike Greve[a], Kristin Masuch[b], Sebastian Hengstler[b], Simon Trang[b] [a]Chair of Information Management, University of Goettingen, Humboldtallee 3, 37073 Göttingen [b]Chair of Information Security and Compliance, University of Goettingen, Platz der Goettinger Sieben 5, 37073 Göttingen
Outlet	Published in the Proceedings of the Forty-First International Conference on Information Systems, India 2020 (VHB A)
Abstract	Companies around the world are faced with challenges in dealing with data breaches. While in Germany companies need to notify the affected and fear losing their valuable customers, in Bolivia, where rapid digital globalization increases vulnerability, data security overall is not a publicly present topic, and customers are directly exposed to the consequences of security incidents. Our study examines the cultural difference in addressing the digital challenge of recovering from data breaches. We investigate through a scenario-based experiment the effect of compensation and remorse on the customer-company relationship. Our results show that German customers are more likely to demand compensation for a data breach as a recovery action, whereas Bolivian customers are satisfied with an apology. We discuss this finding in the context of cross-cultural values and practical implications for countries that are currently undergoing a rapid rise in technology and are therefore exposed to substantial security risks.
Keywords	Data Breach Recovery Action; Compensation; Remorse; Justice Theory; Digital Challenges; Cross-Cultural Analysis

2.1 Introduction

With the goal of digital inclusion, technologically underdeveloped countries are on the way to catching up through rapid growth and the advance of digital technology (Dewan et al., 2004; Nambisan et al., 2017). While this is obviously a positive development to reduce digital inequality, the sudden introduction of internet-related technology is leading to increased security vulnerabilities (Riggins & Dewan, 2005). Countries such as Germany, which have a long history of digitization, have learned over the years to deal with challenges of digitization such as security and have now covered them through regulations such as the General Data Protection Regulation (GDPR) (Broy, 2017; Molnár-Gábor, 2018). However, this learning process is sorely lacking in countries that are experiencing rapid digital growth. While digital convergence has often already been achieved for the technological set-up and processes, there is still a large knowledge gap in addressing digital challenges.

This can especially be observed among South American countries, which lag behind in the world-wide comparison of digital competitiveness (International Institute for Management Development, 2018). Due to a rapid rise in digital technology, businesses are particularly susceptible to cyberattacks in the coming years (Mori & Assumpcao, 2007; Sweetney, 2015; Terranova Security, 2015). Such unauthorized attacks on the confidentiality of data of companies are called data breaches (Collins et al., 2011; Goel & Shawky, 2009; R. C.-W. Wong et al., 2011). Among Latin American countries, there are few reporting requirements for companies experiencing data breaches, and organizations do not face much by way of penalties for failing to protect consumers' sensitive information (Guillamont & Vijil, 2019). For example, Brazil has lost approximately $8 billion as a result of cybercrime but has not yet passed a general data protection law (Sweetney, 2015). While waiting for governmental regulations and expecting a decrease in attacks through better security guidelines, affected customers and companies currently experiencing the consequences of data breaches (Terranova Security, 2015).

Recovery research has shown, that affected companies can apply specific strategies, such as providing compensation or an apology can strengthen the company-customer relationship and even cause a higher trust and loyalty of the customers towards the company than before the incident (Krishna et al., 2014). This paradox suggests, that companies should rather use a recovery strategy and inform their customers than conceal the data breach (McCollough et al., 2000). Therefore, our investigation addresses the impact of two different recovery strategies (compensation and apology) on the customers' attitude (trust and loyalty) and behavior (word of mouth) towards the breached company. Furthermore, cultural differences play a key role in the handling of customer interaction and communication (Dinev et al., 2009; Hui & Au, 2001). Studies have shown that national culture has a powerful influence on individuals' attitudes and behavior (Johnston et al.,

2015). Therefore, Goode et al. (2017) call upon research that investigates the impact of cultural differences on the perception of recovery actions after a data breach. This means that current studies on data breaches lack an in-depth understanding of how impaired customer perceptions of recovery are culturally conditioned. This investigation draws on the identified gap in the data breach recovery action literature, and conduct this investigation in two different countries to explore the following research question:

Should recovery actions following a data breach be tailored to the customers' cultures when investigating their impact on customers' post-breach attitudes and behavior toward the affected company?

The investigation builds upon the example of a data breach in the case of a supplier of fitness trackers. We conducted a scenario-based investigation among 759 people, including 483 participants in Germany and 276 in Bolivia. We refer to the GLOBE dimensions (House et al., 2004) to emphasize the difference in cultural values and to integrate our results into existing research. Our investigation builds upon justice theory, which provides a theoretical lens into the topic of justice, to expand our theoretical framework on recovery actions (Rawls, 1971). Moreover, we rely on the literature on service failure to extend the theoretical background of the cultural context. Our study makes three main contributions: First, we empirically demonstrate how recovery action positively affects customers' loyalty, trust, and word of mouth after a data breach. Second, we evaluate the mediating role of satisfaction with the received recovery action on the effect mentioned above. Third, we show that the positive impact of recovery actions varies across cultures. In our discussion, we set these contributions in the context of the digital challenges among countries and discuss whether companies should disclose data breaches to affected customers without mandatory regulations.

2.2 Conceptual Background

2.2.1 Deriving Compensation and Apology through Justice Theory

The theory of justice (Rawls, 1971) is one of the basic theoretical frameworks in the literature on service recovery (e.g., Hong and Lee 2010; Morrisson and Huppertz 2010; Wan and Zhang 2014). Fairness or justice theory, in general, has three dimensions: distributive justice, procedural justice, and interactional justice. After a data breach, affected consumers may perceive the company and its performance as inadequate (Parasuraman et al., 2005), which can negatively affect the company's reputation and make service recovery actions an unavoidable corporate strategy (Goel & Shawky, 2009). Recovery actions are well addressed in service failure literature (e.g., Baker et al. 2008; Gelbrich and Roschk 2011). Goode et al. (2017) conducted a literature review on recovery of service failure and identified noteworthy trends, including apology and explanation as the cheapest actions for firms, as well as compensation as an effective form of providing recovery (Goode et al., 2017). Both recovery mechanisms can be derived from the theory of justice. First, once a data breach has reached public interest, companies can apologize to their customer about the incident (Baker et al., 2008). This is a form of interactional justice, which is conceptualized as the treatment in which information and decisions are communicated (Bies & Shapiro, 1987). Recent research shows that the perceived recovery by a customer after a data breach is strongly, positively influenced by an explanation with an apology than just the explanation (Bradley & Sparks, 2012) and identifies a positive effect on customer satisfaction through an apology (Wirtz & Mattila, 2004). Second, another possibility of recovering from the damage caused by a data breach is offering compensation to the customer. Thereby the customer perceives the compensation as a form of renewed service provision (Goel & Shawky, 2009). Gelbrich and Roschk (2011) assign compensation mostly to distributive justice, which deals with the perceived fairness of the distribution of resources and decision outcomes (Adams, 1963). In the context of recovery actions, distributive justice can mediate the relationship between procedural and interactional justice as well as lead to satisfaction (Prasongsukarn & Patterson, 2012).

Especially as the number of data breaches is steadily increasing (Ponemon Institute, 2019), apology and compensation belong to the most crucial aspects of an effective recovery strategy (Chang & Wang, 2012). While in Germany the topic of data security is prominent and data breaches often reach public awareness due to the mandatory breach notification law (Broy, 2017; Molnár-Gábor, 2018), there is less awareness of data security in Bolivia (DLA Piper, 2020). So far, very few data breaches are publicly reported in Latin America. However, generally Latin American companies are falling behind in international comparison in terms of cyber insurance adoption, and hence a high number of security incidents can be assumed (Terranova Security, 2015). Table 21 shows a short outline of selected publicly reported data breaches that affected customers in the cultural regions of Germany and Bolivia (Latin America).

The following two data breaches are examples of the use of compensation as a recovery action. On May 24, 2018, unauthorized third parties stole 10 million US dollars and nearly 14,000 credit card numbers from the Banco de Chile. The data theft caused a four-day breakdown of digital services. As a result, the customers received a claim for compensation to make up for the damage they suffered (Sernac, 2018). Due to the intrusion of an unauthorized third party into the Sony PlayStation Network between April 17-19, 2011, a failure occurred. 77 million accounts were stolen, and users were unable to use the services for 23 days. As compensation, Sony introduced a "Welcome Back" package that included selected PlayStation content. The package included 30 days of free PlayStation Plus membership for all affected users, with existing subscribers receiving an additional 30 days. All users also received one year of free identity theft protection. The PlayStation 3 and PSP game offerings varied by region, e.g., affected German customers received access to different games than the affected customers in the U.S. (Caplin, 2011).

Table 21: Compensation and Apology in actual Data Breaches

Theory	Instantiation	Country	Examples	Response Strategy
Distributive	**Compensation**: Material services which the customer receives. *Examples:* Credit note, replacement product, money back.	Chile	Banco de Chile (Sernac, 2018) 24.05.2018, $10 million and 14,000 credit card numbers were stolen.	The bank provided compensation to all consumers affected by the interruption of services after the breach.
		Germany (+North America, Asia)	Sony (Caplin, 2011) 17.-19.04.2011, 77 million personal account data of users of the PlayStation Network were stolen.	The company provided regionally different games for free, as well as free use of exclusive services.
Interactional	**Apology**: Admission of the failure and understanding of the situation in which the customer has got into. *Examples:* Express regret and/or admit guilt.	Latin America	Taringa (Taringa, 2017) 04.09.2017, 28 million user data of the Latin American social media platform were stolen.	The company has publicly informed users about the incident, expressed its deep regret, and explained what action is being taken.
		Germany	Vodafone (BBC News, 2013) 12.09.2013, 2 million data sets of customers in Germany were stolen.	The company made a public statement and informed the affected customers and apologized for the incident.

Alternatively, in the following two examples of data breaches the company apologized as a recovery action. On 1 August 2017, the social network Taringa was hacked, stealing nearly 28.7 million user data. This corresponded to about 94% of all registered users. The stolen data included usernames, email addresses, and hash passwords. In a public statement and personal messages to users, the company apologized. Additionally, future cybersecurity measures were presented, such as improving the systems to detect and prevent unauthorized access to user accounts. A much more robust encryption process for new passwords has also been introduced (Taringa, 2017). On 12 September 2013, almost two million customers of the telecommunications company Vodafone were affected by data theft. The perpetrators stole information on name, address, date of birth, bank code, and account number. In a public statement, Vodafone deeply regretted the incident and apologized to all those affected (BBC News, 2013).

2.2.2 Recovery Research in the Cultural Context

Recent research on data breaches and their disclosure has mainly focused on the aftereffects of economic impacts on equity markets, stock prices, and the market value of an individual company (Campbell et al., 2003; Morse et al., 2011). However, only a few studies have been conducted in the area of data breach recovery actions (Goode et al., 2017; Greve, Masuch, et al., 2020), and this research lacks the component of cultural consideration of the customer. Therefore, we rely on cultural studies from the area of recovery research after a service failure. Such studies show that the same recovery action is perceived differently in different cultures and thus has consequences for customer behavior (Patterson et al., 2006; Prasongsukarn & Patterson, 2012). The influence of culture on this causal relationship can be traced back to the fact that in this process, there is usually a social exchange that takes place with interactions between the company and the customer (Mattila & Patterson, 2004b). As a result of this, the values of both parties involved (company and customer) are each influenced by their cultural background.

In the context of compensation as a recovery action, N.Y.Wong (2004) identifies that compensation affects satisfaction and word of mouth in low power distance and high individualism cultures. The higher appeal of compensation in individualist cultures than collectivist cultures is also supported through a causal higher effect on perceived justice (Hui & Au, 2001). Similarly, Mattila and Patterson (2004a) show that compensation seems to drive customers' fairness perceptions, in particular with American consumers, as an example of an individualist culture. Furthermore, this is directly linked to an effect on post-recovery satisfaction (Mattila & Patterson, 2004b). In comparison, studies about the effects of apologies are rather controversial. Studies address the Asian culture and show that apology improves satisfaction for Singaporean and Australian people (N. Y. Wong, 2004), and Taiwanese customers perceive apology to be more just than US customers (Wang & Mattila, 2011). However, Hui and Au (2001) cannot support a difference among cultures in the effect of apology on perceived fairness. Regardless of the recovery action, Wong (2004) highlights the cultural dimension of uncertainty avoidance as a significant factor on the repurchase intention, as individuals would seek to minimize the potentials for failure. Overall, the cross-cultural studies often limit their results to the focus on one specific cultural aspect (Hui & Au, 2001; Mattila & Patterson, 2004a). Furthermore, there is currently little insight into cultural differences of digital mechanisms in African or Latin American cultures (Arage et al., 2015).

2.2.3 Cultural Uniqueness: Germany and Bolivia

For globally operating companies, cultural differences in the markets represent a major challenge concerning their strategic orientation. Information systems research shows that national culture, corporate culture, and individual cultural factors (sub-cultures) influence the behavior of a person (Leidner & Kayworth, 2006). Related studies point out that national culture can influence people's behavior in various aspects, such as information security compliance behavior, technology adoption, or the strategic direction of a company (Connolly et al., 2019; Srite & Karahanna, 2006). Different approaches have been established in IS research to explain and quantify differences on a national and cultural level. The most widely used basis for distinguishing between national cultures is Hofstede's cultural dimensions (Hofstede, 2001; Leidner & Kayworth, 2006). Despite their introduction about 30 years ago, the application of these dimensions in IS research still provides valid results today (Dinev et al., 2009). Hofstede characterizes national cultures using five different aspects: power distance, uncertainty avoidance, individualism (and collectivism), masculinity, and long/short-term orientation. Other studies, such as the GLOBE study (House et al., 2004), build on Hofstede's dimensions and extend them to other aspects in a more organization-centric approach. Generally, the orientation among cultural dimensions has the advantage of transferable results from the country level to the broader culture class.

Table 22: GLOBE Dimensions

Source: Globe (2020); House et al. (2004)

GLOBE Dimension	Description	Bolivia	Germany
Uncertainty Avoidance	The extent to which a society, organization, or group relies on social norms, rules, and procedures to alleviate the unpredictability of future events.	3.35	5.22
In-group Collectivism	The degree to which individuals express pride, loyalty, and cohesiveness in their organizations or families.	5.47	4.02
Humane Orientation	The degree to which a collective encourages and rewards individuals for being fair, altruistic, generous, caring, and kind to others.	4.05	3.18
Assertiveness	The measure of acceptance in society to confirmation, aggressiveness, and assertiveness. This is indicated through direct communication and the value of power.	3.79	4.55
Power Distance	The degree to which members of a society who lack power are comfortable with the unequal distribution of power.	4.51	5.25
Future Orientation	How individual gratification is delayed, and society engages in planning and investment.	3.61	4.27
Performance Orientation	The way that members of the group are encouraged to improve and perform.	3.61	4.25
Gender Egalitarianism	The degree to which society promotes gender equity and allows opportunity regardless of gender.	3.55	3.10
Institutional Collectivism	The degree to which institutional practices reward the distribution of resources and collective action.	4.04	3.79

Note: The GLOBE Dimensions are measured on a 7-point Likert scale, from 1= very low to 7=very high

For the cultural distinction in our approach, we use the GLOBE study for the following reasons: First, the GLOBE study is mainly used to describe cultural differences in organizational processes and strategies. As we are investigating the influence of national culture on data breach recovery actions, which is a part of an organization's information security strategy, our context fits into the target group for the use of the GLOBE dimensions (Hadwick, 2011). Second, we compared data conducted in Germany and Bolivia, and only the GLOBE study provides data to define the national culture of both countries (House et al., 2004). We distinguish cultural uniqueness based on the GLOBE dimensions of social practices (see Table 22). It is generally assumed that the higher the difference in the values of the respective dimension, the more the compared cultures differ. The nine dimensions show that Bolivian and German cultures differ significantly. Especially in the dimensions of uncertainty avoidance and in-group collectivism, increased differences between the Bolivian and German cultures can be identified.

2.3 Hypotheses Development and Research Model

A research model was developed to study the effects of compensation and apology as data breach recovery actions. On the one hand, it considers the customers' perception of the recovery action by measuring their satisfaction with the recovery action. On the other hand, it addresses the customers' attitude and behavior towards the company through measures such as trust, word of mouth, and loyalty (see Figure 16). Based on the justice theory, we firstly propose to investigate the impact of compensation as instantiations of distributive justice as a recovery action. Driven by recovery research, customers tend to request a refund, replacement, or repair when they issue a complaint (Goode et al., 2017; Morrisson & Huppertz, 2010).

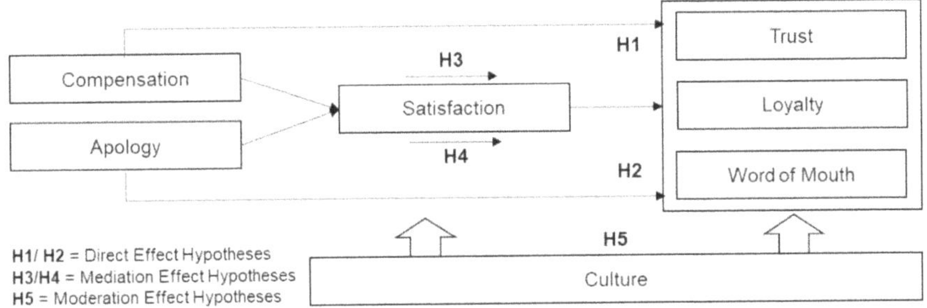

Figure 16: Research Model

Earlier research demonstrates how compensation generally remains a vital strategy (Walster et al., 1973) and positively influences customers' perception (Bradley & Sparks, 2012; Smith et al., 1999). Applied to our piece of research, we focus on the customer attitude and behavior towards the fitness tracker provider after receiving compensation. As previous research has shown the reception of compensation affects the trust (Lii & Lee, 2012; Mattila, 2009), the loyalty towards the company (Gelbrich & Roschk, 2011), as well as word of mouth (Baker et al., 2008; Lii & Lee, 2012; N. Y. Wong, 2004). Therefore, we hypothesize that compensation as a recovery action after a data breach can influence the customers' loyalty, trust, and word of mouth.

H1: *In case of a data breach, customer loyalty, trust, and word of mouth are positively influenced when the company offers compensation as a recovery strategy.*

Secondly, we suggest that an apology as an instantiation of interactional justice should be investigated as a recovery action after a data breach. An apology can be considered as a reward that disturbs esteem and concerns (Walster et al., 1973). Therefore, an apology can enhance justice perception and positively affect the customers' attitude. This has been shown by previous research that investigated how an apology by the company affects the loyalty towards them (Wang & Mattila, 2011), the trust in the company (Mattila,

2009), as well as word of mouth (Baker et al., 2008; N. Y. Wong, 2004). Therefore, we hypothesize:

H2: *In case of a data breach, customer loyalty, trust, and word of mouth are positively influenced when the company offers an apology as a recovery strategy.*

Besides the effects of compensation and apology on trust, loyalty, and word of mouth, previous research investigated the effect on customer satisfaction with the recovery strategy (del Río-Lanza et al., 2009; Maxham & Netemeyer, 2002, 2003). An apology has a positive effect on the satisfaction that people feel when receiving the recovery (Karatepe, 2006; Smith et al., 1999). Studies found that an increase in satisfaction usually shapes post-experience attitudes and thereby improves desirable business-oriented variables such as the perception of the company (Oliver, 1980). For instance, satisfaction was found to significantly affect trust, loyalty, as well as word of mouth (Flavián et al., 2006). Studies, such as Kim et al. (2004) and Avram et al. (2015), demonstrate the mediating role of satisfaction. Thus, in the context of our study, we argue that the recovery actions compensation and apology both have a positive effect on satisfaction, which in turn makes consumers more likely to overall increase the attitude (trust and loyalty) and the behavior (word of mouth) towards the breached company.

H3: *The satisfaction with the recovery action mediates the effect of compensation on customers' long-term perception.*

H4: *The satisfaction with the recovery action mediates the effect of an apology on a customers' long-term perception.*

The few studies in recovery research that analyze the influence of culture (discussed in the previous section) enhance its influence. We argue that culture has a moderating impact on all previous hypotheses. This moderation effect is supported by several studies (Hui & Au, 2001; Mattila & Patterson, 2004a; Prasongsukarn & Patterson, 2012; N. Y. Wong, 2004). As previous studies vary in their results, we follow the structure of Dinev et al. (2009), by including an exploratory hypothesis into our research model to generally address the moderating effect of culture in our model.

H5: *Culture moderates the mediation of satisfaction on recovery action on long term perception.*

2.4 Research Design

2.4.1 Experimental Design and Context

An online experiment tested the defined hypotheses. Compensation and apology were introduced through a 2x2 between-subject, full-factorial design. The survey was conducted independently in Germany and Bolivia. A fictitious data breach of a fitness tracker was described to the participants. We utilize a fitness tracker's data breach because consumers have accepted to collect their data to enjoy the benefits of using a fitness tracker.

Besides, fitness trackers collect personal health data; however, they do not officially belong to the category of health apps and therefore, do not need to follow strict security guidelines (Behne & Teuteberg, 2020). Also, interconnectivity with other devices has made fitness tracker vulnerable to data breaches (Mills et al., 2016). Both aspects enhance the risk of a potential data breach, which is already shown by an increasing number of unauthorized data accesses (M. Lee et al., 2016). To ensure that the participants could imagine the fictitious situation only persons wearing a fitness tracker or using a fitness tracker app were surveyed. In Germany, people were surveyed during a local live sports run (July 2019), and in Bolivia, the survey was mainly conducted among university students in Santa Cruz de la Sierra in November 2019. The university offers many opportunities for sports activities, and the survey participants are regularly involved in the activities. In both countries, the participants were personally approached and asked to conduct the online survey on a provided tablet. The survey was conducted in the German and the Spanish language.

2.4.2 Procedure

The survey started with an introduction that requested the participants to relate to the context of the study by imagining that they regularly use a fitness tracker as a tracking tool for running. To encourage the participants to relate to the context, examples of fitness trackers in the form of apps such as Runtastic, Nike Run Club, and Strava, as well as fitness trackers in the form of Smart Watches such as Fitbit, Apple Watch or Samsung Galaxy Fit were stated. The introductory text continues by explaining that the fitness tracker initially requires personal data such as e-mail address, date of birth, height, weight, running behavior, and similar data for set-up configurations. Additionally, during tacked activities, the fitness tracker automatically saves live-tracked GPS data. Building upon this background information the participants were asked to imagine that they would like to go for a run and when starting the fitness tracker, the following message informing about a data breach by an unauthorized third party pops up on the screen:

"Dear user, we discovered a security incident in your Fitness Tracker account on June 25, 2019. An unauthorized third party has stolen some of your personal data."

The message continued by providing information about the kind of data that was breached. With this, we differentiated between name, e-mail address, date of birth, and the number of runs that were affected by half of the participants. While the other half received that besides the data mentioned above and including information that live-tracked GPS data was breached. This differentiation is considered as the data breach severity with the binary characteristic "low" and "high." The manipulated variable is considered as a control variable in the analysis to ensure that recovery actions hold independently of the severity level of the breach. The customer then received one of four randomly selected messages representing different reactions.

Table 23: Conditions of Recovery Actions

		Compensational Condition	
		Neutral	Compensation Offered
Apological Condition	Neutral	*"If you have any questions, please contact us."*	*"As compensation, we offer you to use our premium version free of charge for 3 months. (There are no further obligations. Your account will then automatically switch back to the standard version.) If you have any questions, please contact us. "*
	Apology Offered	*"We deeply regret the incident and are endeavoring to address it to ensure that such inconvenience does not recur. We apologize for the inconvenience. If you have any questions, please contact us. "*	*"We deeply regret the incident and are endeavoring to address it to ensure that such inconvenience does not recur. We apologize for the inconvenience. As compensation, we offer you to use our premium version free of charge for 3 months. (There are no further obligations. Your account will then automatically switch back to the standard version.) If you have any questions, please contact us. "*

Either the customer received the apology as a reaction of the provider. This was instantiated by a message containing an apology from the provider, including regrets about the incident and a promise that the company would work on the issue to prevent it from happening again. Alternatively, the customer receives a compensation offer. The provider offered the customer the opportunity to use the premium version free of charge for three months (there were no further obligations. The account will automatically reset to the standard version). Table 23 shows the reactions to the scenario with their respective characteristics. Subsequently, each participant received the same questionnaire with manipulation control.

2.4.3 Dependent Variable Measures

All constructs described in the hypotheses were operationalized using established scales from previous research and adapted to the context of this work. In this research context, the items were selected for their consistency with the construct definition and the quality of measurement. The items were then translated into German and Spanish and cross-checked by the authors. A seven-point Likert scale from 1 ("fully disagree") to 7 ("fully agree") was used to measure the items, which is also used in the related literature. All constructs were reflective. As we collected our data from two different sources (Germany and Bolivia), it was necessary to show that the same constructs were measured in both samples. Accordingly, we tested for configural and metric measurement invariance (Steelman et al., 2014). By using the same item (see Table 24), we separately estimated two models and could not find any significant differences in the factor loadings. Moreover, the comparison of the path coefficients is stable among the two groups.

Table 24: Operationalization of Latent Constructs

Constructs and Items	Loadings	
	Germany	Bolivia
Satisfaction (Kantsperger & Kunz, 2010)		
The reaction of the Fitness Tracker provider fully meets my expectations.	.886	.837
Looking back, I perceive the response of the fitness tracker provider as a good experience.	.849	.778
Looking back, the decision to use this fitness tracker was right.	.705	.785
The reaction of the Fitness Tracker provider corresponds to my ideas.	.862	.832
Trust (J. K. Choi & Ji, 2015)		
I think the fitness tracker is safe.	.924	.912
I find the Fitness Tracker trustworthy.	.953	.937
All in all, I trust the Fitness Tracker.	.957	.929
I find the Fitness Tracker reliable.	.878	.925
Word of Mouth (S. S. Kim & Son, 2009)		
I will tell other positives about the fitness tracker.	.933	.899
I will recommend the Fitness Tracker to anyone who seeks my advice.	.957	.915
I will advise my friends and acquaintances to use this fitness tracker.	.960	.933
Loyalty (Kau & Loh, 2006)		
I will continue to use this fitness tracker.	.886	.849
I will not change my Fitness Tracker provider after the incident.	.862	.819
I consider myself to be a loyal customer of this fitness tracker provider.	.874	.852

Note: All items were translated into German and Spanish for the survey.

2.5 Analysis and Results

2.5.1 Sample Description and Perceived Recovery Action

The survey was conducted in Germany and Bolivia independently. After deleting invalid answers, in Germany, a sample size of n = 483 participants aged 19 to 80 years (M=29.94, SD= 9.04 years) and 53.21% men and 45.54% women were collected. In Bolivia, a sample size of n = 276 participants aged 19 to 59 years (M=24.51, SD= 5.97 years) and 35.51% men and 63.04% women were collected. Overall, the respondents stated that they train or engage in other sports activities 3.8 times a week on average and run 1.69 times a week on average. In addition, 52.04% of respondents stated that they "occasionally" or more frequently (20.55% always) use a fitness tracker for sports.

Between the countries, the participants were approximately equally distributed among the four experimental conditions. To measure the perceived received recovery action, we included two single items into the survey. Both statements had to be evaluated by the participants on a 7-point Likert scale. The first statement regarded apology by stating that the company expresses its regret in its reaction to the incident. For both countries, the results differ significantly between the participants that received the apology condition and the others (Germany: $t(478)=-12.57$, $p<.001$; Bolivia: $t(270)=-4.43$, $p<.001$). The second statement regarded the compensation condition by stating that the company offers compensation as a reaction after the incident. The results for the participants that received the compensation are statistically significantly different from the other participants for both countries (Germany: $t(478)=-20.44$, $p<.001$; Bolivia: $t(270)=-4.51$, $p<.001$).

2.5.2 Measurement Validation

A potential problem for this study is the common method bias due to its single-informant approach. To detect a common post hoc method bias, we applied Harman's single-factor test and ran an exploratory factor analysis (Podsakoff et al., 2003). We included all measurement items. The result indicated that no single factor is emerging from the computation that accounts for most of the variance. Hence, we argue that common method bias is of concern for this study.

All dependent variables (satisfaction, trust, word of mouth, and loyalty) are latent variables measured by constructs with items, as shown in Table 24. We included all items in the analysis as the factor loadings were larger than .7, as suggested by Gefen and Straub (2005). The validation of the validity and reliability of these constructs is supported through the criteria composite reliability (CR) and average variance extracted (AVE) (see Table 25).

Table 25: Correlations and Measurement Validation

	CR		AVE		COMP		APOL		SAT		LOY		TRU		WOM	
	GER	BOL	GER	BOL	GER	BOL	GER	BOL	GER	BOL	GER	BOL	GER	BOL	GER	BOL
COMP	n.a	n.a	n.a	n.a	1	1										
APOL	n.a	n.a	n.a	n.a	.352	.366	1	1								
SAT	.902	.892	.697	.674	.432	.217	.428	.293	**.835**	**.821**						
LOY	.917	.895	.786	.740	.197	-.021	.277	.172	.649	.642	**.887**	**.860**				
TRU	.962	.960	.862	.857	.181	-.001	.205	.113	.536	.541	.709	.718	**.928**	**.926**		
WOM	.965	.940	.903	.839	.259	.034	.274	.199	.694	.614	.753	.718	.699	.638	**.950**	**.916**

AVE = Average Variance Extracted; CR = Composite Reliability; GER = Germany; BOL = Bolivia; COMP = Compensation; APOL = Apology; SAT = Satisfaction; LOY = Loyalty; TRU = Trust; WOM = Word-of-mouth

Both requirements are met when all the construct has a CR value higher than .7 and an AVE value higher than .5 (Urbach & Ahlemann, 2010). In our model, all values are clearly above the threshold. To assess the discriminatory validity, (Fornell and Larcker (1981) offer an approach where the square root of the AVE is compared with the correlations between the constructs. The comparison shows that all constructs retain a higher value for the square root of the AVE than for the correlation with other constructs. It can be said that our model has acceptable and significant measurement characteristics.

2.5.3 Partial Least Square Analysis

The research model was tested using structural equation modeling with the partial least square analysis. The analyses were carried out with SmartPLS3. We used the bootstrapping re-sampling method with 5000 samples to assess the significance of the paths. All p-values that indicate a significance at $\alpha < .05$ are indicated in bold. We assess the measurements for Germany and Bolivia separately before conduction a multi-group analysis to compare the results of both countries (Hair et al., 2014; Sarstedt et al., 2011). The suggested research model is a moderated mediation model that incorporates recovery actions as the independent variable. Compensation and apology as the recovery actions influence trust, loyalty, and word of mouth as dependent variables though satisfaction as a mediator. Culture is included as a moderator variable upon the entire mediation model. To find out the mediation effect, we follow the structure of Hair et al. (2014) and conduct a multi-group analysis to test the effect of culture as a categorical moderator on each path.

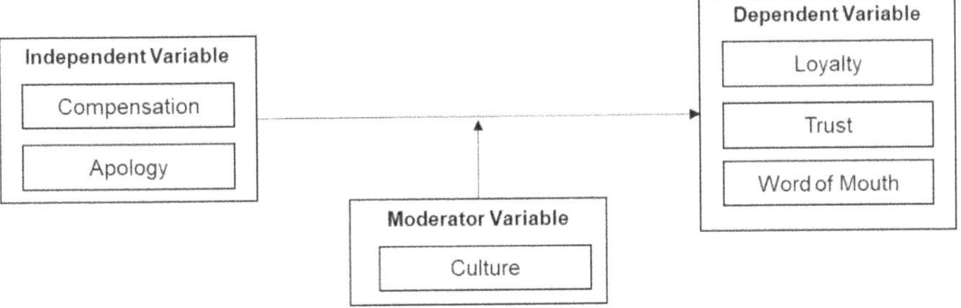

Figure 17: Estimation Model without Mediator

First, the direct effect between the recovery action and trust, loyalty, and word of mouth is analyzed (see Figure 17). We test this by a structural model that does not contain the mediating satisfaction construct. The results of the path analysis are shown in Table 26. The β-value indicated the magnitude of the effect. This effect size is tested by a t-test, whether it is statistically significantly different from zero (t-value and p-value of this test are provided). The direct effects show that in Germany, both recovery actions have a significant positive effect on all dependent variables, while in Bolivia, only apology has a statistically positive effect. In context with our hypotheses, this result shows that H1 is supported for both countries, while H2 is supported for Germany but not for Bolivia. The cultural difference is supported by the Welch-Satterthwaite-Test (Henseler, 2012) for comparison between the two country samples. If the test shows a significant result, it can be concluded that the path coefficients differ along with the two investigated cultures. As we conclude that there is a direct effect, we can analyze whether the effect may be mediated (Baron & Kenny, 1986).

Table 26: Results of the Model Estimation without Mediator

Path	Germany			Bolivia			Comparison	
	β-value	t-value	p-value	β-value	t-value	p-value	t-value	p-value
Total Effect: Independent Variable → Dependent Variable								
Compensation → Trust	0.114	2.371	**.018****	-0.096	1.389	.165	2.494	**.013****
Compensation → Word of Mouth	0.124	2.793	**.005*****	-0.050	0.696	.486	2.069	**.039****
Compensation → Loyalty	0.185	4.125	**<.001*****	-0.043	0.698	.485	2.991	**.003*****
Apology → Trust	0.238	5.101	**<.001*****	0.207	3.068	**.002*****	0.380	.704
Apology → Word of Mouth	0.162	3.521	**<.001*****	0.132	1.968	**.049****	0.362	.718
Apology → Loyalty	0.209	4.595	**<.001*****	0.216	3.401	**.001*****	0.090	.928

Note: ** p<0.05; *** p<0.01; all p-values that indicate a significance at α <.05 are bolded

Second, we include the mediator satisfaction into the structural model (see Table 27). We test the direct effect between the recovery actions (independent variables) and the satisfaction with the received recovery action (mediator) (see Figure 18). Then we test the direct effect between the satisfaction (mediator) and after-breach trust in the company, loyalty towards them, and word of mouth (dependent variables). The indirect effect from the independent variable to the dependent variable via the mediator can be directly derived by multiplying the effect size of the two direct effects. The results of the indirect effect are considered to evaluate H3 and H4. Additionally, for the sake of completeness, the direct effect between the recovery action and the three dependent variables is tested. The total effect of the mediation model is the sum of the last-mentioned direct effect and the indirect effect. This total effect equals the effect between the recovery action and the dependent variables without the mediator. Hence the results are the same as in Table 26.

Table 27: Results of the Mediation Model Estimation

Path	Germany			Bolivia			Comparison	
	β-value	t-value	p-value	β-value	t-value	p-value	t-value	p-value
Direct Effect *a*: Independent Variable → Mediator								
Compensation → Satisfaction	0.322	7.815	**<.001*****	0.127	1.835	.067	2.415	**.016****
Apology → Satisfaction	0.314	7.576	**<.001*****	0.247	3.440	**.001*****	0.821	.412
Direct Effect *b*: Mediator → Dependent Variable								
Satisfaction → Trust	0.568	12.485	**<.001*****	0.570	10.238	**<.001*****	0.023	.982
Satisfaction → Word of Mouth	0.722	22.283	**<.001*****	0.623	12.112	**<.001*****	1.635	.103
Satisfaction → Loyalty	0.687	17.682	**<.001*****	0.670	16.448	**<.001*****	0.300	.764
Indirect Effect a × b: Independent Variable → Mediator → Dependent Variable								
Comp. → Sat. → Trust	0.183	6.241	**<.001*****	0.073	1.746	.081	2.174	**.030****
Comp. → Sat. → Word of Mouth	0.232	7.219	**<.001*****	0.079	1.788	.074	2.799	**.005*****
Comp. → Sat → Loyalty	0.221	6.780	**<.001*****	0.085	1.804	.071	2.368	**.019****
Apology → Sat. → Trust	0.179	6.369	**<.001*****	0.141	3.301	**.001*****	0.750	.454
Apology → Sat. → Word of Mouth	0.227	7.105	**<.001*****	0.154	3.180	**.001*****	1.271	.205
Apology→ Sat → Loyalty	0.216	6.679	**<.001*****	0.165	3.381	**.001*****	0.868.	.386
Direct Effect *c'*: Independent Variable → Dependent Variable								
Compensation → Trust	-0.059	1.408	.159	-0.121	2.080	**.038****	0.870	.385
Compensation → Word of Mouth	-0.047	1.290	.197	-0.124	2.312	**.021****	1.195	.233
Compensation → Loyalty	-0.108	2.693	**.007*****	-0.182	3.610	**<.001*****	1.155	.249
Apology → Trust	-0.017	0.411	.681	-0.010	0.168	.866	0.097	.923
Apology → Word of Mouth	-0.018	0.512	.608	0.062	1.075	.282	1.186	.236
Apology → Loyalty	0.022	0.544	.586	0.042	0.779	.436	0.305	.761

Note: ** p<0.05; *** p<0.01; all p-values that indicate a significance at α <.05 are bolded

Overall, the mediation model explains 29% of the variance for trust, 43.1% of the variance of loyalty, and 48.4% of the variance of word of mouth for the German sample. The results of R^2 are similar for the Bolivian sample (R^2=.286 for trust, R^2=.427 for loyalty, R^2=.480 for word of mouth). The results of the mediation model show that the indirect effect is positive for all tested paths. For the German sample, all compensation and apology statistically significantly positive effect trust, loyalty, and word of mouth through satisfaction with the recovery action. While for the Bolivian sample, only apology as a recovery action is mediated through satisfaction on the three tested dependent variables. The difference in compensation as an input variable significantly differs between cultures. In summary, H3 can only be confirmed for Bolivia, while H4 can be confirmed for both countries. This result is in line with the results of H1 and H2. The multi-group analysis indicated that there is a cultural difference in post-breach customer attitudes depending on recovery actions (H5).

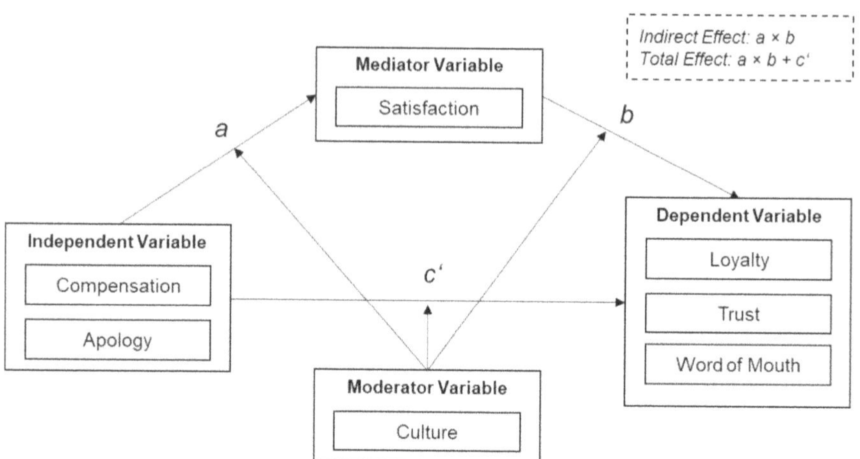

Figure 18: Estimation Model with Mediator

Therefore, both effects in sum reduce the total effect by canceling each other out. Such a case is called a suppression effect and indicated that only direct paths could be interpreted (Cheung & Lau, 2008; Zhao et al., 2010). As we analyzed three dependent variables, the β-variable indicates the estimated effect size. It can be seen that the effect size of the indirect effect on word of mouth is slightly greater for both recovery actions in German, compared to trust and loyalty, while in Bolivia the effect size on loyalty has the highest effect size. We also analyzed the effect of the control variables (data breach severity age, gender, sports activity) on the latent variables. Significant paths include gender to satisfaction ($\beta = 0.13$, $p = .031$), and gender to trust ($\beta = -0.15$ $p = .002$) for the Bolivian sample.

2.6 Discussion

2.6.1 Practical Implications for Cultural Customization of Recovery Actions

The purpose of our study was to examine whether the influence of recovery actions after a data breach on the post-breach attitude and behavior of customers is culturally dependent. We considered Bolivia and Germany as two example countries with distinct cultures (House et al., 2004). The GLOBE study magnified this difference among several dimensions. We hypothesized to find this distinction also among the effect of recovery actions. Our results show that apology affects loyalty, trust, and word of mouth in Germany and Bolivia. However, compensation only positively affects the three dependent variables in Germany and not in Bolivia. Thus, recovery actions are not culturally neutral perceived. We further found that the causal relation between recovery actions and customer attitudes and behavior is fully mediated by satisfaction with the recovery action. This mediation effect further shows that the higher the satisfaction with the recovery action, the higher the trust in the company, the loyalty towards the company, and word of mouth for Bolivians and Germans. However, the direct effect of the recovery action on satisfaction is culturally dependent. Compensation only has a significant positive effect on satisfaction in the German sample, while the Bolivian sample shows no significant from compensation to satisfaction. In contrast, both culture samples show a significant effect from apology to satisfaction. The sample results were found for the indirect effect from recovery action to satisfaction to trust, word of mouth, and loyalty. Connecting the study results to the difference in cultural dimension could imply that the lower value of in-group collectivism implies the individualism of the German culture, which could cause the acceptance of compensation as a recovery action. As found in recovery research of service failure, customers in individualistic cultures prefer to keep a distance between themselves and the supplier. Material values can create this distance. Therefore, it is possible to ensure such a distance by compensation. This is because compensation or reimbursement of costs compensates for the customers' loss and, at the same time, avoids a dispute with the customer. Furthermore, the difference in uncertainty avoidance in both countries, can in accordance to the literature be the reason for an overall critical attitude of Germans towards the overall recovery of a data breach. This could explain the high sensitivity and hence effect of both evaluated recovery mechanisms.

Overall, the identified results help organizations optimize their strategies towards future recovery actions after comparable data breaches. Companies should consider the cultural background of their customers and customize their recovery strategies, as the focus should be set on the customers' satisfaction with the recovery action. Our results indicate that German in comparison to Bolivian customers are more likely to demand compensation for a data breach as a recovery action. While Bolivian customers are satisfied with an apology instead of compensation. As our results show that customer relations are strengthened through an apologizing notification, we support companies, that currently on the rapid rise of digitalization to disclose data breaches and use these strategies which is virtually at no cost, even if they are not inferior to mandatory regulations. By doing so, companies take responsibility for the digital inclusion by addressing the arising digital challenges by themselves.

2.6.2 Implications for Justice Theory and Contributions to Literature

Even though of the practical nature of this research, our investigation considers implication for theory. As a theoretical lens, we build upon the justice theory to provide an understanding of different recovery strategies. Our investigation shows that the perception of the causes of two instantiations of justice theory, namely compensation and apology, differs concerning culture. This result is an indication of culturally dependent justice perception and therefore supports research that evaluates this aspect (Patterson et al., 2006; Prasongsukarn & Patterson, 2012). Besides, our study contributes to the existing literature. Firstly, our research contributes to recovery actions research of service failures, as we were able to show that the service failure literature has applicability and thus transferability to data breaches (Goode et al., 2017). Thus, our paper can also contribute by investigating the impact of recovery actions and satisfaction with the recovery actions on customer attitudes and behavior after a data breach. We thereby, conversely, draw new conclusions for the service recovery literature. Secondly, we add to the so far limited research agenda of data breach recovery actions. This is achieved by investigating two different data recovery actions for a data breach through experimental research, thus complementing the existing security literature. It can illustrate how further research can explain customer responses to help companies determine recovery actions such as compensation and apology in response to a data breach. Third, our research adds to the cross-cultural studies in the context of recovery actions. So far, there is limited research in this area, especially when considering the increasing number and, therefore, the importance of data breaches worldwide. Our contribution to previous cross-cultural studies is twofold: First, we explicitly consider the recovery after data breaches, following the future research call by Goode et al. (2017). Second, we consider the Latin American culture, which so far has gotten little attention, as the cultural comparison of recovery action, even though they have a rapid rise in digital technology and high risk of potential breaches (Terranova Security, 2015).

2.6.3 Limitations and Opportunities for Future Research

Our study has some important limitations that need to be considered when interpreting the results, but it also provides opportunities for future studies. The experiment was based on a fictitious data breach situation in which the participants had to empathize with the given situation. In the ideal case, future studies also offer a comprehensive validation of the measurements of real adopters that are affected by a data breach. Thereby further dependent measures that evaluate the actual post-adoption behavioral consequences, such as usage continuance should be addressed. Besides, only compensation and apology were applied as recovery actions in the present work. It should be considered that different formulations could have had another effect. This means that in the future, different formulations of apologies, as well as different forms and levels of compensation, should be evaluated. Furthermore, additional aspects such as response time, the form of explanation, or interpersonal communication, should be added to the research agenda. Besides, the cross-cultural experiment contains some limitations. By considering the GLOBE dimensions to indicate the difference in the two considered cultures, it is automatically implied that the participants of the study reflect the generally evaluated culture if the country by the GLOBE study. Furthermore, such studies assume homogeneity of societal values and behaviors. Such generalizations can obscure important information (Martinsons & Ma, 2009). However, our study only considered the GLOBE dimensions as an indication of cultural differences. Future studies should address these dimensions independently to provide insights into the direct relationship between single cultural aspects and their impact on post-recovery customer behavior. Besides, our investigation results are based on the study of two culture samples. Future studies should validate the results by comparing other different, but also similar cultures to generate more precise statements about cultural differences.

2.7 Concluding Remarks

Our paper deals with the challenges posed by digital inclusion. While equal opportunities and the benefits of digitization should be pursued, it is important to prepare those who are on the rise for the digital challenges ahead, such as security risks (Riggins & Dewan, 2005). Therefore our research deals with the recovery after data breaches, A key concern of affected companies is to strengthen the customer-company relationship and not to lose any customers after a breach (Aivazpour et al., 2018; Goode et al., 2017). In this study, we explore the relation of recovery actions and customer attitudes and behavior towards the breached company. The research agenda is addressed in the context of customers' cultural values. Through a 2x2 scenario-based investigation with 483 participants in Germany and 276 participants in Bolivia, we find empirical evidence for the cultural difference in the effects of recovery reaction. Besides, our results show that satisfaction with the recovey action mediated the effect on trust, loyalty, and word of mouth.

III. Synthesis of Knowledge

This section presents a single study (Study 4) which holistically builds upon the gathered knowledge and puts mHealth initiatives in the focus of the investigation. While the previous section conducted individual studies aiming for research on the utility, the focus is now broadened towards the long-term effect of mHealth on the health systems in the Global South. Thereby the scalability and the sustainability of interventions are targeted outcomes, which are depicted through a process model which aims to support mHealth projects to exceed the pilot phase by analyzing the roles and actions of stakeholders in this process. The study answers RQ 3 and tackles the practical problem of pilotitis and project failure at early stages.

1. Study 4: Healing the 'Pilotitis' in mHealth

Table 28: Fact Sheet of Study 4

Title	Healing the 'Pilotitis' in Mobile Health – A Holistic Stakeholder Perspective on Making Interventions Scalable and Sustainable in Low-Resource Environments
Authors	Maike Greve[a], Alfred Benedikt Brendel[b], Milad Mirbabaie[c], Lutz Kolbe[a] [a]Chair of Information Management, University of Goettingen, Humboldtallee 3, 37073 Göttingen [b]Chair of Business Information Systems, esp. Intelligent Systems and Services, TU Dresden, Helmholtzstraße 10, 01069 Dresden [c]Chair of Information Systems & Digital Society, Paderborn University, 33098 Paderborn
Outlet	Under Review in the Information Systems Journal (VHB A) Previously received valuable feedback in the Revision (2nd round) at the European Journal of Information Systems (VHB:A) and invited for Resubmission in the Journal of the Association of Information Systems (VHB A)
Abstract	Mobile health (mHealth) facilitates the provision of healthcare services via mobile technology and improves the quality and accessibility of healthcare for citizens in a cost-effective manner. This is especially valuable in low-resource environments, such as countries of the Global South. However, many mHealth projects do not proceed beyond the pilot phase. This article aims to explain how projects can exceed the pilot phase and successfully scale up and sustain. We conducted an interpretive stakeholder analysis by investigating mHealth initiatives via interviews with practitioners involved in mHealth project management in low-resource environments. Our interview data guided us towards a three-phase process model with two inflection points and four aggregated domains of challenging areas that require specific actions to facilitate the scaling up and sustaining of mHealth interventions. Our results provide a processual model for overcoming the pilot phase and achieving sustainability from the outset of mHealth projects by describing the stakeholder involvement and actions needed at the four domains economy, environment, technology, and users. Overall, our holistic process model of mHealth project phases may trigger new ways of looking at the pilotitis phenomena, which currently bogs down projects in the pilot stage and limits the general health development towards the targets formulated by the Sustainable Development Goals. This contributes to further theorizing and research by academics regarding the scalability and sustainability of emerging technologies as mHealth, and more considered action by practitioners to assist with long-term intervention management and design to realize value and impact.
Keywords	mobile health, pilotitis, sustainability, scalability, low-resource environments

1.1 Introduction

The use of digital technology to enable or support healthcare and disease prevention has increased significantly in low-resource environments (LREs), such as countries of the Global South, where health services and healthcare infrastructure are sparse (Latif et al., 2017). In particular, mobile health (mHealth) interventions (e.g., via smartphone applications) have become popular healthcare tools (Chib et al., 2015; Mechael, 2009; Sondaal et al., 2016). In the Sustainable Development Goals (SDGs), they are considered catalyzing and revolutionary healthcare delivery tools that contribute to 'ensuring healthy lives and promoting well-being for all at all ages' (UNDP, 2015). Given the reported advantages of mHealth technology, the discussion of *whether* it should be used in the area of development has been replaced by the question of *how* it should be used (Walsham et al., 2007).

However, the current mHealth landscape shows that interventions are implemented as pilot projects and are frequently discontinued after the initial phase (F. Huang et al., 2017). Such short-term pilot projects can be seen as a 'drop in the bucket' because mHealth interventions need to be at a scale and provide long-term sustained service to have an impact on a health system (Braa et al., 2004; Motamarri et al., 2014). As a result, practitioners in LREs complain about widespread 'pilotitis'—i.e., the failure of digital health pilot projects to progress to full implementation (Fanta & Pretorius, 2018; F. Huang et al., 2017)—because a lot of money is spent on project funding, but few to no healthcare improvements are realized long-term (F. Huang et al., 2017).

While prior research on mHealth has focused on technology introduction and improvements to healthcare processes (Chib et al., 2015), comparatively less attention has been given to the scale-up and sustain phases after a technology pilot (Heeks, 2017). The information and communication technology (ICT) for development (ICT4D) research agenda strongly focuses on the link between ICT and development. However, there is still a need to understand the transformative process of how ICT can foster development (Sein et al., 2019). It is argued that exceeding projects towards scalability (reaching as many people as possible) and sustainability (providing long-term support which persists over time) are essential factors in this development process towards 'health for all' (Braa et al., 2004). To date, researchers have analyzed the barriers to the uptake of mHealth (Mechael et al., 2010; van Olmen et al., 2020), the factors that influence the dissemination of mHealth applications (Sanner et al., 2012; Sundin et al., 2016; K. Wilson et al., 2014) and developed frameworks to evaluate the success of technology-supported health programs (Leon et al., 2012). A holistic understanding of phases, tasks, stakeholders, and challenges within the process, from pilot to scaling up and sustainability, and how to address these factors to reach a successful and sustainable state, is still missing. Against this background, we aim to answer the following research question:

How can mHealth initiatives be scaled and sustained in low-resource environments?

To answer this research question, we build on the interpretive stakeholder analysis methodology (Pouloudi et al., 2016) by interviewing 17 stakeholders (including researchers, digital health consultants, and health funds) about their experiences, lessons learned, and best practices in the context of piloting, scaling up, and sustaining mHealth projects. Subsequently, we developed a framework that includes actions pertaining to the four domains of economics, environment, technology, and usage at three distinct phases. Our findings highlight the importance of inflection points, i.e., the periods at the end of one phase and the beginning of another (i.e., pilot to scale-up and scale-up to sustain). At these inflection points, the tasks and expectations of stakeholders change. These changes must be taken into account to effectively prepare for and eventually execute transitions from one phase to the next.

Hence, the purpose of this paper is to demonstrate the holistic actions and influences of stakeholders in the different project phases which move mHealth pilots to scale up and sustainability in LREs. This supports the exceedance of pilot projects to overall health development aimed for by the SDGs. From a research perspective, this study contributes to theorizing and investigating the scalability and sustainability of emerging technologies, such as mHealth. For practitioners, this study provided a starting point to more thoughtful action to support long-term intervention management and design to achieve the value and impact of mHealth.

1.2 Background

In the following sections, we summarize the literature on mHealth pilotitis in LREs and the scalability and sustainability of such projects. In addition, we outline stakeholder theory, the theoretical framework for our investigation.

1.2.1 The Phenomenon of mHealth Pilotitis in LREs

mHealth, as a subclass of digital health (Mechael, 2009), describes the use of mobile ICT (e.g., smartphone applications) to enable and support health information and services (Nacinovich, 2011). In recent years, from a technological perspective, the use of digital artefacts in LREs has shifted towards the use of mobile technology (i.e., phones and tablets). Thereby, digital ICT has shifted from a peripheral to a core role, especially in the Global South (Heeks, 2020), where basic access to healthcare and reaching people in rural areas are challenging because health facilities are scarce (Chib et al., 2015; Motamarri et al., 2014). For instance, community healthcare workers (i.e., citizens with a rudimentary education who provide basic healthcare in remote areas of LREs) can be supported in their primary health delivery via portable digital services that enable data monitoring and/or provide informational materials (e.g., videos) (Greve, Lichtenberg, et al., 2020; Motamarri et al., 2014; Thondoo et al., 2015). The enormous potential for overcoming spatial, temporal, and even structural constraints in healthcare is greatly strengthened through mHealth projects in LREs (Baird et al., 2018). Accordingly, the number of mHealth interventions is steadily growing in the Global South, such as sub-Saharan Africa (Chib et al., 2015; Latif et al., 2017).

The implementation of mHealth initiatives usually starts on a small scale with a so-called pilot study to test procedures, principles, design, and strategies and to assess how feasible a scale-up would be (Moore et al., 2011). A pilot is characterized by a preliminary initiative to test and evaluate an intervention in a controlled setting (Batchelor & Norrish, 2005). Most commonly, a pilot intends to provide technical proof of concept or a single problem's solution (WHO, 2011). Particularly in the mHealth context, a small-scale pilot is the starting point since stakeholders often have little technology experience, and the cost of such a proof of concept is manageable and, thus, often funded (Hosman, 2011; Matavire & Manda, 2014).

However, the proliferation of discontinued mHealth pilots has become so severe that many have criticized this 'pilotitis' (Bhatia et al., 2020; Fanta & Pretorius, 2018; F. Huang et al., 2017). The term describes dissatisfaction with the small number of mHealth applications that make it from pilot to full-scale implementation (Fanta & Pretorius, 2018; Tomlinson et al., 2013). An example of dissatisfaction with the 'early death' of pilot mHealth projects is illustrated by the actions of the Government of Uganda, which stopped all new mHealth projects in 2012, demanding that future mHealth applications be interoperable, sustainable, and in compliance with laws and regulations rather than proceeding as before (Huang et al., 2017).

The literature identifies several possible barriers to the uptake of mHealth pilots (e.g., Aranda-Jan et al., 2014; Istepanian & AlAnzi, 2020; Kruse et al., 2019). Such barriers, which hinder the achievement of the anticipated goal of mHealth implementation (C. Kruse et al., 2019), include political factors (e.g., a lack of governmental support and interference from laws and regulations), economic factors (e.g., scarce funding and a lack of cooperation between initiatives), social factors (e.g., user-specific characteristics, such as language barriers and a lack of health literacy), and technological factors (e.g., the high cost of mobile data and a limited supply of electricity for charging devices) (see Appendix, section II.1.9 for a detailed review). In sum, the literature presents a diverse and multifaceted picture of the barriers to mHealth interventions experienced in LREs. However, a comprehensive understanding of how barriers are interrelated and how they can be overcome is missing, warranting various calls for investigation on how to overcome these barriers and facilitate the scalability and sustainability of interventions (e.g., Heeks, 2014; Walsham, 2017).

1.2.2 Lessons from Sustainability and Scalability Research

The scalability—i.e., 'the ability of a health intervention, shown to be efficacious on a small scale (pilot) and/or under controlled conditions, to be expanded under real-world conditions to reach a greater proportion of the eligible population, while retaining effectiveness' (Milat et al., 2013, p. 289)—and sustainability—i.e., the potential 'to make an information system work, in practice, over time, in a local setting' (Braa et al., 2004, p. 338)—of initiatives in LREs, such as Global South countries, have been core themes of interest to information systems (IS) researchers in the ICD4D community for years (e.g., Braa et al. 2004; Sahay et al. 2013). In the early 2000s, the first attempts to computerize healthcare in the Global South were donor-based projects that were discontinued when the funding period ended (Baark & Heeks, 1999), and the challenges of introducing ICT in the Global South became apparent (Sahay, 2001). Now, twenty years later, the number of projects and initiatives has grown considerably, and the topic of scalability and sustainability is more timely than ever, though the central challenges remain (Heeks, 2014; Mthoko & Khene, 2018). The current research agenda of ICT4D highlights this challenge by emphasizing the importance of understanding and articulating how ICT interventions contribute to development (Sein et al., 2019; Walsham, 2017).

This interlinkage of ICT and development is especially vital in the context of mHealth because SDG 3 formulates the global need for development to ensure healthy lives and promote well-being for all (UNDP, 2015). Therefore, investigating how mHealth, as a technological tool, can support SDG 3 in the long term is a key criterion of the ICT4D agenda. However, so far, research on the process of reaching scalability and sustainability in mHealth initiatives has been limited (Aranda-Jan et al., 2014). Currently, short-term failure factors influencing the implementation and adoption of mHealth applications (Marcolino et al., 2018; Steinhubl et al., 2015) are discussed because of the widespread availability of examples and related data. Only recently has the opportunity for an in-depth analysis of scaled-up and sustained mHealth projects emerged due to the slowly but steadily increasing number of them, which is still low in comparison to the vast number of discontinued pilots (Bhatia et al., 2020). Hence, earlier studies were naturally limited in scope and could not develop a comprehensive understanding of how to foster scale-up and sustainability.

In the following paragraphs, we briefly describe the current research on the scalability and sustainability of digital health and mHealth pilots. We describe the chasm between the potential of mHealth as a technology to improve healthcare in LREs and contributing to the SDG of good health and well-being for everyone by eluding to the phases of pilot, scale-up, and sustain. (based on Hosman, 2011 and Braa et al., 2004) (Figure 19).

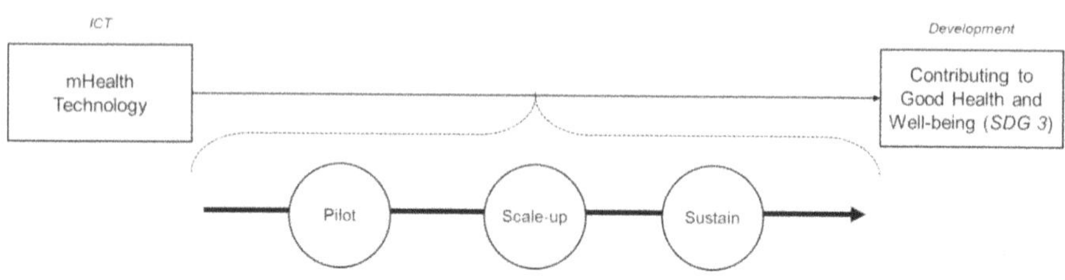

Adopted from Braa et al. (2004) and Sein et al. (2019)

Figure 19: The Chasm of mHealth Technology and Contributing to Good Health

The extant research focuses on factors that affect scalability (Sanner et al., 2012; Sundin et al., 2016; K. Wilson et al., 2014). Braa et al. (2004) state that scalability relates not only to technological proliferation but also to 'how to reproduce and translate the necessary learning processes alongside the spreading of artifacts, funding, and people' (p. 338), while Miscione and Sahay (2007) emphasize that systems need to be 'embedded into existing practices and enact new routines' (p. 7) to be scaled. Furthermore, Sahay et al. (2013) take up the transformation process, especially for global scalability, and explain that it not only consists of constant gains and expansion, as is often assumed but must include losses. This means that pure replication does not cause scalability; rather, a translation process is required. Although research has examined the concept to some extent, examining actual mHealth interventions shows that, so far, the number of interventions that have scaled up to a large nationwide implementation is low (Chib et al., 2015). Overall, the interrelationship between pilots, scale-up, and sustain is still open to discussion. While Hosman (2011) emphasizes that both concepts should be planned from the beginning, Braa et al. (2004) refer to scalability as a strategy or, as they call it, a 'prerequisite' for the sustainability of local action.

Research seeking to explain sustainability emphasizes a variety of problematic conditions in LREs and indicates a high risk of failure in the long term (Avgerou, 2008). Braa et al. (2004), who investigated large-scale IS, concluded that the challenge of scalability 'involves shaping and adapting the systems [technological sustainability] to a given context [environmental sustainability], cultivating local learning processes [social sustainability], and institutionalizing routines [institutional sustainability] of use that persists over time (as well as when the researchers leave and external funding [financial sustainability] is over)' (p. 338). Besides these five types, they identify researchers as influencing stakeholders who may end their support after the pilot, which can be detrimental to the scale-up of a pilot. Overall, sustainability research suggests that any digital technology must be appropriately interwoven with organizational practices and secure the necessary financial and knowledge resources, political commitment, and long-term stakeholder commitment (e.g., researchers), for its continued maintenance and growth (Braa et al., 2004).

Taken together, existing research suggests that multiple dimensions and stakeholders intervene in the complex nature of the phenomenon, influencing and hindering long-term and large-scale success. Existing models and analyses (e.g., G. B. Fanta & Pretorius (2018), Greenhalgh et al. (2017), Leon et al. (2012)) focus heavily on failure and related barriers but pay little attention to overcoming them or anticipating a transformation process that bypasses the barriers (see Appendix for a summary of extant literature). This highlights an important theoretical and practical gap in defining the holistic process that links the scalability and sustainability of mHealth initiatives in LREs. This process should not discuss each phase as an isolated construct, but it should include how to reach from one phase to the next phase (e.g., what tasks within a pilot are necessary to reach the subsequent phase of scale-up).

1.2.3 The Roles of Stakeholders

The complex nature of scaling up and sustaining mHealth initiatives that are often built around consortia or project teams involves a multitude of intervening stakeholders. The intertwining of actors, institutions, and international global players complicates project execution (Aklilu et al., 2020; Ali & Bailur, 2007). In LREs, the challenges caused by this complex network of stakeholders are increased because projects are often financed externally and require international and national partnerships to acquire such funding (e.g., project consortia) (Kaur & Ahmed, 2019). The healthcare sector involves additional stakeholders—patients, healthcare workers, nurses, doctors, clinics, hospitals, and policymakers, among others, which adds to this complexity (Kohli & Tan, 2016; Pouloudi et al., 2016). The involvement and commitment of stakeholders play a significant role in a project's success (Bailur, 2007; Eze et al., 2020). Previous research has emphasized that stakeholders' roles are among the factors that can contribute to ensuring sustainability (Heeks, 2014) and scalability (Sæbø & Thapa, 2012) of ICT4D projects. In addition, it has been argued that stakeholder perspectives on ICT and development have been insufficiently investigated (Kaur & Ahmed, 2019).

Against this background, our view of the problem of pilotitis is based on stakeholder theory (Freeman, 2010). At its core, stakeholder theory emphasizes the interrelationship between a company and its stakeholders. While the theory has evolved as a management and organization theory (Brenner & Cochran, 1991; Jawahar & McLaughlin, 2001; Preston & Sapienza, 1990), recent approaches consider the complexity of inter-organizational relations of stakeholders in a wider socio-economic context (Pouloudi et al., 2016).

Overall, the literature on stakeholders in the context of mHealth in LREs and ICT4D is scarce. Eze et al. (2020) synthesized existing research on individual interactions between mHealth stakeholders in the Global South. These individual interactions are built around four main stakeholder groups: patients, healthcare workers, system developers, and facilities. The analysis indicated that many studies provide findings from pilot projects (e.g., Hao et al., 2015; Lemay et al., 2012; van Dam et al., 2017) where the maturity and reach of the system implementation are limited. Based on their analysis, the literature barely focuses on how stakeholders may, for example, shift their positions over time from principal project drivers to long-term supporters. Therefore, there is a limited perspective in the literature on the long-term role of stakeholders within mHealth projects—from pilot to sustainability.

1.3 Research Approach

Our study follows a qualitative approach to generate a nuanced understanding of the stakeholders, challenges, and processual steps involved in managing an mHealth project in LREs, from pilot to scale-up and sustainability. In line with our objective of advancing a holistic view, this qualitative approach facilitates the recognition of different perspectives, stakeholders, and interests and generates a process model that can provide rich insight into the pilot, scale-up, and sustainability phases of mHealth projects in LREs. Our main research method is an interpretive stakeholder analysis (Freeman, 2010; Pouloudi et al., 2016)[13] comprising exploratory problem-centered expert interviews (Döringer, 2021) with a variety of stakeholders involved in mHealth projects in LREs. As shown in Figure 20, we collected and analyzed data in parallel to the interviews. In accordance with the concept of theoretical saturation, we stopped the search for interview participants when the content did not further inform the derived concepts and themes in the data analysis (Glaser & Strauss, 1999). For the data analysis, we followed the theory-informed interpretive approach of Pouloudi et al. (2018). The following sections describe the methods applied for data collection, data analysis, and synthesis.

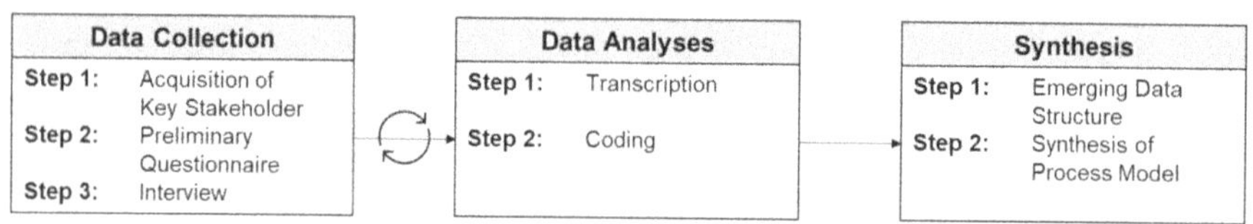

Figure 20: Research Approach

1.3.1 Data Collection

Given the exploratory nature of this research, we adopted a qualitative research design. Interviews were conducted with a diverse set of mHealth practitioners, which afforded us a more complete understanding of the phenomenon based on the data collected. We identified people at organizations that implement or participate in mHealth initiatives—

[13] Ontologically, the study takes an idealistic stance, assuming that reality is subjective and cannot be understood independently of the actor. Epistemologically, we take an interpretive stance, assuming that social reality is relative.

including researchers, technical managers, and project managers at non-governmental organizations (NGOs) or health institutions—as key stakeholders when considering mHealth projects from a practical and holistic stance. Thus, we conducted 17 interviews with mHealth practitioners from different institutional and organizational backgrounds. This ensured the consideration of various voices (Myers & Newman, 2007). Furthermore, the stakeholder theory emphasizes that key stakeholders come from a heterogeneous group and have different values, roles, and perspectives (Pouloudi et al., 2016). To ensure this quality of data, every interviewee had at least participated in the implementation of one mHealth project. Finally, the sample included interviewees who have been responsible for decision-making and gathered specific knowledge regarding the project process. Thus, this sample group could assess the process of reaching scalability and long-term sustainability. This allowed us to collect rich data regarding perceptions of structural elements and practices. This, in turn, enabled us to discern patterns and uncover diverse and potentially conflicting perceptions regarding stakeholder participation and interaction (Pouloudi et al., 2016), resulting in a deeper and more comprehensive understanding of how stakeholders influence the mHealth process from pilot to sustainability.

We recruited interviewees by selecting and requesting potential participants based on personal contacts, social and career networks, internet research, and recommendations. Fortunately, as part of an international consortium for an EU-funded mHealth project in a country in Sub-Sahara Africa (eSwatini), we had access to an extensive network of contacts and potential interviewees. To foster participation, emphasize our credibility, and address potential concerns, we sent participants an email that outlined the purpose of the study, stated our academic affiliations, and assured confidentiality and anonymity. We also sent a preliminary questionnaire and a privacy statement to the interviewees. The preliminary questionnaire included questions regarding the job positions and employers (including the number of employees, type, goals, and countries of operation) of the interviewees and the mHealth tools (including their names, field of use, and the number of users) they used. Selected information about the 17 interviewees is summarized in Table 29.

Table 29: Description of Interviewee Sample

No.	Stakeholder Subgroup	Professional Position	Field of mHealth	User Group of mHealth	Countries of Operation
I1	Global Health Fund	Managing Director	Symptom Checking / Monitoring	Patient	Ghana, South Africa, Ethiopia
I2	NGO	Head of Operations	Financial Health Cost Transaction	Patient	Madagascar
I3	NGO	Head of Operations	Symptom Checking / General Education	Patient	South Africa
I4	Global Health Fund	Medical Specialist	Education and Live Teleconsulting for Disabled Children	Healthcare Workers	28 Countries in Africa and Asia, especially India and Bangladesh
I5	NGO	Project Manager	Education on Disabilities / Health Promotion	Healthcare Workers	Ethiopia, Nigeria, Uganda, Zimbabwe, Cameroon
I6	NGO	Medical Specialist	Data Collection / Education	Midwives	Ethiopia and 40 other countries
I7	NGO	Medical Specialist	Financial Health Cost Transaction	Pregnant Women	Madagascar
I8	NGO	Project Manager	Education/Health Promotion	Pregnant Women / Healthcare Workers	Suriname, Ethiopia
I9	Global Health Organization	Project Manager	Prevention Education / Patient Management	Healthcare Workers	Eswatini
I10	Global Health Organization	Project Manager	Supply Chain	Health facilities	Nigeria, Sierra Leone, Chad
I11	Global Health Organization	Project Manager	Data Collection / Patient Management	Healthcare Workers	Nigeria
I12	NGO	Technical Specialist	Data Collection / Patient Management	Healthcare Workers	South Sudan, Cambodia, Myanmar, and Thailand, among others
I13	NGO	Technical Specialist	Data Collection / Patient Management	Healthcare Workers	27 African Countries
I14	NGO	Technical Specialist and Project Manager	Digital Health Ecosystem/Platform	Healthcare Workers / End-Users	Mozambique, Rwanda, South Africa, and Zimbabwe
I15	Global Health Organization	Technical Specialist	Data Collection / Family Planning	Healthcare Workers	Mozambique
I16	Research Institution	Assistant Professor	Health Insurance	Patient	Burkina Faso, Indonesia
I17	Research Institution	Associate Professor	Health Promotion	Patient	Indonesia, Pakistan

Note: (IX) refers to 'interview X' and is used as a reference to map the quotes to the interviews.

We conducted semi-structured interviews via online voice chat from February to September 2020 and followed established guidelines for qualitative interviews (Myers & Newman, 2007). Interviews lasted between 28 and 66 minutes (mean: 45 min) and were recorded (with the interviewees' consent after they signed a privacy statement) and then transcribed.

The interview included open-ended and follow-up questions structured via a topic guide to support the interview process (for exemplary questions, see Appendix). This guide included questions asking interviewees to describe their work experiences and the application area of the mHealth tool. We also asked them to identify other stakeholders and describe their involvement in the mHealth projects, the mHealth development and evolution process regarding scalability and sustainability, and the mHealth tools' impacts, efficiencies and inefficiencies, and successes and failures. Interviews concluded with questions about the potential benefits of mHealth. Furthermore, we preserved flexibility to adjust the interview guide based on individual responses (Gioia et al., 2013). Following Yin (2016), the interview questions were designed to be free of suggestive elements to avoid influencing the interviewees. To avoid imposing our own worldview and language on respondents (Myers & Newman, 2007), we first elicited perceptions indirectly by asking open-ended questions about the mHealth project and views on project evolution and barriers encountered in the process and only then asked interviewees directly about their perceptions of specific barriers and stakeholder roles that emerged from the literature and previous interviews. While it is undeniable that we, as researchers, are biased due to prior knowledge derived from the literature and previous interviews, we strived for open-minded data collection.

1.3.2 Data Analysis

We collected and analyzed data in parallel, which allowed us to gain deeper insights by formulating new or more nuanced questions in later interviews. This approach made it possible to reflect on the ongoing data collection and cleanse it for possible blind spots (Miles et al., 2014). Acknowledging the nascent nature of stakeholder theory in the context of mHealth projects in the Global South, we adopted a predominantly inductive interpretive approach (Klein & Myers, 1999; Pouloudi et al., 2016). Therefore, the consideration of stakeholder roles and perspectives was used to guide the study setup and later to articulate our findings. However, it was not used to limit our data analysis. Consistent with this approach, we analyzed the transcripts using iterative descriptive examination, and making sense of our data in a grounded theory manner. We performed the initial data coding by preserving the integrity of the so-called first-order concepts, closely aligning them with the underlying information without accumulating it (Gioia et al., 2013). The second-order analysis then focused on aggregating first-order concepts based on similarities and differences to reduce the number of codes and classify them into conceptual themes (Gioia et al., 2013).

In line with the described coding approach, we sequentially followed a mixed top-down and bottom-up approach (Lansing et al., 2018). We started with a top-down approach guided by stakeholder theory and the informed interpretive approach of stakeholder analysis developed by Pouloudi et al. (2018). We followed a bottom-up approach by developing and validating first-order coding concepts during the data analysis. The sequential phases of the process model (pilot, scale-up, sustain) were contextualized by the qualitative data and aligned with the previous coding (Pentland et al., 2020) after reviewing the literature to understand the problem setting better. Then we refined and validated the findings along with the second-order themes through the interviews and finally synthesized the findings into a process model that docks with the existing theoretical discourse and terminology.

1.3.3 Syntheses

The coding process resulted in the emergence of a data structure that illustrates the progress of aggregation from raw data to an empirical structure (Gehman et al., 2018). Two researchers synthesized the data structure and model after independently using continuous analysis of the transcripts, followed by an assignment of the codes to the core topics (Gioia et al., 2013). After the derivation of concepts and themes, we refined the inductively derived findings with existing knowledge and terminology from the literature. We thereby defined the sequential structure of pilot, scale-up, and sustain (see Section 2). The findings were refined in the context of the phases. The so-far static results were transformed to a processual dynamic model (Gioia et al., 2013). This model is based on an additional consultation with literature to redefine interrelationships and articulation of time dimensions of the emergent concepts. Along with the unfolding patterns of relationships between the phases, we identified the action domain and linked steps between the dimensions. The importance of phase transitions became apparent, which we call 'inflection points.' In the entire syntheses process, we constantly iterated between the data and the emerging themes and compared the themes to the literature and theory for validation. Throughout this process, a holistic dimensional process model evolved along with the sequential project phases and the referenced action domains. Each phase and domain configurations characterize the underlying actions and stakeholder roles that need to be considered among project managers and demonstrate the complexity that currently causes failure and pilotitis. The corresponding findings are outlined below.

1.4 A Holistic Stakeholder Perspective on the mHealth Intervention Process

The proposed perspective of the process—from the pilot stage to scaling up and sustainability of mHealth interventions in LREs—is holistic and dynamic (see Figure 21). At all phases of the process, action is needed in four domains: economics, the environment, technology, and usage. The domains identified through the data analysis have some resemblance to extant macro-environmental conceptualizations (e.g., PEST; see Peng & Nunes, 2007). The data has identified respective stakeholders for each of these domains, which roles and participation are essential. In the economy domain, this includes funders such as donor organizations and the local government. In the environment domain, this includes stakeholders with a thematic interest and substantive stakes in the project, such as the ministry of health, NGOs, and research institutions. In the technology domain, the stakeholders include system developers and IT facilitators. In the usage domain, the stakeholders include end-users, such as patients or health workers.

As suggested in the literature (e.g., Braa et al., 2004), the derived process model recognizes that the scale-up phase follows the pilot and provides a 'prerequisite' for sustainability. Developed from the data, the transition from one phase to another, which we refer to as inflection points, are the critical areas where mHealth projects struggle (Ali & Bailur, 2007; Hosman, 2011; F. Huang et al., 2017; K. Wilson et al., 2014). In particular, stakeholders' roles and expectations change at inflection points, and it is crucial to understand the relevant tasks before and after inflection points that facilitate transitions between phases and to provide insights into how stakeholders can help projects traverse these inflection points.

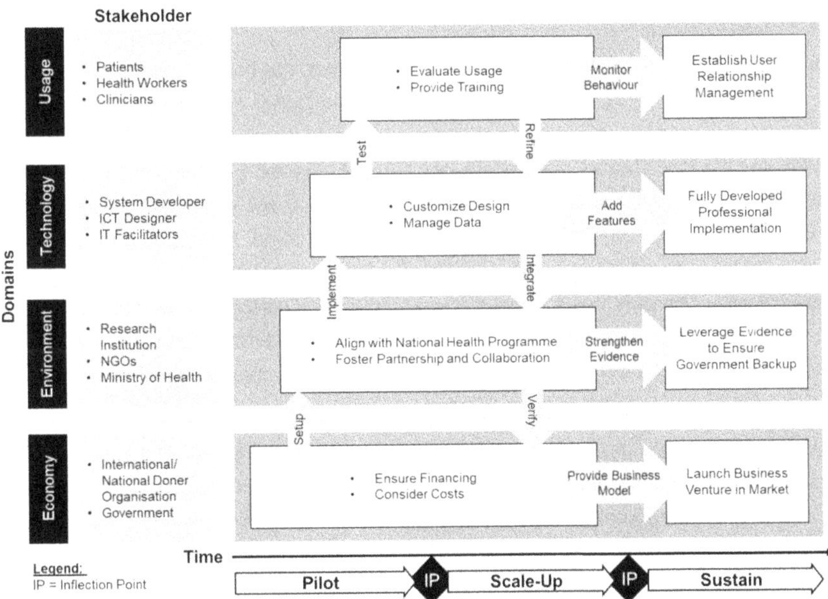

Figure 21: The Process from Pilot to Scale-Up and Sustain of mHealth Projects

In the following sections, we present the chronologically proceeding for mHealth projects in LREs from the pilot to the scale-up and sustainability phases in terms of the four aforementioned domains and their stakeholders. The requirements of this process were derived from the interviews and are related to the barriers identified in the literature (Section

2). As the requirements are derived from key stakeholders who are in a position to make decisions and steer the project, they also refer to them. Since this can include a variety of people, as our interview partner sample shows, we refer to this key stakeholder group in the following as project management. However, the general perspective on the holistic process includes the identification of roles of various stakeholders and how they shift at inflection points. For each phase, we describe the four domains individually, starting with a discussion on the requirements within the phase for this domain, then moving towards the requirements needed to be addressed to prepare for the infection point in this domain and transition to the next phase.

1.4.1 Pilot Phase: Set-up to Scale-up

1.4.1.1 Economy

The economic domain constitutes the foundation of an mHealth project because it addresses the primary requirement, namely sufficient financing. The initial pilot project is often financed through fundraising or earmarked funding from external organizations, such as the US Aid (I14) or European Union (I9).

> *I think the most common model is that piloting [...] is financed by [internationally donated] projects.*[14] *(I1)*

Funding is usually limited to the scope of the pilot and, therefore, limits the stakeholder contribution of donor organizations to this time frame. Donor organizations require a detailed cost breakdown to verify the donations needed. In this regard, project management addressed the costs before the actual project start. However, this calculation needs to be based on an insightful environment analysis that addresses the local conditions (e.g., smartphone penetration). This enables a valid cost estimation, as the purchase of devices (due to limited smartphone penetration in the user group) or costs for charging (e.g., purchase of solar chargers due to limited power supply and electricity) need to be included. During the pilot, the financial support is provided through donors; therefore, the government does not play a major role in this sense but has an important role in the context of their thematic stakes (environment domain).

It is essential to consider the transition to scale-up in the pilot phase. Because the financial support of donor organizations is limited to the pilot, the costs should be reconsidered by the project management to prepare for the pilot–to–scale-up inflection point. It is essential to know how and what costs need to be covered after the pilot phase. The project's management should communicate with donors during the pilot phase to discuss long-term financing. If donors stick to the limitation of the budget to the pilot phase, other financing stakeholders need to be considered (e.g., government, other national/international donor organizations, and partner networks). However, before starting negotiations

[14] The quotes were slightly adjusted in wording for better readability.

for scale-up financing with new stakeholders, their role needs to be anticipated. This mainly includes the needed financial support, estimated through the long-term costs. The costs need to be distinguished between initial and recurring costs and fixed and variable costs. In particular, variable costs—which depend on the number of users (i.e., the number of devices purchased)—should be considered, as they increase during scale-up, and recurring costs—such as maintenance services—should be considered, as they need to be covered in the long-term. In this phase, the cost savings should be discussed to reduce the long-term costs.

> *Our main goal has been to ensure that we work with partners where field workers either already have smartphones or are given smartphones for a specific project. (I5)*

> *The problem was that we had to pay for airtime. Every time we sent a voice message or a text message, we were paying. And of course, without limited funding [through donor organization], you cannot cover these costs as an NGO [project management].(I8)*

1.4.1.2 Environment

A crucial requirement for a pilot is the value of the mHealth intervention for users and the (local) health system. It is essential to understand the needs, pain points, and expectations of the local health system and the government's demands. This becomes especially vital if the mHealth device or application is designed to be used by professional healthcare suppliers (e.g., healthcare workers or clinicians). To successfully design an mHealth intervention at a pilot scale, the local conditions need to become familiar and well understood; this includes understanding the technological environment (such as mobile network conditions), awareness of existing digital health interventions, and identifying corresponding stakeholders (e.g., network provider and other facilitating organizations). The contact and engagement of stakeholders who have a thematic interest in the project must be ensured in the pilot phase.

> *For this pilot phase, we have only chosen one region, and for that, we have the validation of the ministry of health and all the hierarchy down to the very person who is in charge of every single hospital we work with. (I2)*

Furthermore, at the inflection point, the role of thus far passive, supportive in-country stakeholders changes from pure support to being demanding. For example, the government expects a scale-up, health facilities expect a health impact, and users expect professional technology. Similarly, some stakeholders (e.g., researchers) may end their engagement and activity because they got their intended 'pay out' (e.g., data for a publication). This changes the entire dynamic within the stakeholder network and is one major obstacle to reaching the scale-up phase. If this dynamic is not anticipated, losing the support of local authorities or other key stakeholders because of miscommunication of expectations can end a promising pilot. Therefore, it is important to communicate early on about expectations and long-term objectives. For instance, the ministry of health is an essential partner; hence, mHealth project management needs constant communication with officials to gather their feedback on requirements and needs. Some examples are ensuring compliance with national technology standards and aligning with national programs and the national health information system to react promptly to changing demands. It is necessary to comply with the preconditions of a country's government to implement an mHealth application. Before reaching an inflection point, it is essential to search for and establish new contacts and support networks. For instance, local partners can provide contacts to other institutions or public hospitals that might be willing to join the project to replace leaving stakeholders and facilitate a successful scale-up.

> *[...] we work with local partners in [name of country]. For example, with [name of local partner]. They digitize pharmacy shops and are therefore a very natural contact because, on the one hand, they have a direct link to the provider side, but on the other hand, they also have direct patient contacts where they can introduce new digital solutions [to extend the user base]. (I1)*

1.4.1.3 Technology

Once the economic and environmental domains have been addressed, the technology can be implemented. The requirements already in the pilot phase in the technology domain are the design that needs to be altered to be suitable for the target group and the collection and management of data. In the context of the design, it is necessary to avoid overwhelming users; the interviewees emphasized simple applications that follow a user-centric design approach.

> *So the design has to be foolproof so that you know exactly—I can only press here, there, or there. And then it has to happen on its own. So that was the biggest challenge: to break it down and to switch off one's own ability to abstract. Of course, it's a question of habit, of education, of culture, of what can be handled and what cannot. What works and what doesn't. (I3)*

Starting with a simple application in the pilot phase ensures operability and ease of use. While a user-centric application is important to ensure adoption, stable background functionality ensures retainment. Limiting factors include poor networks, limited mobile internet connections, and the use of old operating systems. Therefore, the application should incorporate a design that considers such environmental factors. To ensure that all aforementioned requirements are met, the system designers and developers are the key stakeholders of this domain. From the projects' beginning, they need to be closely entangled with the environment to be aware of the environmental conditions to manage their expectations and address challenges early on. Assumptions and experiences from other settings should not be transferred without elaboration and testing.

> *[The app development company] understands now because we really talked to them a lot about the situation in Africa. So, we told them, for example, 'Okay, we need this app to work on like the lowest iPhone or Android version you can think of.' That is not something they do every day [...]. They tested the app with the oldest phone they could find. I am really happy with this partner that they went so far as to find this phone [...]. So in that regard, they are a bit more than just the executor. (I8)*

To be able to shift to a scale-up, prototypical technology needs to shift to professional implementation. This includes considering increasing server capacity, planning large-scale maintenance and updates, and large-scale data management. In the pilot phase, the researchers may have been sufficient to develop a small-scale or prototypical tool; however, new stakeholders, such as technical service providers and local technical assistants, need to be contacted and involved before the first inflection point to be able to handle the technology in the scale-up phase. Furthermore, designs should be reconsidered so that they can accommodate more users and greater complexity. System developers need to balance innovative functionality and standardized core functions, such as data management.

1.4.1.4 Usage

The usage domain becomes relevant when the mHealth application has been tested by a relatively small number of users in the field. Already in the pilot phase, user acceptance lays the groundwork for the dissemination of the application. Training and involvement of users should be regarded from the outset. Participatory design procedures, such as human-centered design (Holeman & Kane, 2020), where the system designer and user closely collaborate on the iteratively developed version of the tool, ensure usability, and meet user requirements.

> *We talk to the users, the end-users, to understand their feedback and what can be changed: what is good, what is not. Because, of course, we realize that this is just the first version, and based on feedback, we can, of course, change it and make it better. (I8)*

When working with groups of stakeholders, it is important to consider their relationships. For example, when evaluating a tool supported by a government, whether users are, for example, government employees should be taken into account, as their feedback may be biased due to the power hierarchy between stakeholder groups. Hence, frequent sensitive qualitative evaluations with individual users may help circumvent this bias. Training users can also provide a point of interaction between various stakeholders (e.g., patients, healthcare workers, implementing facilitators such as NGOs, governmental representatives, health organizations, nurses, and doctors) and ensure that the project facilitator is aware of various stakeholders' understandings of the mHealth intervention.

> *The [certain population] considers it impolite to say critical things so directly. So when you do a feedback session, it's appropriate for them to say what they think, what we expect, what they should say. Such an open feedback session is not possible with them. They would never sit down and say, 'Well, that would be nice, and I would like to have that,' or something. (I3)*

Furthermore, the transition towards scale-up includes considerations of automated evaluations and standardized training. Hence, project management must ensure that the mHealth tool is tested with different evaluation and training methods throughout the pilot phase. For example, they can test how users use the tool with and without training. The pilot phase needs to be seen as a learning phase that helps one understand the user groups.

So that's also where feedback is really important, in making sure that we are connected to field workers, and we listen to them and understand what they really need from such an application. Because if we don't meet those needs, then you can be sure that the app will never be used. (I5)

1.4.2 Scalability Phase: Scale-up to Sustain

1.4.2.1 Usage

Beginning with the usage domain, meeting the needs of a growing number of users is a substantial part of the process of preparing the intervention for scaling up. However, while personal interaction with pilot users is desired at small scales, automated evaluations and standardized training must be implemented when crossing the inflection point. For example, this can include evaluating technical metadata, which provides information about interaction patterns and usage time. These standardized metrics can be automatically analyzed and serve as indicators for usability issues. The interviewees explained that collecting and analyzing technical usage data leads to a better understanding of user behavior and needs. Incorporating this information into the service by refining the design and focusing on the commonly used features can address this problem and serve as a response strategy. This can be achieved by requesting data entries and collecting metadata about how and when a user interacts with the application. This is incredibly effective for circumventing the cultural habits of users who are unaccustomed to providing negative feedback.

But just by having a look, for example, at when someone opens up the app and for how much time they spend on the app, we have found amazing information. For example, they are not using it during their office hours; they're using it between six o'clock and eight o'clock in the morning and after seven o'clock at night. They are not using it as a guide; they are using it to read up on information or refresh their memories. So by feeding that information back to the content providers, we say to them, 'Don't aim this as a quick reference guide. Aim this as a tool that people are using after hours, and we build a simple function that allows them to create favorites. So if you open up an app, you can click on a page and mark it as a favorite.' That has become such a hit because we understand how the user is using the app. (I14)

Nonetheless, in the scale-up phase, personal contact with a sub-group of users is desired to analyze the indicated usability issues closely. Careful consideration and detailed evaluation of usage behavior should be conducted when user groups with new characteristics join (e.g., a different mother tongue or different education). For such groups, the knowledge gained from the pilot users cannot simply be transferred.

We currently do some rounds of field testing with people in African countries and Asian countries, get some different feedback and then revise the content according to the field workers' feedback. (I5)

In the pilot phase, standardized training procedures need to be established. While for some interventions, the user group may include professionals (e.g., healthcare workers or clinicians), personal training can seldom be conducted on a large scale (however, training should be standardized to be conducted by several people). Interventions for a broad end-user group should be designed to be used without personal training but could, for example, include digital guidelines within the tool.

1.4.2.2 Technology

Fueled by the usage domain, the digital tool may need additional refinement according to the growing knowledge and changing needs of the enlarged user group (e.g., multi-language options). Those refinements should ideally be made as a result of the inflection point but before starting the scale-up phase. In the pilot phase, the design should be simple; however, as users adopt the initial design, additional features can be added.

> *[...] based on that, we learned to make simple apps, to do one thing very well: make a simple app that works perfectly, and from there, you can add features. And that's why [name of the application] is so simple, and it works. (I8)*

The technology tool needs to be adaptable enough to handle the heterogeneity of users and manage more data in a standardized manner. It is essential to ensure that continuous maintenance and updates of the application are provided. System developers need to be aware that the task of continuously refining and updating the tool becomes essential during the scale-up phase to ensure long-term usage. Updates need to be supplied quickly and frequently to guarantee the stability and availability of the application while allowing incremental refinements to follow the dynamic environment. Whereas during the pilot phase, maintenance and support could be conducted by the implementing organization or the system developers themselves, a service needs to be provided, for example, via an external service provider (e.g., to provide a service hotline) to increase efficiency during the scale-up phase.

> *So, if we don't keep these teams working and maintaining the apps, within a year or two years, whatever it is, the app will just stop working. And then, to run... to try and get that working again requires a huge amount of money. (I14)*

The interplay and collaboration of stakeholders are very important if these tasks are split among various actors. To anticipate the infection point for transitioning towards the sustainability phase, the tool should be prepared for integration, and the initiating organization must remain open to innovations (e.g., new systems and organizations).

1.4.2.3 Environment

Ideally, coming out of the inflection point and the pilot phase, a network with collaboration partners for the scale-up is established. This network includes a heterogeneity of partners, with, on the one hand, can provide specific tasks (e.g., clinics provide access to patients or researchers conduct scientific impact evaluation) and on the other can have sufficient resources and experience to deal with large-scale operations (e.g., governments have decision power over healthcare facilities or large private-sector firms such as insurances which can include service in the insurance program). The interviewees emphasized the advantages of nationwide scaling, which enables a fair and wide reach of healthcare provision or service. However, this is often only possible through intense government engagement and the integration of the project with existing infrastructure. For example, governments and other partners offer programs (e.g., health IS systems) and information infrastructures (e.g., or existing text message services) that can be leveraged to extend an application's use.

> *[...] because there is this kind of core foundation of a client management information system in the country, like a government-owned one, we anticipated that in the long term, the work we are doing on the mHealth intervention could integrate with that system. (I9)*

This underlines the importance of aligning an mHealth application with the environment, i.e., to ensure its ability to integrate with the existing system. Thus the application becomes part of the national health service and is embedded in the national health strategy. To anticipate the sustainability phase, close collaboration between health officials and implementing organizations is key to overcoming the scale-up phase, where evidence and health outcomes are still limited. To prepare for the shift towards the inflection point of reaching sustainability, the initial evidence of an mHealth tool's impact and success should be reported, monitored, and communicated to other stakeholders.

> *We used the first evidence and showed this to the ministry of health. So the ministry of health was very much interested in seeing the evidence and how we can scale the use of the app which is also in their interest. (I6)*

> *The department of health [government] typically will say "We will pay you" or "We will work with donors to pay you to support the app because we see value in it." If they don`t see value in it or if they don`t get value after a year the department of health can literally just switch their support off. (I14)*

1.4.2.4 Economy

As for the economic domain, when coming out of the inflection point, running costs should be known, and a source for financing the scale-up through the respective stakeholders has to be found.

> *There are other [funding opportunities]. We are in contact with politicians. There are ideas on how to get funding from politics for the scaling program. (I3)*

Often a new stakeholder enters the project for financial support at this stage. The time frame of this support varies depending on the stakeholder. For example, donor organizations may limit their funding to a specific period, similar to the pilot funding. At the same time, governments may provide long-term financial support already at this stage. However, in the scale-up phase itself, developing a business model that fits the intervention ensures the long-term continuity of the mHealth project and is independent of short-term, limited funding. The interviewees outlined possible approaches include transitioning the mHealth application to the state after ensuring its buy-in in the scalability phase (I5), handing over the project to other stakeholders (e.g., healthcare or telecommunication provider) (I1), integrating with an insurance plan to ensure reimbursement through insurance companies (I16), receiving compensation from the user of the application (I1).

The continuous financing is sustained via compensation or a business model that is either consumer-based so that specific parties pay for it directly or that you can get into insurance plans. And that is something where mixed models are also possible. In South Africa, for example, we see that telco providers are increasingly financing offers and refinancing them from their normal mobile phone contracts, so to speak, and the mHealth service is an extra offer. (I1)

To prepare for the inflection point and reach sustainability, the long-term participation and support of shareholders have to be generated. This support in consultation with the business model ensures cost coverage and perhaps even the generation of profit which is essential to reach sustainability. Many interviewees critique the limited engagement of the government in this regard. The interviewees describe the need for local parties (especially the government) to take over the long-term responsibility and enable a local independent mHealth service. This role change needs to be anticipated in the inflection point to reach the sustainability phase.

Actually, of course, one wants the countries to be independent in this respect and to finance it themselves. [...] The long-term goal should be to cooperate as much as possible with the local governments. Because at the end of the day, it is not a model that somewhere in the West [in developed countries] they keep delivering money for some projects [in the Global South].(I4)

1.4.3 Sustainability Phase: Sustain for Long-Term Success

1.4.3.1 Economy

Coming out of the second inflection, the goal is to reach economic sustainability. The interviewee proposed two equally reasonable actions for this. First, the business venture with the subsequent business model needs to be launched in the market and can cover its costs or even generate profit without any additional financial support through stakeholders. Second, the government (or another stakeholder) takes the role of ensuring the long-term financing of the costs and covers costs themselves or prioritizes the various donations and funding pools for this project.

Every end of the year the government will sit down and plan their whole workplan for next year. So during the compilation of that workplan, they list up all the projects or internal donation support for the next year. So even if [several names of donation organization] want to fund it, that is where the government says, we use the donation for these projects. So the funds could have come from anywhere but it is constantly provided for the costs of this specific project through the government. (I10)

If the financing is sustained, the business venture can even consider further expansion (e.g., other countries or extension of platforms) to generate earnings. However, the business model has to stay flexible to be adjusted according to needs and environmental conditions and the cost coverage has to be ensured.

So, it all isn't to make a profit; it's just to get people to see the value of it if indeed it is valuable and then to take it up themselves and to invest. Not necessarily big amounts of money but just enough for maintenance and to update content. (I5)

1.4.3.2 Environment

In addition to a successful business model, another focus is on strengthening health impacts and evidence to ensure long-term environmental sustainability. The generation of evidence provides transparency in the overall value of this intervention. Therefore, this evidence of, for example, individual health impact needs to be provided to all stakeholders, including governments, who rely on it to make informed decisions regarding the nation-wide health provision Collecting meaningful data further increases the validity and quality of these decisions.

Thus, superior reports and encompassing evidence provided to governments and partners increase reaction time and improve the supervision and monitoring of healthcare service provision. By building and providing governments with dashboards, the project's impact can be continuously monitored. Reporting of data can often be done in real-time, increasing the quality and pace of decisions, and enabling governments to react to incidents in a timely fashion. Furthermore, these dashboards can even ensure the harmonization of data (e.g., throughout various projects) and conduct analyses and generate visualizations for reports further increases the value of tools to governments. Furthermore, the continuous evidence can also increase the relevance of the mHealth project as the data provides additional value for partners, especially governments which ensures their long-term backup as a stakeholder.

> *And I hate to use the word win-win, but it is win-win. The department of health [government] is happier because they know that the health metrics that they are interested in are now reported across the whole country. The dashboard now provides harmonized information, and so data can be monitored consistently and metrics can be pulled out in a bundled way. It's really a good solution for all stakeholders to build a unified ecosystem. (I14)*

1.4.3.3 Technology

To reach technological sustainability, the tool has to be embedded in the environment—i.e., integrated with existing systems, aligned with rules and norms, and incorporated into the culture and values of users. Furthermore, the final product or service has to stay flexible and open so that changes can be made to the portfolio if needed. However, while the pilot and scalability phases were of an agile prototypical nature due to continuous improvements to the design, in the sustainable phase, a fully professional development is reached, which is nonetheless updated regularly and contains a maintenance and support service.

> *I am also pushing the fact that apps need to be updated all the time. You know, you regularly get on your mobile device a whole bunch of messages that say, 'These apps need to be updated.' And you don't even think about it. You click on the thing, and it updates those apps. And you have to update those apps because this landscape is moving very quickly. The operating systems on the mobile devices, hacking, all of that stuff moves very quickly. So if you don't keep on maintaining the applications, very soon, they'll stop working. (I14)*

Furthermore, to provide a sustainable technology ecosystem, technology-based services should closely collaborate (e.g., network of digital health interventions) and be built on the same infrastructure (e.g., provided via the same app store) to simplify the usage for end-user, but also to guarantee technical standards and raise awareness of existing services.

> *So for patient apps we put them in the Google PlayStore but for healthcare workers we put them into their own app store. What also happens is the healthcare worker when they register, they register on the app store. So it means that every app that they download they don`t have to re-register every time they download an app for example. (I14)*

1.4.3.4 Usage

Users also play a vital role in the sustainability phase. To achieve usage sustainability, behavior should be automatically monitored, tracked, and analyzed.

> *We are going to get more data, about more things, in a more reliable way that is going to be easier to analyze; and therefore, we have an expectation that it's going to make our oversight and service design and service reform easier and more impactful. (I9)*

The data can be used to improve the provided services and ensure long-term usability and utility. The tool needs to be aligned to the needs of users, generate additional value, and continue to be useful for them. This also ensures a user-centric design and further increases the commitment of users.

Furthermore, the overall objective is to establish a long-lasting user relationship, which on the one hand continuously attracts the user to the tool and guarantees usage but, on the other hand, offers a source for feedback whenever the monitoring of behavioral data indicates possible optimizations. The project management has to constantly work and emphasize the engaging role of the users as stakeholders. The interviewees suggest that a user relationship should be built personally. This provides a personal "face" to the technology, which can be provided through personal training or personal contact via health centers or health facilities.

> *So [name of app] has a face. There are people from the township who go to the huts. We work with the people; we work with the kindergarten teachers and with the parents. They know... they know this Health Education Centre, which is in the middle of the community. (I3)*

1.5 Discussion

This paper aimed to investigate the factors that influence the successful scaling and sustaining of mHealth initiatives in LREs. Based on a qualitative approach, we derived a holistic perspective on the actions that can help mHealth initiatives move beyond the pilot phase. We employed a stakeholder analysis to show that stakeholders are embedded and entangled in the pilot, scale-up, and sustain phases, and change their positions or stakes at the inflection points between the phases. We articulated a model that identifies a processual perspective for project management to prepare for the inconsistent involvement of various stakeholders. We thereby provided a roadmap of action points in four domains to overcome the inflection points that currently keep mHealth initiatives from moving from pilot to scale-up and from scale-up to sustainability. In the following section, we discuss our model and gather insights in light of the 'bigger picture'. Our model aims to structure and communicate knowledge along the trajectory of a single project, but it also has implications for the entire system of selecting and funding consortia to implement innovative ideas.

1.5.1 Regrouping Stakeholders and Building Capacity

While ICT4D has a long-standing research agenda on social networks and the interactions and knowledge sharing of different stakeholders (Andrade & Urquhart, 2010; Braa et al., 2004; Cho et al., 2008), our interviewees confirmed strong collaboration between stakeholders in one initiative. However, they also pointed out that capacity building and knowledge transfer between projects are limited; that is, learning from failure rarely extends beyond the participants of the project.

> *The main issues [of the first project] were that it was a very complicated app [...]; we learned to make simple apps, to do one thing very well, make a simple app that works perfectly, and from there, you can add features. And that's why [name of the second project] is so simple, and it works. That's all. (I8)*

While some of our interviewees emphasized the desire for cross-initiative capacity building, they all pointed to the uniqueness of the value of the knowledge they gained along the way to overcoming obstacles. One of the interviewees, who worked at a global health fund, explained the hesitation around sharing knowledge: knowledge gathered during a pilot phase is seen as a unique selling point for new funding, and such sharing could sabotage the chances of success when applying for funding in the future.

> *[Knowledge transfer] is always a bit tricky because we are also their donors, and we also notice that some of our [funded project] partners don't like to share what the success factors are. Because then they know that the other programs [based on this knowledge] can also somehow get the money, which is then no longer provided to them. (I4)*

However, even the attempt to learn from past experience by deriving guidelines (e.g., the Principles of Digital Development) that are publicized and promoted tends to intensify competition for funding. Publishing these lessons learned and good practices also leads to previously exclusive knowledge becoming generally accessible, which is expected to lead to simplification of the application process. However, the standardization of the mHealth deployment process has led to an increase in the requirements of funding bodies because the following of such guidelines is now required for new projects. This tightens the market, and initiatives have even greater problems fulfilling the complex formal requirements of funding organizations. One interviewee alluded to the complexity of the funding application process:

> *These reports and also the application... Well, they're really half doctoral theses. So, I don't know. For €10,000 you sit there for weeks if you haven't done it before, to answer all these questions that you have to answer. (I3)*

Funding bodies focus on the experience of applicants, as well as their collaboration and long-term perspectives. One interviewee emphasized that the actual project idea, and hence the application field and feasibility of the mHealth initiative, become secondary.

> *[...] in the future, it will certainly always be about the team. That means that in the mHealth area, you have a wide range of people who are involved, and we always look at—do the people understand healthcare at all, and are the people able to implement and support possible solutions in this market in the long term? There are many who on paper have made a theoretically good solution, but in the long term, we simply don't believe in the assertiveness [of participants and the project at the market]. (I1)*

In summary, funding bodies face the challenge of finding the best ideas and the best consortia to pilot, scale up, and sustain them. However, existing means to increase the number of applications (e.g., transparent application guidelines) lead to a higher number of applications to sort through and also an increase in standards for applications. Our proposal to address the competition for funding and the limited exchange of knowledge is to decouple the idea from the stakeholder network. Current funding conditions require unique ideas, multi-faceted stakeholder consortia (from local implementation partners to research partners), and extensive formal processes. In practice, we would expect a market of ideas that brings experienced consortia and stakeholders with good ideas and problem knowledge together to apply for funding. The decoupling of the idea and the stakeholder network would cause the following: a) project ideas (e.g., from local parties based on practical relevance or from researchers based on scientific rigor) can be pursued even if the initiating party does not have a suitable stakeholder network; b) inexperienced stakeholders (e.g., governments or system developers) that would like to enter the market can be integrated with networks and, thus, contribute to an initiative; and c) experienced stakeholders (e.g., those who have already carried out projects and/or have learned from their failures) are coupled with less experienced stakeholders, facilitating the transfer of knowledge and gathering of experience. Eventually, a cycle of new stakeholders will be trained by more experienced stakeholders until the new ones can, in turn, provide training. Moreover, good ideas will have a fighting chance against worse ideas from more experienced consortia.

1.5.2 Rethinking the Funding Scope

While the competition for financing is one aspect of an mHealth initiative, those that receive funding still struggle to achieve scalability and sustainability. Several interviewees reported that they had just ended a project after the initial funded pilot phase.

> *"The first [mHealth] service that we launched was in Africa. We work in [time-limited] projects and receive funding for these [time-limited] projects, which means that if a project ends, the service also ends, which is very sad. That happened in Ethiopia after four years." (I8)*

The situation described by the interviewee is common. The project funding usually covers a limited period regardless of the project's impact and results. As the derived process model shows, in the current setup, project stakeholders are expected to acquire extended funding options during the project's actual duration to ensure smooth continuation after the end of the funding period. This is emphasized as a hurdle, especially for projects that are not well entangled in the local environment.

> *You are there [in the LREs as an international organization] for such a short time, financed, and then you cannot make all the connections you need in such a period. (I8)*

Moreover, we suggest that funding organizations reconsider their scope of funding by including the phases that a project has to go through (pilot, scale-up, and sustain). Our interviewees reported that common practice is to slightly change the project idea or the scope, such as an expansion of users—e.g., starting the project with pregnant women (maternity health) before extending to everyone (general health) (I7)—or a change of operation domain—e.g., from Ethiopia to Suriname (I8)—to suit the currently pilot-oriented funding calls and receive new financial support for an established project. We suggest that funding organizations provide scale-up funding calls for projects for which project consortia can apply in the course of the pilot phase to get stable financial support during the inflection point and proceed to the scale-up phase. If funding organizations expect similar requirements for scale-up or sustain project proposals as for pilot proposals, they help consortia to prepare for inflection points instead of merely attempting to get additional funding.

Most of the interviewees mentioned that their projects are funded by development agencies outside of Africa (e.g., the United Nations, European Union, World Bank, and USAID), which support the agenda of the SDGs and call for project proposals that pertain to digital technology. Therefore, local governments in LREs are in a position in which externally funded money is often the first choice when starting initiatives.

> *In Africa, it is often like that when you come from abroad; the expectation [of the government] is often that you bring money with you. That's simply due to experience. So if every development project is funded by [names of international development agencies] money, then they often expect that they are quite happy to look at it and make approaches, but in return, they expect the costs of the program to be covered externally. They simply say, 'Yes, we like to try things out,' but the expectation is that they will not finance the pilot and that these funds will be acquired elsewhere. (I1)*

This makes it even more difficult when governments are required to provide financial and organizational support for scale-up. During the pilot phase, they are passive actors who have made their infrastructure (e.g., healthcare workers) available and, ideally, have been able to observe an initial impact of the project. In the scale-up phase, the government is expected to take on a new role for which it is usually unprepared in terms of both technological know-how and financial readiness. Thus, governments are caught in a chasm between projects' ambitions and need to scale up on the one hand and their limited resources and knowledge on the other. To bridge this chasm, we propose the following: First, funding agencies could require the inclusion of proportional government funding from the start. This would hold governments accountable for health development in their respective countries, but it would already preselect projects (as not all good project ideas can get support by a government), which would limit the diversity of mHealth interventions and give a lot of decision-making power to governments. Second, governments should establish stable collaborations with digital facilitating organizations if they cannot take on the task themselves. Facilitating organizations must manage and standardize digital tools for governments (e.g., digital platforms with government-approved health apps). However, such facilitating organizations should be financed by governments in the long run.

1.5.3 Fostering Reverse Innovations and Synergistic Research

While Walsham (2012) shaped the research agenda of ICT4D with his question, 'Are we making a better world with ICT?', we would like to discuss the relevance of this call not only for Global South countries in low-resource settings but also for high-income countries. The need for mHealth does not exclusively apply to LREs. It can be argued that, on the one hand, the insightful research findings from such settings can be used to inform IS 'mainstream' research (Sahay et al., 2017), and on the other hand, the innovative products and artifacts may be of value to high-income countries. In IS research, the discrepancy between 'mainstream' researchers and the ICT4D community has been discussed. Sahay et al. (2017) recognized the parallel discourses of both streams and highlighted the similarities of theories, gaps, and problems to emphasize the need to contribute to both streams. Sein et al. (2019) further proposed that the characteristics of LREs can also be found in high-income countries and that ICT4D research should not only take place in the Global South.

We would like to emphasize that not only the synergy of research findings should be addressed, but also the synergy of practical results of interventions. The advantages of mHealth become especially apparent in LREs with scarce healthcare facilities and the need to bring healthcare to the people rather than arranging healthcare provision around a centralized infrastructure. One interviewee emphasized that, in the long term, their mHealth intervention, which provides health education about naturopathy and conventional medicine, should be cross-financed via a rollout in high-income countries.

> *In the future, one idea is that we say we want to launch this app in the European or German market as well, with slightly different content, of course. [...] I think there are also... many people that say, 'We would also like to have this app. Why can't it be made so that it fits our needs?' It could also be made in a slightly more advanced version. A bit of counseling, telemedicine, and distribution of in-app purchases, and so on, would partly finance the project. That would be my favorite idea, as this would be something self-sustaining. (I3)*

This example shows that lessons and innovative ideas from LREs can have the potential to be transferred to high-income countries. Hence, we would like to direct the IS research community's attention to this phenomenon of developing mHealth technology for LREs but finding implications and transfer potential for other non-LREs. To the best of our knowledge, there has not been an intensive discourse on how to approach this opportunity. Specifically, it would be valuable to understand how such a transfer potential can be identified during a pilot and how it should be realized. We imagine that this transfer could be a work package within a project, but questions remain on how to conduct it.

1.5.4 Limitations and Future Directions

Our study is not free of limitations, which indicates opportunities for future research. Our analysis aims to provide a holistic view of the practical process of mHealth initiatives, from pilot to scale-up and sustainability. However, this view is based on data from the perspectives of stakeholders who are involved in decision-making processes and in a position to steer and guide projects. Hence, the derived process is based on 'hearsay' about mHealth users. Future research should investigate the usage domain based on a close investigation of users of mHealth pilots. Topics on individual usage include individual capabilities, personal human development, and the improvement of people's well-being and health as effects of ICT usage (Qureshi, 2015).

Furthermore, our developed framework was implicitly evaluated by reaching a state of theoretical saturation, meaning that the framework took shape during the progression of the interviews and reached its final form before the last interview. However, an explicit evaluation of the framework, i.e., by applying it to conduct an actual project, could provide valuable insights into shortcomings and areas of improvement. Thus, we hope that future research will adapt our framework and refine it.

Lastly, our research is built upon the assumption that mHealth has a positive impact on health development goals, such as universal healthcare coverage and the well-being of all at all ages (UNDP, 2015). While the general research agenda does not question the interlinkage of ICT and development overall (Walsham et al., 2007), there is still a gap in the understanding of how this development process emerges from ICT interventions (Sein et al., 2019). Hence, this article contributes to the literature by providing a holistic stakeholder perspective on the practical transformative process from mHealth pilot projects to scalability and sustainability. However, the scope of this analysis does not include the impact evaluation of health and development outcomes through mHealth interventions. We leave this agenda to others (e.g., Gurman et al., 2012; Krah & de Kruijf, 2016; Marcolino et al., 2018) and further call for research on the development outcomes of individual stakeholders by addressing questions such as 'How do mHealth tools improve working conditions or enable increased productivity for healthcare workers?', 'Do mHealth interventions enable access to a new market or generate new jobs for organizations?' or 'Are there cases where mHealth interventions are detrimental to healthcare, and if yes, why and how could this be prevented?'.

1.6 Conclusion

mHealth interventions are promising when it comes to facilitating and improving healthcare in settings with sparse infrastructure and resources. However, the literature indicates barriers to such interventions that lead to high failure rates of pilot projects, which is known as pilotitis. In the SDG agenda, health interventions require wide reach and long-term service. In this article, we explored how mHealth interventions can be scaled and sustained to support healthcare in LREs. Based on a holistic stakeholder perspective, we derived a phased process and a need for action in four areas that guide the intervention from the pilot phase to scaling and sustainability. We highlighted the existence of inflection points between the phases as critical due to the shifts in stakeholders' roles and support. The failure of mHealth should not be a devastating disease to fight; rather, mHealth projects should be able to reach scale-up and sustainability to support the actual health concerns of LREs. It is our contention that the formulated process can be used as a practical roadmap for future projects and a theoretical lens for understanding the pilotitis affecting mHealth interventions in LREs and thus be the medicine that heals it.

1.7 Appendix

1.7.1 Barriers to mHealth in LREs

Table 30: Summary of Key Barriers

Domain	Barriers	Exemplary Reference
Political	Political instability	(Aranda-Jan et al., 2014; Lester et al., 2010)
	Lack of governmental support	(Leon et al., 2015; O' Connor and O' Donoghue 2015)
	Regulations, laws, and policies	(Kiberu et al., 2017; Mechael et al., 2010; Vesel et al., 2015)
Economic	Scarce funding from doners	(Barnett & Gallegos, 2013; Chirambo et al., 2019; Folaranmi, 2014; E. Lee et al., 2011)
	Limited health budgets of governments	(Stephani, 2019)
	No cooperation between initiatives	(Tomlinson et al., 2013)
Social	Users' lack of health literacy	(Czaja et al., 2006; Hur et al., 2015)
	Language barriers	(Sundin et al., 2016)
	Users' and stakeholders' lack of technical knowledge	(Kiberu et al., 2017; Medhanyie et al., 2015; Sundin et al., 2016)
	Data privacy concerns	(Bigna et al., 2013; Greve, Lichtenberg, et al., 2020; Källander et al., 2013; Nhavoto et al., 2017)
	Sharing of devices	(Rana et al., 2015; Wesolowski et al., 2012)
	Loss of devices due to criminality	(Ginsburg et al., 2015; Leon et al., 2012; Littman-Quinn et al., 2013)
Technological	Insufficiency of networks	(Albabtain et al., 2014; David et al., 2020; Littman-Quinn et al., 2013; Thondoo et al., 2015)
	High costs of mobile data	(Barnett & Gallegos, 2013; Hellström, 2010; Ngabo et al., 2012; Tamrat & Kachnowski, 2012)
	Limited electricity supply	(Emmanuel et al., 2019; Ginsburg et al., 2015; E. Lee et al., 2011; Thondoo et al., 2015)
	Integration to health information systems	(Barkman & Weinehall, 2017; Leon et al., 2012; van Olmen et al., 2020)
	Usability	(Leon et al., 2012; Rowland et al., 2020)

We reviewed articles focusing on mHealth barriers and obstacles in LREs and structured them (Table 30) according to the categorical factors of the political, economic, social, and technological (PEST) framework (Buchanan & Gibb, 1998; Peng & Nunes, 2007). The framework enables one to outline the environment of the considered mHealth initiative. Relying on the PEST analysis offers a holistic analysis of the general environment while also allowing one to yield a health-related context (Gupta, 2013). We identified articles through a keyword search. Articles focused on the following three domains: a) mHealth, health apps b) barriers, obstacles, and hurdles; and c) low-resource environments, the Global South. The review of the relevant articles indicated several noteworthy trends among the framework's factors.

First, some barriers to mHealth consist of political factors. Political instability in a country (e.g., war) hinders the delivery of health services (David et al. 2020; Folaranmi, 2014). Chi et al. (2015) found this to be particularly true for maternal and reproductive health, which are among the most common uses of mHealth interventions. However, even when a policy situation is stable, dealing with outdated or muddled regulations, for example, hinders the adoption of mHealth (van Olmen et al., 2020; Tamrat & Kachnowski, 2012; Wallis et al., 2017), as regulations, laws, and government policies are often not aligned with technological advances (Kiberu et al., 2017; Mechael et al., 2010; Vesel et al., 2015). In particular, when a country has few precedents in healthcare sector digitization (e.g., no electronic health records or hospital information systems), there is a lack of appropriate legislation aligning mHealth applications with the health IS infrastructure (Stroetmann, 2018). In addition, governments seldom see the need for action in the absence of evidence of the impact of mHealth interventions. Often, the available evidence is ambiguous—e.g., health impacts but no economic evidence (Iribarren et al., 2017)—or insufficient (Istepanian & AlAnzi, 2020) and prevents governments from making informed investment decisions and allocating a limited budget to even the most promising health interventions (Mechael et al., 2010). Even when evidence is provided, governments can be barriers in the form of a lack of support for mHealth interventions due to organizational constraints; for example, unclear hierarchical structures inhibit support (Aranda-Jan et al., 2014; O' Connor & O' Donoghue, 2015).

Second, economic barriers can be identified. Most mHealth projects are donor-funded, which limits available financial resources in terms of time and budget (Barnett & Gallegos, 2013; Chirambo et al., 2019; Folaranmi, 2014). To date, governments have had little to no involvement in funding mHealth initiatives (Chirambo et al., 2019; Istepanian & AlAnzi, 2020; Tamrat & Kachnowski, 2012). This is largely due to the limited health budgets available to governments in LREs (Stephani, 2019). Due to the tight overall budget, primary healthcare facilities lack adequate training, supervision, vital supplies, and basic infrastructure (H. Y. Lee et al., 2012). Attempts to sustain funding through advertising-based business models have thus far failed (Botha & Booi, 2016). There is now a variety of mHealth applications in the Global South, but most projects work in isolation and do not consider their environments (Tomlinson et al., 2013). This lack of collaboration inhibits the sharing of experiences (Barkman & Weinehall, 2017; Braa et al., 2004), resulting in the repeated meager developments of similar applications, which not only consumes valuable resources but also requires time and expertise, thus inhibiting progress.

Third, are the societal barriers to the adoption of mHealth. Here, the technology user (i.e., patient, healthcare worker, clinical staff, etc.) has been the focus of research to date. Health literacy is an important factor for mHealth, because to use a health-related application, the user—especially if the mHealth intervention is patient-centered—must be able to understand and interpret the information provided (Waruingi & Underdahl, 2009). Low levels of education combined with low health literacy are barriers to mHealth applications (Albabtain et al., 2014; Waruingi & Underdahl, 2009). Low literacy in general also limits the use of mHealth (Lund et al., 2014). This problem is compounded when multiple local languages exist, making it difficult and costly to translate the application according to local conditions (Sundin et al., 2016). A similar barrier is that the technical knowledge and experience, and thus, the technical affinity of users and stakeholders are low (Kiberu et al., 2017; Medhanyie et al., 2015; Sundin et al., 2016). Healthcare workers are often unable to use mobile devices and applications as intended (Istepanian & AlAnzi, 2020). An important issue in the context of personal health data is privacy. Users have reservations about the use and security of their data and may therefore reject an application (Greve, Lichtenberg, et al., 2020; Istepanian & AlAnzi, 2020; Källander et al., 2013; Nhavoto et al., 2017) Local habits of sharing cell phones in households or among multiple people make it difficult to ensure data privacy (Rana et al., 2015; Wesolowski et al., 2012). There is also a fear of data breaches due to insecure servers and applications (Littman-Quinn et al., 2013). Another issue concerns the possible loss of the user's mobile device due to theft. This particularly affects mHealth applications for healthcare workers who are provided with a gadget in the context of a project (Ginsburg et al., 2015; Leon et al., 2012; Littman-Quinn et al., 2013).

Fourth, many barriers discussed in the research relate to technological factors. A commonly cited barrier is the lack or the inadequacy of network or internet connectivity (Albabtain et al., 2014; Istepanian & AlAnzi, 2020; Ngabo et al., 2012; Tamrat & Kachnowski, 2012). Mobile internet access and data transfers are limited and expensive in the Global South (Barnett & Gallegos, 2013; Ngabo et al., 2012; Tamrat & Kachnowski, 2012). When projects bear this cost, users may abuse this access by using mobile credit for private calls or sharing it with friends (Medhanyie et al., 2015). In addition, power outages hinder the use of mHealth (Iribarren et al., 2015). These outages affect not only charging capabilities but also technical infrastructure, such as servers, resulting in downtime for the entire vital ecosystem (Barnett & Gallegos, 2013). Another barrier is the integration of mHealth with existing government hospital information system (HIS). This is challenging and requires compliance with technological and regulatory requirements (Barkman & Weinehall, 2017; Leon et al., 2012). Often, mHealth interventions are not designed to ensure easy and rapid integration with HIS, or the existing digital infrastructure is already outdated and thus unable to integrate externally developed applications with new forms of data or other inputs (Mechael et al., 2010; Wallis et al., 2017). Finally, the usability of an application can constitute a barrier. Patients are seldom involved in the application development process and accompanying policies; therefore, mHealth interventions lack assurance of suitability for users (McCurdie et al., 2012; Rowland et al., 2020). This results in barriers due to complex application designs and low adaptability (Wallis et al., 2017).

1.7.2 Sustainability and Scalability Frameworks

Table 31: Overview of Topic-Related Sustainability and Scalability Frameworks

Framework (Reference)	Description
Framework for conceptualizing program sustainability (Shediac-Rizkallah & Bone, 1998)	The framework identifies that the factors of the community environments, project design, and implementation factors, and factors within the organizational setting influence a program's sustainability. While the original framework does not consider scalability in the mHealth context, Dharmayat (2019) applies the framework in the context of an mHealth project in Malawi. Stakeholder support is identified as an essential success factor for scalability.
Layered implementation model for scalability (Broens et al., 2007)	The paper introduces a layered implementation model based on product lifecycle, stating that mHealth interventions undergo different stages, from a prototype for small-scale pilots to large-scale pilots and finally to operational products. In each of these phases, different dimensions are the main influence on the successful scale-up of the project. The dimensions considered are technology, acceptance, financing, organization, and policy and legislation. Their literature review also identifies the key stakeholders in the telemedicine system as patients, healthcare professionals, regulators, financiers, technology providers, and healthcare organizations. However, the study does not concern sustainability or low-resource environments.
Health systems framework for decision-making about mHealth for community-based health services (Leon et al., 2012)	The study develops a framework to assess the challenges for mHealth scale-up in South Africa. They found four factors to be considered in the process of decision-making about mHealth that should be scaled for community-based health services: organizational, technological, financial, and stewardship. Stewardship mostly deals with government and policy issues, organizational factors include culture and capacity, technological factors pertain to usability and sustainability, and the financial dimension relates to long-term funding. However, their framework provides a static representation of scalability components that should be considered in the decision-making process to appraise the challenges of scaling up.
The NASSS framework for considering influences on non-adaptation (N), abandonment (A), spread (S), scale-up (S), and sustainability (S) of patient-facing health and care technologies (Greenhalgh et al., 2017)	The study developed a framework to evaluate the success of UK-based digital health programs that not only considers the adoption of the technology but also incorporates the possibility of non-adoption, abandonment, spread, scale-up, and sustainability of health and care technology. To determine the correct option for each case evaluated, they established seven domains, each consisting of various questions. Further, they classified the different challenges of each dimension into three categories: simple, complicated, or complex. While simple challenges are solvable, complicated challenges are difficult to handle, and complex challenges lead to failure.
A conceptual framework for sustainable eHealth implementation (Fanta & Pretorius, 2018)	The paper provides a conceptual framework for the sustainability of eHealth implementation in Global South countries. They argue that sustainability depends on not only technological factors but also interrelated organizational, economic, and social factors. The framework uses an input-process-output-outcome-impact approach and extends this approach by adding feedback loops to underpin the interdependency of components and non-linearity in achieving sustainability. The framework identifies seven reinforcing and two balancing loops for sustainable eHealth implementation. Fanta et al. (2019) used the framework to assess the readiness of hospitals to implement sustainable mHealth solutions.

1.7.3 Qualitative Interviews

Table 32: Leading Questions of Interview Guideline

Overview of mHealth use	How does [name of company] use mHealth apps? How does [name of mHealth app] function in detail? How is the [mHealth intervention] project funded?
mHealth Adoption Process and Stakeholder Involvement	Why did you choose [mHealth app] and how did the different stakeholders support the adoption of the mHealth app? What factors influence the adoption of [mHealth app] by the users? How do stakeholders collaborate and support each other?
Observed reasons for mHealth success and failure	What are the advantages and opportunities of using [mHealth app]? What are the challenges or risks of using [mHealth app]? What obstacles are created by outside factors for [mHealth app]? How do outside factors support the use of [mHealth app]? How do Stakeholder contribute to these obstacles and advantages How would you change [the mHealth app] if you could?
Use of mHealth in the future	Which contribution does mHealth make to health development in the Global South? What and how do stakeholders play a role in the long-term success of reaching healthcare goals, especially in the context of mHealth?

C. Contributions

This cumulative thesis aims to further explore the phenomenon of mobile technology as an assent to address the development agenda regarding healthcare in the Global South. The objectives were to investigate the design and action which needs to be considered to guide interventions towards utility, scalability, and sustainability. To achieve this, research questions were derived with a focus on organizing and assessing existing knowledge (RQ1), investigating the design of mHealth to cope with the challenges of the Global South (RQ2), and subsequently, prong together a guiding framework for mHealth projects to reach scale and sustain (RQ3).

The first section in this final part of the thesis (C.I) recapitulates the findings from each study conducted to answer the core research questions presented in Section A.I.2. Moreover, it synthesizes the results and relates the findings into an overarching view on mHealth4D. The implications for practice and research and the limitations of this thesis are presented in section C.II. Finally, this thesis closes with concluding thoughts about mHealth4D (section C.III).

I. Findings and Synthesis

This section summarizes the results and contributions of each study included and provides answers to each research question posed in section A.I.2. Moreover, the findings are related to one another and support a holistic understanding on an abstracted level.

I.1 Findings for the Status Quo of Health IS Research

The first research question (RQ1) aimed to assess the existing body of research, synthesize prescriptive knowledge, and identify research gaps of the broader body of digital health literature. This "zoomed out" understanding is needed to provide a guidance lens for "zooming in" (Gaskin et al., 2014) by exploring specific interventions of mobile technology to support healthcare in the Global South. Study 1 (Table 33) addresses this question by organizing the current landscape of knowledge through an analysis of the different levels of engagement (i.e., micro and macro-levels) and research paradigms (i.e., behavioral and design research).

Table 33: Findings of Study 1

Title	Framing Research Questions Intersecting Information Systems and Health: A New Research Perspective at Micro- and Macro-Level
Addressed RQ	RQ 1: What is the status quo of IS research on health, and what future research opportunities can be revealed?
Main Contribution	Comprehensive overview of Health IS research through a micro-macro lens concerning belief formation, actions, and outcomes. Six research questions were derived to expedite the development and adoption of IS in healthcare, reveal hitherto underexposed research aspects, and thus guide future research.

Through a systematic literature review (Brendel et al., 2020; vom Brocke et al., 2009; Webster & Watson, 2002) of 46 research papers on healthcare interventions published in the Basket of Eight (Franklin Liu & Myers, 2011; Lowry et al., 2013), the first study organized and structured the existing status quo of Health IS research using the BAO framework as a lens for analysis (Melville, 2010). Building on this framework, the study structures existing knowledge among the macro and micro-levels, connecting social and organizational context with belief, action, and outcome formation, to analyze the impact of digital health interventions. The role of IS in empowering and changing feasible practices was set into focus to examine IS in the changing environment of healthcare.

Based on this analysis, it can be summarized that in Health IS studies, scholars focus slightly more on behavioral research (in contrast to design research) and macro-level investigations (in comparison to micro-level investigations).

The few studies that address the micro-level are concerned with the role of individuals in relation to technology (e.g., user engagement, user behavior, or user interaction). In addition, this individual action is linked to belief formation promoted by organizations, such as eHealth kiosks in India to raise individual awareness about infant care (Venkatesh, Bala, et al., 2016), and outcome assessment, such as studying the impact of individual behavior on the village and society in the context of eHealth kiosks (Venkatesh et al., 2020). While this is one of the few studies looking at the societal outcome, it is worth noting that micro-level studies show very limited interaction with the macro-level, especially concerning societal impact, while interaction with specific organizational outcomes is at least to some extent considered. Further, studies on the micro-level are limited in design focus and rather investigate individual behaviors.

Studies primarily concerned with macro-level outcomes align digital health and organizational structure, for example, by considering design aspects that affect organizational behavior. This includes studies that examine general conditions and challenges in the implementation process, identify specific application areas, and examine the overall impact of IS in the health context. In addition, macro-level research focuses on the linkage between digital health and societal structure. In particular, the focus is on the impact on social system behavior through studies of online communities (e.g., Goh et al. (2016)). Further, research on the macro-level connects the organizations and society at the outcome level; here, the focus is mainly on the implementation of electronic health records (e.g., Adjerid et al. (2018)). It is worth noting that most studies at the societal level take a country-specific perspective (e.g., Liwei Chen et al. (2019)), as health ecosystems vary widely due to different economic and political backgrounds.

Building on the synthesis and organized status quo in Health IS research, several opportunities for future research are identified. In view of the general thesis theme, three specific research opportunities are worth emphasizing. First, the individual belief formation should be triggered. Dadgar and Joshi (2018) investigate how the design of mHealth services influences the self-management of diabetes patients. This is a great example of addressing the opportunities and solutions that technology can offer to influence belief formation, which affects individual action formation, positively. Second, the synthesis reveals that the influence of institutional, societal, and organizational structures on individual health-related beliefs is strongly underrepresented. However, as beliefs are a powerful instrument in the process of long-term sustainable changes, they should receive more attention, specifically by investigating how societal, institutional, and organizational structures influence individual actors' health-related beliefs. Third, research generally shows the positive impact of IS on health outcomes (e.g., clinical studies where it is shown that specific interventions have certain health results), particularly in LMIC. In addition, researchers agree on the need to align institutional and organizational goals (Klecun et al., 2019). However, there is a lack of research that addresses the structures necessary to overcome such obstacles. Therefore, research needs to address how institutional structures foster the adoption of digital health systems at the organizational level.

In summary, the analysis of the broad domain of Health IS research through micro and macro lenses provided insights and research opportunities for informing beliefs, enabling actions, and transforming outcomes that guide exploratory mHealth in the Global South. The six derived research questions hitherto reveal underexposed research aspects and thus illustrate how researchers might begin to tackle complex problems arising at the nexus of IS, healthcare organizations, and society. In the notion of "zooming in and zooming out" (Gaskin et al., 2014), Study 1 provides a "zoomed out" orientation map of the promising research directions (vom Brocke et al., 2015), which motivated the "zooming in" investigation of conducted mHealth research in the Global South. The following studies aim to address these research opportunities by investigating the design of an mHealth app (Study 2), the outcome assessment of the interaction between an organization and individual mHealth users (Study 3), and the organizational and societal structure to enable long-term mHealth adoption (Study 4).

I.2 Findings through Research in the Global South

The second overarching research question aimed to conduct studies that create knowledge while addressing actual health problems in the Global South. Thereby focusing on the need-based design to cope with the challenges and conditions in the environment. This is further subdivided into the design of an mHealth app for CHWs (RQ 2.1) and the investigation of coping with security challenges of mHealth in a culturally sensitive way (RQ 2.2.)

I.2.1 Findings for Designing an mHealth for Community Health Workers

To better understand how mHealth interventions need to be designed to cope with the challenges and conditions of the Global South, Study 2 conducts an action-design research study considering an mHealth app for CHWs to support NCD prevention and counseling in eSwatini. The main contribution of the study is summarized in Table 34.

Table 34: Findings of Study 2

Title	Fostering Non-Communicable Disease Prevention in The Global South: An Action Design Research Project of a Mobile Health Intervention in eSwatini
Addressed RQ	RQ2.1: How can an mHealth app be designed to support decentralized health systems and be usable for community health workers?
Main Contribution	The mHealth app as a fully functional, field-tested, and ready-to-use artifact for CHWs in eSwatini to support their counseling in hypertension and diabetes. Design principles for the generalized problem class of decentralized NCD prevention in the Global South.

Study 2 designs an mHealth app as a supportive tool for NCD counseling of CHWs in eSwatini that fosters personalized risk calculation and overall prevention of hypertension and diabetes. Based on the ADR approach by Sein et al. (2011) and informed by the IS success model (DeLone & McLean, 2002, 2003), the app is iteratively developed based on evaluation cycles with healthcare experts, policymakers, and CHWs. Each iteration contributes to refining the final artifact and the design knowledge generation. Based on seven meta-requirements, a final set of three design principles is derived to theorize the gained knowledge for the generalized problem class (Gregor et al., 2020). The findings of the study are of two abstraction levels. First, the contribution is the developed mHealth artifact itself, which is situated to the practical situation in eSwatini. This means that contextual factors such as the cultural and educational context of the CHW cadre are highly dependent on the selected environment of the country eSwatini. This may also affect the evaluation and specific design features. Second, the design process is finalized by generalizing reflections and learning to provide knowledge (Iivari, 2015) through design principles for the abstracted problem class (Gregor et al., 2020; Gregor & Hevner, 2013). This generalizable knowledge is described in the following.

The derived prescriptive design knowledge is separated into three design principles. The first principle regards the content presentation. At the core is the objective of presenting the content in a comprehensible manner for the CHWs, who have different educational backgrounds, so that they clearly understand the functional content (i.e., how to navigate the app) and the health-related content (i.e., how to prevent NCDs). Mechanisms to support this principle include the use of icons, culturally appropriate semiotics, visualizations (e.g., images and videos), and signal statements. The second design principle addresses workflow automation, aiming for consistent, long-term oriented, and comparable NCD counseling for people through CHWs. The mechanism to attempt this principle includes functions and information along the existing workflow, automated workflow logic, diagnostic functions, the execution of such diagnostics at every visit, and an automatic record of health data history. The third principle emphasizes the need for mobile counseling. The objective of location-independent and data-secured counseling of CHWs can be reached via mobile and tailored ICT. The mechanism supporting this principle includes a personal login, individualized data access for CHWs, an IS tool functional on a mobile device, data storage on the device itself, and asynchronous data backup.

In summary, Study 2 showcases how such an mHealth app can function as an important catalyst for digitally enhanced technology solutions in healthcare; it emphasizes a design tailored to the needs (e.g., information along the existing workflow) and requirements (e.g. comprehensible for illiterate people) of CHWs as an integral part of decentralized health systems and acknowledges the need for research on institutional and organizational change (i.e., task-shifting) to understand the potential of mHealth in various structural forms of development. Further, the ADR methodology enables an iterative redesign of the mHealth app by considering theory and practice simultaneously. The continuous evaluation in the real world and, therefore, consideration of organizational conditions and user feedback support the needed user-participation and contextual considerations.

The design principles enable generalizable knowledge for app designers and support the use of mHealth as an asset for NCD education in the Global South. The findings indicate that countries with a similarly structured decentralized healthcare system can consider developing an mHealth app based on the provided design principles.

I.2.2 Findings for Coping with Security Challenges in a Culturally - Sensitive Way

Research has indicated the high sensitivity of healthcare data and the resulting privacy and security challenges that are explicitly dominant for mHealth. In this regard, RQ2.2. is dedicated to the need of addressing such challenges in a culturally sensitive way. Study 2 is a scenario-based, empirical, cross-cultural investigation of the user perception of recovery communication after a data breach. Table 35 summarizes the findings of the study.

Table 35: Findings of Study 3

Title	Overcoming Digital Challenges: A Cross-Cultural Experimental Investigation of Re-covering from Data Breaches
Addressed RQ	RQ2.2: How can the security challenges of mHealth be addressed and dealt with in a culturally sensitive way?
Main Contribution	The perception of recovery actions offered by an mHealth company after a data breach is dependent on the user's culture.

Study 2 examines people's perception of the design of the announcement of a data breach in which personal health information is breached from a mHealth device. This study has been conducted among Bolivian and German fitness tracker users to investigate the impact of two distinct cultures (House et al., 2004) on the users' perception and reaction.

The study offers three key findings. First, the study examines whether recovery actions (compensation and apology) after a data breach have an influence on mHealth service users' perception and behaviors that is culture-dependent. The results show that an apology influences loyalty, trust, and word of mouth for German and Bolivian users. However, compensation has a positive effect on the three dependent variables only for the German sample. Thus, recovery actions are perceived differently across cultures.

Second, a link between the study's findings and differences in the cultural dimension could indicate that the lower value of in-group collectivism (low in German and high in Bolivia) implies the individualism of German culture, which could cause the acceptance of compensation as a recovery action. Individuals from individualistic cultures prefer to keep a distance between themselves and others. Material assets can create this distance.

Therefore, it is possible to provide such distance through compensation. Furthermore, the different uncertainty avoidance of the cultures (high in Germany and low in Bolivia) may be the reason for an overall critical attitude of Germans towards recovery communication.

Third, the study generally shows that mHealth providers need to take responsibility for digital inclusion by addressing the emerging security challenges themselves. Since the results show that relationships are strengthened by apologetic communication, especially mHealth providers that are currently on the rapid rise of digitalization (such as in the Global South) should disclose the data breaches to their users, even if it is not legally required. An apology that costs virtually nothing can be a strategic way to inform users when a data breach has occurred while ensuring user satisfaction and loyalty.

In summary, Studies 2 and 3 provide in-depth insights into the specifics of mHealth in the Global South. Both emphasize the user-specific design of a) an mHealth app and b) recovery communication after a security incident.

I.3 Findings for Fostering Scalability and Sustainability

Building on the organized knowledge base, identified research opportunities, and investigations of specific mHealth contexts in the Global South, the last research question (RQ 3) aims to provide a holistic perspective on mHealth interventions in the Global South through an investigation of projects' process towards scalability and sustainability (see Table 36).

Table 36: Findings of Study 4

Title	Healing the 'Pilotitis' in Mobile Health – A Holistic Stakeholder Perspective on Making Interventions Scalable and Sustainable in Low-Resource Environments
Addressed RQ	RQ3: How can mHealth interventions reach scalability and sustainability?
Main Contribution	A holistic processual model for overcoming the pilot phase and achieving sustainability from the outset of mHealth projects by describing the stakeholder involvement and actions needed at the four domains economy, environment, technology, and users.

The current mHealth landscape shows that interventions face many challenges, especially in the Global South. As a result, the pilot projects are frequently discontinued after their initial phase. This problem is of high practical relevance and is already rigorously embedded in research (e.g., Braa et al., 2004). However, there is a need to generate findings so that stakeholders and the general public can benefit from them (Ilavarasan, 2017; Schelenz & Pawelec, 2021). Study 4 provides this holistic perspective by synthesizing the experiences, best practices, and learnings of mHealth interventions in the Global South. The study is built on the interpretive stakeholder analysis methodology

(Pouloudi et al., 2016) and expert interviews with 17 mHealth stakeholders (including researchers, digital health consultants, and health funds).

The main finding of the study is a procedural model to cover the steps towards mHealth initiative sustainability. The process divides the phases according to the need for action of the respective stakeholders into four areas: economy, environment, technology, and usage. In the economic domain, the respective stakeholders are funders such as donor organizations and the local government. In the environmental domain, these are stakeholders with a thematic interest and a substantial stake in the project, such as the Ministry of Health, nongovernmental organizations, and research institutions. In the technology area, stakeholders include system developers and IT funders. In the usage domain, stakeholders include the end users such as patients, CHWs, or medical staff.

The model identifies the scale-up phase as subsequent to the pilot phase and a prerequisite (antecedent phase) for sustainability. The transitions from one phase to another are referred to as inflection points, as these are identified to be the critical areas where mHealth projects experience difficulties and fail. In particular, stakeholder roles and expectations change at inflection points, and it is essential to understand the relevant tasks before and after these points to gain an understanding of how stakeholders enable the transition from one phase to another.

The offered holistic perspective on interventions helps individual mHealth projects to move beyond the pilot phase. As a result, the embedding and involvement of the various stakeholders in the pilot, scale-up, and sustain phases and the engagement or role allocation at the inflection points between the phases are of interest. The process perspective helps project management prepare for the conflicting involvement of the various stakeholders. In this way, the model provides a roadmap with action items that structure along the development of a single project. It also shows the implications for the entire system, from the selection and funding of consortia to the implementation of innovative ideas.

I.4 Synthesis of Findings

In the following, the findings of the four studies are summarized (see I.4.1) and synthesized by deriving a holistic, socio-technical view to conceptualize mHealth4D (see I.4.2). Building on this, the findings are reflected by discussing the relevance and value in a practical manner (see I.4.3).

I.4.1 Summary of Findings

Having summarized and recapitalized the findings of the four studies included in this thesis, the main findings are synthesized in Table 37 for each of the four research questions.

Table 37: Main Findings for Research Questions

Section	Research Question	Main Findings
I. Assessing the status quo: structuring Health IS research	RQ 1: What is the status quo of IS research on health, and what future research opportunities can be revealed?	- The status quo of Health IS research offers insight for the research agenda on mHealth4D. - Current knowledge indicated the different levels of research engagement in the health environment. - Overall, design research, research at the micro-level and its interaction with the macro-level, as well as the influences of macro-level structures to enable long-term mHealth adoption are underrepresented.
II. Research in the Global South: fostering design and action towards utility	RQ2.1: How can an mHealth app be designed to support decentralized health systems and be usable for CHWs?	- The content of an mHealth service needs to be presented in a comprehensible manner that ensures that all CHWs understand it. - The existing workflow of the CHW counseling has to be supported by the automated diagnostic service. - The device has to be mobile, to allow flexible, location-independent, and data-secured counseling.
	RQ2.2: How can the security challenges of mHealth be addressed and dealt with in a culturally sensitive way?	- mHealth in the Global South is explicitly affected by security risks and hence vulnerable to data breaches. Regions (such as the Global South) that have been rapidly introduced to internet-related technology, lack data protection regulations, and mature infrastructure. - mHealth providers in the Global South are affected by the consequences of data breaches. Recovery communication offers a possibility to rebuild the relationship with affected users. This communication needs to be culturally tailored. - Due to the high in-group collectivism of culture, Bolivian do not positively perceive an offered compensation, while apology affects loyalty, trust, and word of mouth of users.
III. Synthesis of knowledge: towards scalability and sustainability	RQ3: How can mHealth interventions reach scalability and sustainability?	- The pilot phase is a starting phase for mHealth4D initiatives followed by the scalability phase and the sustainability phase. - The transition from one phase to the other is highly critical, these inflection points are often the reason for project failure. - The stakeholder involvement can be separated into four categories: economy, environment, technology, and usage. The roles and responsibilities of the stakeholder change at inflection points.

The four studies provided new insight into the design and action of mobile technology as an asset for healthcare development driven by SDG3 in the Global South, thereby adding to the growing knowledge base for the emerging use of mobile technology in this agenda and geographical-specific context. The research opportunity was addressed through the overall research agenda of Health IS research from micro/macro-level perspectives (Study 1). The studies that were conducted on specific aspects in the Global South underlined the potential of mHealth in this environment. Moreover, they provide insight on how to generate utility through design (Study 2) and a culturally sensitive response to security challenges (Study 3). Building on this utility, Study 4 synthesized the findings through a processual model that drives mHealth interventions towards scalability and sustainability. However, while the potential of mHealth4D is evident, all studies indicate the challenging nature that the healthcare environment in the Global South provides. Research and practice are just at the beginning of investigating and tackling this complex environment.

I.4.2 Deriving a Socio-Technical Conceptualization of mHealth4D

Viewing the technology itself as just one component of a socio-technological system offers a lens to understand what mHealth4D is and what it may become in the future. The IS discipline is primarily concerned with the interplay of humans and digital information or technology to conduct specific tasks (Recker, 2021). Therefore, the socio-technical perspective considers the technology and the individual equally in social contexts and interprets the outcomes as a result of their interaction (Sarker et al., 2019). In this notion, Varshney (2014) depicted mHealth as an interplay of *healthcare professionals* as the main decision-makers in medical care, the *IT* in the form of a mobile device, the *service* (application) as the healthcare provided, and the *patient* as the user of the IT and receiver of the healthcare service (see section A.II.2.). Adopting and extending this framework and thus considering the general notion of socio-technical systems (Sarker et al., 2019) allows for organizing and a better understanding of what mHealth4D is and how this phenomenon needs to be designed, taken into action, and further explored.

To conceptualize mHealth4D, it is helpful to derive the full model in a stepwise manner. First, an understating of the social components and how in an analog manner the task is performed by these is needed (see I.4.2.1). This means how healthcare services are provided by healthcare professionals and offered to patients. This is depicted generally and then discussed under the constraints of the Global South. Second, an understanding is generated of how mobile technology can facilitate the task of healthcare provision (see I.4.2.2). Thereby, the technical components are introduced, and their influence on social components is described. This is, again, first described in a general manner and then contextualized to the setting of the Global South. Lastly, building on this understanding, a holistic socio-technical view of mHealth4D is derived and discussed (see I.4.2.3).

I.4.2.1 The Task of Providing Healthcare

The task is to provide a *healthcare service* (e.g., diagnosis, prevention, and treatment). In the initial analogous context, this task is performed by a *healthcare professional* on a patient (Silva et al., 2015). Since the service can be multifaceted, we refer to the person receiving the service as "*people*" since "patient" refers to someone suffering from a disease, which is not necessarily the case (e.g., for prevention services). However, in the Global South, healthcare professionals are generally located in urban areas (de Carvalho et al., 2021). Therefore, *CHWs* are facilitators who receive limited training but visit people in rural areas to provide basic healthcare to people who cannot see healthcare professionals (Olaniran et al., 2017). Hence, the actor involvement varies when considering the context of the Global South. The context, including environmental, economic, and social factors, further influences the desired and necessary healthcare service (de Carvalho et al., 2021). For example, diseases are context-specific, but diagnostic and therapeutic opportunities depend on local infrastructure and healthcare equipment (Islam et al., 2014).

I.4.2.2 Facilitating Healthcare Provision via Mobile Technology

By including a mobile device as a facilitator for mobile services in this interplay of actors, a holistic socio-technical perspective on mHealth is gained. The *mobile device* itself only serves as the IT tool to provide the *healthcare service*. The service can be a compliment or a substitute to the analog healthcare provision, but it also offers the possibility of fully innovative services (Akter et al., 2013; Miah et al., 2017). In the Global South, mHealth services often provide opportunities for new services that could not be conducted analogously (e.g., NCD risk calculation in Study 2) (Motamarri et al., 2014). The mobile device and healthcare service are thereby interacting and interlinked in both directions. Further, the remaining role of the *healthcare professional* is highly dependent on the service. In the Global South where healthcare professionals are very scarce, the objective of mHealth is to provide a service that can so far not be offered by healthcare professionals to people, e.g., at a scaled level or in rural areas. Therefore, the function of the healthcare professional is extended through technology. To achieve this, healthcare professionals are involved in the design process to define and inform the service in light of medical experience and knowledge (Mechael, 2009). This role can, for example, be supplemented by the Ministry of Health or international healthcare experts (Study 2, Study 4). The interaction is one-directional, as the healthcare professional only informs and directs the design and functionalities of the service. In most cases, a continuous interaction of healthcare professionals with the service is not intended to relieve the load on the professionals (as in Study 2). However some services are built on exactly this interaction, i.e., telemedicine (Hailemariam et al., 2010; Ndlovu et al., 2014). Lastly, the user (*people* or *CHW*) interacts with both the healthcare service and the mobile device. As described before, the role of the CHW as a mediator of healthcare is very unique in the Global South and hence offers a high potential to address the CHW as the primary user of mHealth (as in Study 2) (Early et al., 2019; Källander et al., 2013). However, there are also mHealth projects in the Global South that aim at the people as the direct users (Eze et al., 2020).

I.4.2.3 A Holistic Socio-Technical View on mHealth4D

Building on this understanding of the interplay of social actors and technical components, Figure 22 visualized this holistically. In the following, the role of context and explicitly of the contextual factors of health agenda-driven development in the Global South are discussed.

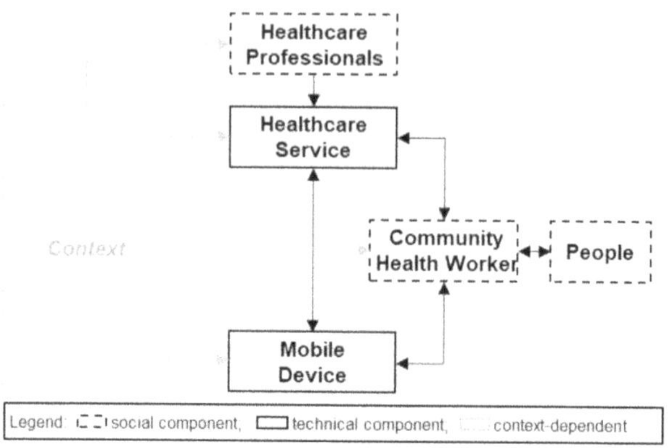

Figure 22: A Holistic Socio-Technical View on mHealth4D

Concerning the first component, the *mobile device*, the presented studies, and further research have highlighted that on the one hand, the selection of device is highly dependent on the health context (see section A.II.2). However, this selection is limited through infrastructural and technical constraints of the local environment (Istepanian & AlAnzi, 2020). While several studies emphasize the wide spread of mobile technology among people in the countries of the fGlobal South (Akter & Ray, 2010; Heeks, 2020), the devices are usually of the older generation, limiting the processing power and functionalities (Study 4). Further, special devices such as fitness trackers and sensors are only slowly emerging (Heeks, 2020). Therefore, building an mHealth project on such devices needs consideration of acquisition costs. Further, the context determines the operability of such devices. In the Global South, mobile data access is often unavailable in rural areas, compounded by power outages and connection failures (Albabtain et al., 2014; Istepanian & AlAnzi, 2020; Ngabo et al., 2012; Tamrat & Kachnowski, 2012). The obstacles of this environment are addressed in Study 4. Further Study 3 investigates the specific security challenges that are generally alluded to the mobile device, however, contexts such as regulations, laws, and policies highly influence this (Kiberu et al., 2017; Mechael et al., 2010; Vesel et al., 2015).

The second component, the *healthcare service*, refers to the service provided through the mobile device, such as the content and utility provided by a smartphone app (e.g., Study 2). This service is highly context-dependent but offers great potential for development (Latif et al., 2017; Niemöller et al., 2016). While Study 4 aimed to guide mHealth project, independent of the healthcare service offered, Study 2 emphasizes the need to design mHealth in dependence of the service and the user group. Overall, it is important to gain an understanding of the existing ecosystem with its particular structures and needs. This is especially important to capture the complexity of the healthcare context.

Further, political structures, interests of involved stakeholders, and roles of decision-makers are aspects that influence the healthcare service (Waugaman, 2016)

The social actors –*healthcare professionals,* and *CHWs*— are also influenced by the context. Factors such as education (relevant for the health training of CHWs (Early et al., 2019)) and experience with technology (affecting trust in technology and usability (Leon et al., 2012) are context-specific. The context is especially relevant for an understanding of the user interaction and user acceptance (Hoque, 2016; Venkatesh et al., 2012). As Middleton et al. (2014) point out, users can take on different roles that are highly dependent on the context. CHWs are in the professional role when they use mHealth as an asset to their work. This is influenced by organizational context (e.g., job need, trust in employer) and the professional context (e.g., loyalty to job, desire to serve the community). Furthermore, as highlighted in research on human-computer interaction, social actors as humans have specific characteristics in terms of demographics and disposition that need to be taken into account when interacting with technology (P. Zhang & Li, 2004). This further acknowledges the need to include the user through a participatory design process (e.g., Study 2).

In summary, the view on mHealth4D extends the conceptualizations of mHealth (e.g., (Varshney, 2014)) for the Global South context and completes the processual model of mHealth4D initiatives on pilot, scalability, and sustainability of Study 3 particularly by holistically viewing at technical and social components and depicting the role of context on such. In the following, the practical guidance for mHealth initiatives is discussed.

I.4.3 Contextualizing the Findings to Understand Relevance and Value

The implementation bottleneck of mHealth interventions has made it increasingly obvious that context matters (Holeman & Barrett, 2017) and that there is a need for coherent, alternative perspectives on more appropriate ICT4D design and action. As this thesis results in a processual view on mHealth intervention scale-up and sustainability (Study 4) and a socio-technical perspective on mHealth4D (see section I.4.2.3), a theoretical and structured lens is provided which is of high value for practitioners involved in mHealth projects as well as researchers.

Study 2 presented one specific mHealth project (the use case of supporting NCD prevention), which can serve as an example of the practical value generated through the theoretical findings. To emphasize and utilize the relevance and value of these findings, in the following the derived theoretical conceptualizations are applied in the practical context of NCD prevention in eSwatini. While Study 2 solely focused on the design and initiation, the conceptual and theoretical findings of this thesis enable practical guidance for the long-term utility, scalability, and sustainability of the initiative.

As described in Study 2, the initiative introduces an mHealth app to support hypertension and diabetes prevention in the context of CHW counseling in eSwatini. While the technical result is a fully developed app, the project is a typical example of a funder-initiated intervention with a multidisciplinary and international project consortium. Hence, stakeholder engagement is limited to the project scope and the intervention is limited in scale. Therefore, the aspect of scale-up and sustainability to extend the original project scope is needed to be considered to overcome the risk of pilotitis (i.e. discontinuance of mHealth service after project end). Following the processual perspective of Study 4, the project endeavors the inflection point between the pilot and scale-up phase. Considering the current status of the mHealth intervention for NCD prevention in eSwatini, the findings suggest three main considerations.

First, it becomes apparent that to reach the scale-up phase, the project must achieve an expansion of the user base. This mainly concerns the technical components, especially the number of mobile devices. Since only a certain number of CHWs have been equipped with tablets under the project budget, funding opportunities for additional devices need to be leveraged through stakeholders (e.g., government or international donors). In addition, partnership and collaboration with other mHealth projects are desirable so that technology initiatives do not compete and synergies (e.g., multiple mHealth services through one device) can be exploited.

Second, social actors play an essential role in long-term use and acceptance. Study 2 primarily involves CHWs in the design process of the app in a participatory manner. However, user co-creation is also essential for scaling and sustainability. Since the CHWs are used as intermediaries in this context, continuous training of this target group is necessary to evaluate usage and user behavior. In addition, the acceptance and trust of the people who receive the counseling must be evaluated. Thereby, medical evidence is also a factor, which should be continuously verified by experts (international and national).

Thirdly, the health development process is the main objective of an mHealth initiative. Thus, the mHealth service must be implemented as part of the national health program. This is mainly possible through government support. To achieve this, the Ministry of Health must receive long-term, demonstrable validation of the effect and added value of the initiative (e.g., on a data basis).

The three mentioned aspects are examples for the relevance and practical value of the theoretical lens provided by the findings of this thesis. Further, the limitations are mentioned, before the overall implications for research and practice are discussed.

II. Limitations and Implications

This thesis contains four studies that explore the phenomenon of mobile technology as an asset of health development in the Global South. The findings of the individual studies were presented and a synthesized view was derived in the previous section. Building on this, the following section discusses the limitations (see II.1) and resulting implications for research and for practice (see II.2).

II.1 Limitations

Researchers and practitioners should consider the following limitations when interpreting the findings of this thesis.

First of all, the thesis relies heavily on a practice-driven phenomenon, which is still in the early stages of academic development. In order to approach the mHealth4D phenomenon, the research of two established IS research streams (Health IS ad ICT4D) is considered. Both, however, are very extensive and broad in their scope and, in turn, are strongly practice-oriented and of a multidisciplinary nature. This means that this thesis, in its explorative dynamic, gives a first approach to the scope of the phenomenon through design knowledge and action guidance, which is not intended to be definite or exhaustive.

In order to address the limitation of broadness, the scope of the underlying research streams was narrowed down. Some steps were taken to substantiate the research background that informed this thesis. First, the broadness of the research streams was made apparent, and, after a conscientious review of the relevant literature, the respective understanding that provides a knowledge base for this work was defined. In this step, for example, the acronym and term mHealth4D was introduced, which did not previously exist in the literature. This also contributed to structuring the terminology. In addition, specific emphasis was placed on the relevant aspects to better capture them. For example, mobile technology was reduced to three core aspects (device, service, and user), which excluded other levels of abstraction. In addition, the work focused on the perspective of the technology interacting with the environment and the adjacent project perspective, which further narrowed down the relevant aspects.

In order to avoid the impression of completeness, it must also be acknowledged that the studies in the second part, which are designated as research conducted in the Global South, are to be understood as two case studies that examine individual aspects (the design for CHW and the communication of security challenges) as examples. At this point, other context-specific aspects could have been addressed, such as the investigation of modern technologies, i.e., artificial intelligence; or mHealth as a supportive tool in health facilities, i.e., clinical decision support. To account for this specificity, mHealth4D was subsequently synthesized as a socio-technical phenomenon. It should be noted, however, that this representation does not concretize the context-specific factors. However, this is attempted to be addressed in Study 4 through the stakeholder perspective.

In addition, there are other limitations. Although the socio-technical perspective is appropriate to consider both the technical artifacts and the individuals who use artifacts in social contexts (Briggs et al., 2010), some limitations need to be mentioned in relation to the perspective and its application in this work. The synthesized view on mHealth4D emphasizes the technical components and limits its view on the involved social actors. This uneven emphasis encounters the technical imperative that implies that technology causes changes in the social world (Robey et al., 2013). Further, the proposed view lacks consideration of outcomes. Sarker et al. (2019) call for the consideration of humanistic and instrumental outcomes. Nevertheless, the individual studies aim to at least partially address the outcome perspective. For example, Study 2 includes both outcome types in the design process of the mHealth app.

Finally, there are significant limitations with regard to the methodology chosen. Study 1 is limited to the status quo of high-ranking IS research on health. This does not take into account the multidisciplinary topic but is limited to the IS perspective. The choice of outlets further restricts the generalizability of the results. The ADR project in Study 2 initiates an mHealth intervention to address the specific problem in eSwatini. On this basis, generalizable knowledge of a more abstract problem class was derived (Iivari, 2015). As the design principles were only derived based on this one intervention, there is a need to test and validate them (Gregor & Hevner, 2013) to ensure generalizability. Study 3, as an experimental study, offers the advantage of the control and precision of variables. However, the replicability of the studies should be checked in order to generalize the results. In addition, only two countries were examined in the cross-cultural study; again, additional countries with other cultural dimensions could strengthen the interpretation of the results. Since Study 4 has an exploratory and qualitative character, the generalizability of its results must be particularly questioned here.

The research environment must also be mentioned as a limitation. This thesis speaks generally about the Global South and tries to generate results that are generalizable to the region. This is a well-known phenomenon that has already been criticized many times (Bai, 2018). Countries in the Global South are diverse in all characteristics. In Studies 2 and 3, one country was selected for each as the specific context setting. Study 4 tries to consider generalizability by interviewing experts in different countries, but here it becomes also clear that diversity cannot be completely covered and still remains limited.

II.2 Implications for Research and Practice

This thesis sheds light on the practical and theoretical relevance of the phenomenon of mobile technology as an asset to the health development agenda in the Global South. Building on the findings and contributions of the individual studies and their synthesis, this section recognizes the theoretical and practical implications of this thesis.

The contributions enabled and advanced the understanding of and knowledge about mHealth4D. However, the utility and usefulness of the contributions will only become clear through the guidance and direction of future research and practices (Corley & Gioia, 2011). Following Ågerfalk & Karlsson (2020), contributions are distinguishable into three types: theoretical, empirical, and artifactual. Further, an implication exists in relation to a contribution and can be directed to research or practice. In the following, the contributions and their implications are discussed and ordered by the type of contribution. An overview of this is provided in Table 38.

The *theoretical contributions*, which include new or modified theories (Ågerfalk & Karlsson, 2020), of this thesis are twofold. First, the synthesis of the studies provides a socio-technical model of mHealth4D (see section I.4.2.) This new perspective on and conceptualization of the phenomenon results in implications for research and practice. As postulated by Varshney (2014), this helps to realize advances in mHealth. There are major challenges that need to be addressed, and a conceptualization supports the structure and guides future research and practice. The challenges are even catalyzed through the complex environment of the Global South (Leon et al., 2012) The socio-technical lens supports this conceptualizing work by emphasizing the interplay of technology and actors, which has been recognized in ICT4D research also (Avgerou, 2017; Sein et al., 2019). Therefore, the derived view in section I.4.2 provides opportunities for ICT4D research to adapt and transfer this perspective to its other domains (e.g., economy and agriculture). This is further supported by theorizing specifically for ICT4D (Tibben, 2015). For Health IS researchers the socio-technical lens provides the opportunity to structure, identify, and tackle challenges of mHealth according to social actors, technical components, and their interplay. This supports the pathway to reach the full advantages of mHealth as an asset for development. For the practice domain, there is the opportunity for stakeholders in decision-making and strategic positions, such as development agencies and governments, to gain a deep and theory-informed understanding of the contextual influences and dependencies between involved entities. This supports informed and guided action-taking and enables the stakeholder to overcome barriers while aiming for long-term development support through scales and sustained mHealth interventions.

Second, Study 4 provides a theoretical contribution through a holistic processual model, which addresses the phased pathway of mHealth interventions from the pilot phase to the scale-up phase to the sustainability phase. Based on this new framework, IS researchers are able to empirically investigate the project management of mHealth interventions (e.g., predicting project sustainability); further, researchers can transfer and adopt the framework to other ICT4D projects (besides mHealth) or generalize for digital health projects. For mHealth stakeholders, the framework is an orientation map for their process and synthesis on challenging domains and the changing nature of the roles of involved stakeholders (Eze et al., 2020). This enables identifying the current situation the mHealth initiative is in, as well as deriving implications and anticipation for future actions to overcome challenges and enable the transformation process towards scalability and sustainability. This is also practical guidance for stakeholders following the Principles for Digital Development that demand practitioners to "design for scale" and "build for sustainability" (Waugaman, 2016).

The *empirical contributions* of this thesis are provided by Study 1 and Study 3. Both studies investigate a phenomenon that has not (or only in limited scope) been covered by research (Ågerfalk & Karlsson, 2020). In Study 1, this phenomenon is Health IS research, which is analyzed based on a new perspective based on the BAO framework (Melville, 2010). Hence the contribution is a comprehensive overview that leads to research questions to expedite the development and adoption of IS in healthcare, revealing hitherto underexposed research aspects and thus guiding future research. This has implications for ICT4D research and Health IS research. On the one hand, the understanding and analysis reveal insights that inform ICT4D researchers on opportunities for the investigation of digital and mobile health in the Global South. On the other hand, Health IS researchers receive guidance to produce pioneering knowledge in their domain to further enable the digital transformation of healthcare.

In Study 3, the empirical contribution is provided through the empirical finding that perceptions of recovery communication after a security incident are culturally dependent. The influence of culture in the context of data breach recovery actions had not been investigated before (Goode et al., 2017). This implies that IS researchers should further investigate the mediating role of culture in the communication of security challenges and perception of justice. The role of culture is important when transferring findings from IS studies conducted in the Global North to the Global South or vice versa (Sahay et al., 2017). The practical implications entail an understanding of user behavior based on cultural dimensions. Further, mHealth providers and involved stakeholders should anticipate communicating security incidents, i.e., data breaches, to affected users through an apologetic message, as this positively affects the customer relationship. The call for digital inclusion and handling of digital challenges is thereby proactively advocated (Riggins & Dewan, 2005).

Lastly, the *artifactual contribution* is provided by Study 2 in the form of a new mHealth app for CHW counseling on NCD prevention in eSwatini. This is resulting from the intervention-oriented ADR research (Sein et al., 2011). The artifact itself results in a contribution based on the change due to the intervention. This is further supported by a theoretical contribution that generalized the design and learnings in the form of design principles and an empirical contribution in the form of a rich description of the design process based on measurements, observations, and descriptions regarding the app in relation to its organizational and social context (Ågerfalk & Karlsson, 2020; Hevner et al., 2004). This provides the opportunity for Health IS and ICT4D researchers to empirically account for the impact on health development based on the app and empirically evaluate the design principles. For the practice domain, the artifact is a blueprint that can be transferred to other countries that face similar decentralized health systems and lack sufficient NCD care, thereby following the principle for digital development "reuse and improve" (Waugaman, 2016). Further, the design principles offer guidance to development agencies and governments for new mHealth solutions of the problem's class. Lastly, the stakeholders in eSwatini that are involved in the intervention take direct advantage of the artifact and can spread it further, extend its scope to other NCDs, or integrate it into their local health data management IS.

Table 38: Overview of Implications

	Contributions	Implications	
		Opportunities for Research	**Opportunities for Practice**
Theoretical	*Overarching:* Socio-technical system perspective explains how the context influences the interplay of users and mHealth in the Global South.	For *ICT4D researchers* to analyze the use of mobile technology in other domains than healthcare in the Global South and for *Health IS researcher* to explain challenges of mHealth based on the components of the socio-technical perspective.	For *development agencies and health ministries/ governments in the Global South* to consider the mHealth' social actors, technical components, and their interplay separately in the cultural context for informed action that leads to scaled and sustained interventions.
	Study 4: A holistic processual model for overcoming the pilot phase and achieving sustainability from the outset of mHealth projects. Stakeholder engagement and their dynamic role in projects must be considered in mHealth project management to reach scalability and sustainability.	For *IS researchers* to predict mHealth4D project sustainability and to transfer the model to general digital health projects or ICT4D projects.	For all *mHealth stakeholders* to identify the situation of their mHealth initiative and their stakeholder role to construct judgments that implicate actions leading to improving their situation (e.g. reaching a new phase).
Empirical	*Study 1:* Comprehensive overview of Health IS research through a micro-macro lens concerning belief formation, actions, and outcomes. Six research questions were derived to expedite the development and adoption of IS in healthcare, reveal hitherto underexposed research aspects, and thus guide future research.	For *Health IS researchers* to conduct pioneering research that refines their perspectives and generates new knowledge to support that the healthcare domain is fully brought into the digital age, contributing to development worldwide. For *ICT4D researchers* to transfer research opportunities of Health IS to investigate mHealth4D.	
	Study 3: The perception of recovery actions offered by an mHealth company after a data breach is dependent on the users' culture. Cultural dimensions provide an understanding of perceptional differences.	For *IS researcher* to theorize about culture as a mediator in communication in the context of IT security challenges and perception of justice in recovery strategies.	For *mHealth providers and involved stakeholders* to understand user behavior and adopt existing (often unregulated) practices in the Global South by proactively communicating security incidents.
Artifactual	*Study 2:* The mHealth app as a fully functional, field-tested, and ready-to-use artifact for CHWs in eSwatini to support their counseling in hypertension and diabetes. Design principles for the generalized problem class of decentralized NCD prevention in the Global South. The ADR methodology supports the dynamic interplay of technical and social components and enables participatory design approaches.	For *Health IS and ICT4D researchers* for empirical accounts regarding the particular health development agenda outcomes (e.g. number of diagnosed NCDs) based on the mHealth artifact itself and its design principles.	For *development agencies and health ministries/ governments in the Global South* to transfer the mHealth app to their specific context. For the *involved stakeholders in eSwatini* to take advantage of the new mHealth app by exposing more CHWs to it, extend the scope to more diseases or integrate the app into the local health management system.

III. Concluding Remarks

The most valuable asset in human life is one's health, yet today's world is still characterized by great inequality in supporting this good. The COVID-19 pandemic is one recent example of this very inequality between the Global North and South, such as in terms of vaccine distribution (Nhamo et al., 2021).

Therefore, a major challenge for us all is to try to create a better world by addressing this inequality. For this, the use of technology must be considered as an indispensable asset (not as a panacea) (Walsham, 2012). This is because technology can enable people from disadvantaged backgrounds to improve their skills and increase their participation in matters that affect their lives, such as their health.

This thesis explores this global issue and focuses on the use of mobile technology for health development in the Global South. This problem-oriented perspective on the mHealth4D phenomenon investigates, on the one hand, the design of mHealth in and, on the other hand, the actions that actors need to take to overcome the challenges of long-term implementation and use.

The four presented studies make a multifaceted contribution to the promising but so far limited nature of mHealth4D investigation in support of the development driven by SDG 3. Taking into account the nexus of research and practice, the focus is placed on research conducted in the Global South concerning individual mHealth initiatives that address a specific development problem within the health sector of individual countries. This is motivated by an analysis of the current knowledge base on health IS, which offers insight into the micro and macro engagement of current research with digital health interventions. The results are brought together in an overarching study that focuses on mHealth initiatives and examines their project management from a stakeholder perspective with the aim of project sustainability. The understanding gained enables an abstract socio-technical view of mHealth4D as a phenomenon.

The objective of this thesis was to emphasize and demonstrate how research can support the challenging nature and still limited utility, scalability, and sustainability of mobile technology interventions in the context of healthcare support and development aid. In conclusion, it is hoped that lessons can be learned from this thesis so that a) future mHealth projects can better utilize the potential benefits of mobile technology and that b) research continues to support this through pioneering practice-oriented research, with both motivated by and aimed at supporting the healthcare situation of the people of the Global South.

References

Adam, M., McMahon, S. A., Prober, C., & Bärnighausen, T. (2019). Human-Centered Design of Video-Based Health Education: An Iterative, Collaborative, Community-Based Approach. *Journal of Medical Internet Research*, *21*(1), e12128. https://doi.org/10.2196/12128

Adams, J. S. (1963). Toward an understanding of inequity. Journal of Abnormal and Social Psychology. *Journal of Abnormal and Social Psychology*, *67*(5), 422–436.

Adjerid, I., Adler-Milstein, J., & Angst, C. (2018). Reducing medicare spending through electronic health information exchange: The role of incentives and exchange maturity. *Information Systems Research*, *29*(2), 341–361. https://doi.org/10.1287/isre.2017.0745

Adu, E. K., Mills, A., & Todorova, N. (2021). Factors influencing individuals' personal health information privacy concerns. A study in Ghana. *Information Technology for Development*, *27*(2), 208–234. https://doi.org/10.1080/02681102.2020.1806018

Agarwal, R., Gao, G. G., DesRoches, C., & Jha, A. K. (2010). The digital transformation of healthcare: Current status and the road ahead. In *Information Systems Research* (Vol. 21, Issue 4, pp. 796–809). https://doi.org/10.1287/isre.1100.0327

Ågerfalk, P. J. (2010). Getting pragmatic. *European Journal of Information Systems*, *19*(3), 251–256. https://doi.org/10.1057/ejis.2010.22

Ågerfalk, P. J., & Karlsson, F. (2020). Artefactual and empirical contributions in information systems research. *European Journal of Information Systems*, *29*(2), 109–113. https://doi.org/10.1080/0960085X.2020.1743051

Aivazpour, Z., Valecha, R., & Chakraborty, R. (2018). The Impact of Data Breach Severity on Post-Breach Online Shopping Intention. *ICIS 2018 Proceedings*.

Aker, J. C., & Mbiti, I. M. (2010). Mobile Phones and Economic Development in Africa. *Journal of Economic Perspectives*, *24*(3), 207–232. https://doi.org/10.1257/jep.24.3.207

Aklilu, A., Lessa, L., & Negash, S. (2020). Understanding the role of stakeholders in fostering sustainability of ICT4D projects: Towards a conceptual framework. *26th Americas Conference on Information Systems*.

Akter, S., D'Ambra, J., Ray, P., & Hani, U. (2013). Modelling the impact of mHealth service quality on satisfaction, continuance and quality of life. *Behaviour and Information Technology*, *32*(12), 1225–1241.

Akter, S., & Ray, P. (2010). mHealth - an Ultimate Platform to Serve the Unserved. *Yearbook of Medical Informatics*, 75–81.

Al-Ramahi, M., Park, I., & Liu, J. (2016). Users acceptance of health behavioral change support systems. *22nd Americas Conference on Information Systems*, 1–5.

Albabtain, A. F., AlMulhim, D. A., Yunus, F., & Househ, M. S. (2014). The role of mobile health in the developing world: a review of current knowledge and future trends. *Cyber Journals: Multidisciplinary Journals in Science and Technology, Journal of Selected Areas in Health Informatics [JSHI]*, *4*(42), 10–15.

Ali, M., & Bailur, S. (2007). The Challenge of " Sustainability " in ICT4D – Is Bricolage the Answer? *Proceedings of the 9th International Conference on Social Implications of Computers in Developing Coutries*, *29*(May), 54–60.

Anderson, C. L., & Agarwal, R. (2011). The Digitization of Healthcare: Boundary Risks,

Emotion, and Consumer Willingness to Disclose Personal Health Information. *Information Systems Research*, *22*(3), 469–490. https://doi.org/10.1287/isre.1100.0335

Andrade, A. D., & Urquhart, C. (2010). The affordances of actor network theory in ICT for development research. *Information Technology and People*, *23*(4), 352–374. https://doi.org/10.1108/09593841011087806

Angst, & Agarwal. (2009). Adoption of Electronic Health Records in the Presence of Privacy Concerns: The Elaboration Likelihood Model and Individual Persuasion. *MIS Quarterly*, *33*(2), 339. https://doi.org/10.2307/20650295

Arage, T. M., Bélanger, F., & Tesema, T. B. (2015). Influence of national culture on employees' compliance with Information systems security (ISS) policies: Towards iss culture in Ethiopian companies. *Americas Conference on Information Systems*.

Aranda-Jan, C. B., Mohutsiwa-Dibe, N., & Loukanova, S. (2014). Systematic review on what works, what does not work and why of implementation of mobile health (mHealth) projects in Africa. *BMC Public Health*, *14*(1), 188. https://doi.org/10.1186/1471-2458-14-188

Arnott, D., & Pervan, G. (2012). Design Science in Decision Support Systems Research: An Assessment using the Hevner, March, Park, and Ram Guidelines. *Journal of the Association for Information Systems*, *13*(11), 923–949. https://doi.org/10.17705/1jais.00315

Asaddok, N., & Ghazali, M. (2017, August 3). Exploring the usability, security and privacy taxonomy for mobile health applications. *International Conference on Research and Innovation in Information Systems, ICRIIS*. https://doi.org/10.1109/ICRIIS.2017.8002472

Asi, Y. M., & Williams, C. (2018). The role of digital health in making progress toward Sustainable Development Goal (SDG) 3 in conflict-affected populations. *International Journal of Medical Informatics*, *114*, 114–120. https://doi.org/10.1016/j.ijmedinf.2017.11.003

Atun, R., Davies, J. I., Gal, E. A. M., Bärnighausen, T. W., & Beran, D. (2018). Diabetes in sub-Saharan Africa: from clinical care to health policy - The Lancet Diabetes & Endocrinology. *Lancet Diabetes and Endocrinology*, *5*(8), 622–667. https://www.thelancet.com/journals/landia/article/PIIS2213-8587(17)30181-X/fulltext

Avgerou, C. (2008). Information systems in developing countries: A critical research review. *Journal of Information Technology*, *23*(3), 133–146. https://doi.org/10.1057/palgrave.jit.2000136

Avgerou, C. (2017). Theoretical Framing of ICT4D Research. In *14th International Conference on Social Implications of Computers in Developing Countries (ICT4D)* (Issue May, pp. 10–23). https://doi.org/10.1007/978-3-319-59111-7_2

Avram, E., Ionescu, D., & Mincu, C. L. (2015). Perceived Safety Climate and Organizational Trust: The Mediator Role of Job Satisfaction. *Procedia - Social and Behavioral Sciences*, *187*, 679–684. https://doi.org/10.1016/j.sbspro.2015.03.126

Ayabakan, S., Bardhan, I., Zheng, Z. (Eric), & Kirksey, K. (2017). The Impact of Health Information Sharing on Duplicate Testing. *MIS Quarterly*, *41*(4), 1083–1103. https://doi.org/https://doi.org/10.25300/MISQ/2017/41.4.04

Baark, E., & Heeks, R. (1999). Donor-funded information technology transfer projects: Evaluating the life-cycle approach in four Chinese science and technology projects. *Information Technology for Development*, *8*(4), 185–197. https://doi.org/10.1080/02681102.1999.9525309

Bai, Y. (2018). Has the Global South become a playground for Western scholars in information and communication technologies for development? Evidence from a three-journal analysis. *Scientometrics*, *116*(3), 2139–2153.

Bailur, S. (2007). Using Stakeholder Theory to Analyze Telecenter Projects. *Information Technologies and International Development*, *3*(3), 61–80. https://doi.org/10.1162/itid.2007.3.3.61

Baird, A., Angst, C., & Oborn, E. (2018). Health Information Technology. In *MIS Quarterly Research Curations*.

Baird, A., Davidson, E., & Mathiassen, L. (2017). Reflective Technology Assimilation: Facilitating Electronic Health Record Assimilation in Small Physician Practices. *Journal of Management Information Systems*, *34*(3), 664–694. https://doi.org/10.1080/07421222.2017.1373003

Baker, T. L., Meyer, T., & Johnson, J. D. (2008). Individual differences in perceptions of service failure and recovery: The role of race and discriminatory bias. *Journal of the Academy of Marketing Science*, *36*(4), 552–564. https://doi.org/10.1007/s11747-008-0089-x

Balasubraman, S., Peterson, R. A., & Jarvenpaa, S. L. (2002). Exploring the Implications of M-Commerce for Markets and Marketing. *Journal of the Academy of Marketing Science*, *30*(4), 348–361. https://doi.org/10.1177/009207002236910

Banker, R. D., & Kauffman, R. J. (2004). 50th Anniversary Article: The Evolution of Research on Information Systems: A Fiftieth-Year Survey of the Literature in Management Science. *Management Science*, *50*(3), 281–298.

Bannon, L. (2011). Reimagining HCI: Toward a More Human-Centered Perspective. *Interactions*, *18*(4), 50–57. https://doi.org/10.1145/1978822.1978833

Bao, C., Bardhan, I. R., Singh, H., Meyer, B. A., & Kirksey, K. (2020). Patient-Provider Engagement and its Impact on Health Outcomes: A Longitudinal Study of Patient Portal Use. *MIS Quarterly*, *44*(2), 699–723. https://doi.org/10.25300/MISQ/2020/14180

Barkman, C., & Weinehall, L. (2017). Policymakers and mHealth: roles and expectations, with observations from Ethiopia, Ghana and Sweden. *Global Health Action*, *10*(sup3), 1337356. https://doi.org/10.1080/16549716.2017.1337356

Barnett, I., & Gallegos, J. V. (2013). *Using mobile phones for nutrition surveillance: a review of evidence*. https://opendocs.ids.ac.uk/opendocs/bitstream/handle/20.500.12413/2602/AGER1.pdf?sequence=1

Baron, R. M., & Kenny, D. A. (1986). The Moderator-Mediator Variable Distinction in Social Psychological Research: Conceptual, Strategic, and Statistical Considerations. *Journal of Personality and Social Psychology*, *51*(6), 1173–1182.

Bashshur, R., Shannon, G., Krupinski, E., & Grigsby, J. (2011). The taxonomy of telemedicine. *Telemedicine and E-Health*, *17*(6), 484–494. https://doi.org/10.1089/tmj.2011.0103

Baskerville, R., Baiyere, A., Gregor, S., Hevner, A., & Rossi, M. (2018). Design science research contributions: Finding a balance between artifact and theory. *Journal of the Association for Information Systems*, *19*(5), 358–376. https://doi.org/10.17705/1jais.00495

Basole, R. C., & Karla, J. (2011). On the Evolution of Mobile Platform Ecosystem Structure and Strategy. *Business & Information Systems Engineering*, *3*(5), 313–322. https://doi.org/10.1007/s12599-011-0174-4

Batchelor, S., & Norrish, P. (2005). Framework for the assessment of ICT pilot projects: Beyond Monitoring and Evaluation to Applied Research. In *infoDev*.

BBC News. (2013). *Vodafone Germany hack hits two million customers - BBC News*. https://www.bbc.com/news/technology-24063621

Behne, A., & Teuteberg, F. (2020). A Healthy Lifestyle and the Adverse Impact of its Digitalization: The Dark Side of Using eHealth Technologies. In *15th International Conference on Wirtschaftsinformatik* (Vol. 1, pp. 584–599). https://doi.org/10.30844/wi_2020_f2-behne

Benbasat, I., & Zmud, R. W. (1999). Empirical research in information systems: The practice of relevance. *MIS Quarterly: Management Information Systems*, *23*(1), 3–16. https://doi.org/10.2307/249403

Bernardi, R. (2017). Health information systems and accountability in Kenya: A structuration theory perspective. *Journal of the Association for Information Systems*, *18*(12), 931–957. https://doi.org/10.17705/1jais.00475

Bernardi, R., & Exworthy, M. (2020). Clinical managers' identity at the crossroad of multiple institutional logics in it innovation: The case study of a health care organization in England. *Information Systems Journal*, *30*(3), 566–595. https://doi.org/10.1111/isj.12267

Bernardi, R., Sarker, S., & Sahay, S. (2019). The role of affordances in the deinstitutionalization of a dysfunctional health management information system in Kenya: An identity work perspective. *MIS Quarterly*, *43*(4), 1177–1200. https://doi.org/10.25300/MISQ/2019/14187

Berner-Rodoreda, A., Geldsetzer, P., Bärnighausen, K., Hettema, A., Bärnighausen, T., Matse, S., & McMahon, S. A. (2020). "It's hard for us men to go to the clinic. We naturally have a fear of hospitals." Men's risk perceptions, experiences and program preferences for PrEP: A mixed methods study in Eswatini. *PLOS ONE*, *15*(9), e0237427. https://doi.org/10.1371/journal.pone.0237427

Berthon, P., Pitt, L., Ewing, M., & Carr, C. L. (2002). Potential research space in MIS: A framework for envisioning and evaluating research replication, extension, and generation. *Information Systems Research*, *13*(4), 416–427. https://doi.org/10.1287/isre.13.4.416.71

Best, M., & Dialogue, A. (2010). Understanding Our Knowledge Gaps: Or, Do We Have an ICT4D Field? And Do We Want One? *Information Technologies & International Development*, *6*, 49–52.

Bhatia, A., Matthan, R., Khanna, T., & Balsari, S. (2020). Regulatory Sandboxes: A Cure for mHealth Pilotitis? *Journal of Medical Internet Research*, *22*(9), e21276. https://doi.org/10.2196/21276

Bhattacherjee, A. (2012). Social Science Research: Principles, Methods, and Practices.

In *Textbooks Collection* (Vol. 3). http://scholarcommons.usf.edu/oa_textbooks/3

Bies, R. ., & Shapiro, D. . (1987). Interactional justice: The influence of causal accounts. *Social Justice Research*, *1*(2), 199–218.

Bigna, J. J. R., Kouanfack, C., Noubiap, J. J. N., Plottel, C. S., & Koulla-Shiro, S. (2013). A randomized blinded controlled trial of mobile phone reminders on the follow-up medical care of HIV-exposed and HIV-infected children in Cameroon: study protocol (MORE CARE). *Trials*, *14*(1), 313. https://doi.org/10.1186/1745-6215-14-313

Blaya, J. A., Fraser, H. S. F., & Holt, B. (2010). E-health technologies show promise in developing countries. *Health Affairs*, *29*(2), 244–251. https://doi.org/10.1377/hlthaff.2009.0894

Botha, A., & Booi, V. (2016). mHealth implementation in South Africa. In P. Cunningham & M. Cunningham (Eds.), *2016 IST-Africa Conference. 11-13 May 2016, Durban, South Africa* (pp. 1-13 TS-CrossRef). IEEE. https://doi.org/10.1109/ISTAFRICA.2016.7530667

Braa, Hanseth, Heywood, Mohammed, & Shaw. (2007). Developing Health Information Systems in Developing Countries: The Flexible Standards Strategy. *MIS Quarterly*, *31*(2), 381. https://doi.org/10.2307/25148796

Braa, Monteiro, & Sahay. (2004). Networks of Action: Sustainable Health Information Systems across Developing Countries. *MIS Quarterly*, *28*(3), 337. https://doi.org/10.2307/25148643

Bradley, G., & Sparks, B. (2012). Explanations: If, when, and how they aid service recovery. *Journal of Services Marketing*, *26*(1), 41–50. https://doi.org/10.1108/08876041211199715

Brendel, A. B., Trang, S., Marrone, M., & Lichtenberg, S. (2020). What To Do for a Literature Review? - Synthesis of Literature Review Practices. *Proceeding of Americas Conference on Information System*, *August*, 1–14.

Brenner, S. N., & Cochran, P. (1991). The Stakeholder Theory of the Firm. *Proceedings of the International Association for Business and Society*, *2*, 897–933. https://doi.org/10.5840/iabsproc1991235

Briggs, R. O., Nunamaker, J. F., & Sprague, R. H. (2010). Special Section: Social Aspects of Sociotechnical Systems. *Journal of Management Information Systems*, *27*(1), 13–16. https://doi.org/10.2753/MIS0742-1222270101

Briscoe, C., & Aboud, F. (2012). Behavioural change communication targeting four health behaviours in developing countries: A review of change techniques. *Social Science and Medicine*, *75*, 612–621. https://doi.org/10.1016/j.socscimend.2012.03

Broens, T. H. F., Huis in't Veld, R. M. H. A., Vollenbroek-Hutten, M. M. R., Hermens, H. J., van Halteren, A. T., & Nieuwenhuis, L. J. M. (2007). Determinants of successful telemedicine implementations: a literature study. *Journal of Telemedicine and Telecare*, *13*(6), 303–309. https://doi.org/10.1258/135763307781644951

Broy, D. (2017). Germany: Starting Implementation of the GDPR - Brief Overview of the Government Bill for a New Federal Data Protection Act. In *European Data Protection Law Review (EDPL)* (Vol. 3, Issue 1). https://doi.org/10.21552/edpl/2017/1/13

Bruns, K., & Jacob, F. (2014). Value-in-Use and Mobile Technologies. *Business & Information Systems Engineering*, *6*(6), 349–359. https://doi.org/10.1007/s12599-014-0349-x

Buchanan, S., & Gibb, F. (1998). The information audit: An integrated strategic approach. *International Journal of Information Management*, *18*(1), 29–47. https://doi.org/10.1016/S0268-4012(97)00038-8

Bukelo, M. F., Kiran, D., Ramakrishna, G. B., Bukelo, M. J., Kiran, P. R., Kulkarni, V., Kumar, N., Kanchan, T., & Unnikrishnan, B. (2015). Risk factors for Non-Communicable diseases among rural adolescents: A school-based cross-sectional study. *Asian Journal of Pharmaceutical and Clinical Research*, *8*(2), 284–287.

Buntin, M. B., Burke, M. F., Hoaglin, M. C., & Blumenthal, D. (2011). The Benefits Of Health Information Technology: A Review Of The Recent Literature Shows Predominantly Positive Results. *Health Affairs*, *30*(3), 464–471. https://doi.org/10.1377/hlthaff.2011.0178

Burton, C., Weller, D., & Sharpe, M. (2007). Are electronic diaries useful for symptoms research? A systematic review. *Journal of Psychosomatic Research*, *62*(5), 553–561. https://doi.org/10.1016/j.jpsychores.2006.12.022

Campbell, K., Gordon, L. A., Loeb, M. P., & Zhou, L. (2003). The economic cost of publicly announced information security breaches: Empirical evidence from the stock market. *Journal of Computer Security*, *11*(3), 431–448. https://doi.org/10.3233/JCS-2003-11308

Caplin, N. (2011). *Details Of The Welcome Back Programme For SCEE Users - PlayStation.Blog.Europe*. PlayStation.Blog. https://blog.eu.playstation.com/2011/05/16/details-of-the-welcome-back-programme-for-scee-users-2/

Chang, D. S., & Wang, T. H. (2012). Consumer preferences for service recovery options after delivery delay when shopping online. *Social Behavior and Personality*, *40*(6), 1033–1044. https://doi.org/10.2224/sbp.2012.40.6.1033

Chaudhuri, A. (2012). ICT for development: Solutions seeking problems. *Journal of Information Technology*, *27*(4), 326–338. https://doi.org/10.1057/jit.2012.19

Chen, Langtao, Baird, A., & Straub, D. (2019a). An Analysis of the Evolving Intellectual Structure of Health Information Systems Research in the Information Systems Discipline. *Journal of the Association for Information Systems*, *20*, 1023–1074. https://doi.org/10.17705/1jais.00561

Chen, Langtao, Baird, A., & Straub, D. (2019b). Fostering Participant Health Knowledge and Attitudes: An Econometric Study of a Chronic Disease-Focused Online Health Community. *Journal of Management Information Systems*, *36*(1), 194–229. https://doi.org/10.1080/07421222.2018.1550547

Chen, Liwei, Baird, A., & Rai, A. (2019). Mobile health (Mhealth) channel preference: An integrated perspective of approach-avoidance beliefs and regulatory focus. *Journal of the Association for Information Systems*, *20*(12), 1743–1773. https://doi.org/10.17705/1jais.00584

Cheung, G. W., & Lau, R. S. (2008). Testing Mediation and Suppression Effects of Latent Variables. *Organizational Research Methods*, *11*(2), 296–325. https://doi.org/10.1177/1094428107300343

Chi, P. C., Bulage, P., Urdal, H., & Sundby, J. (2015). Perceptions of the effects of armed conflict on maternal and reproductive health services and outcomes in Burundi and Northern Uganda: a qualitative study. *BMC International Health and Human Rights*, *15*(1), 7. https://doi.org/10.1186/s12914-015-0045-z

Chiasson, M. W., & Davidson, E. (2004). Pushing the contextual envelope: developing and diffusing IS theory for health information systems research. *Information and Organization*, *14*(3), 155–188. https://doi.org/10.1016/j.infoandorg.2004.02.001

Chib, A., Van Velthoven, M. H., & Car, J. (2015). MHealth adoption in low-resource environments: A review of the use of mobile healthcare in developing countries. *Journal of Health Communication*, *20*(1), 4–34. https://doi.org/10.1080/10810730.2013.864735

Chipidza, W., & Leidner, D. (2017). ICT4D Research – Literature Review and Conflict Perspective. *Proceedings of the 23rd Americas Conference in Information Systems*.

Chirambo, G. B., Muula, A. S., & Thompson, M. (2019). Factors affecting sustainability of mHealth decision support tools and mHealth technologies in Malawi. *Informatics in Medicine Unlocked*, *17*(August), 100261. https://doi.org/10.1016/j.imu.2019.100261

Cho, S., Mathiassen, L., & Nilsson, A. (2008). Contextual dynamics during health information systems implementation: an event-based actor-network approach. *European Journal of Information Systems*, *17*(6), 614–630. https://doi.org/10.1057/ejis.2008.49

Choi, B., Kim, S. S., & Jiang, Z. (Jack). (2016). Influence of Firm's Recovery Endeavors upon Privacy Breach on Online Customer Behavior. *Journal of Management Information Systems*, *33*(3), 904–933. https://doi.org/10.1080/07421222.2015.1138375

Choi, J. K., & Ji, Y. G. (2015). Investigating the Importance of Trust on Adopting an Autonomous Vehicle. *International Journal of Human-Computer Interaction*, *31*(10), 692–702. https://doi.org/10.1080/10447318.2015.1070549

Cobos Muñoz, D., Merino Amador, P., Monzon Llamas, L., Martinez Hernandez, D., & Santos Sancho, J. M. (2017). Decentralization of health systems in low and middle income countries: a systematic review. *International Journal of Public Health*, *62*(2), 219–229. https://doi.org/10.1007/s00038-016-0872-2

Cohen, J., Coleman, E., & Abrahams, L. (2015). Use and impacts of e-health within community health facilities in developing countries: A systematic literature review. *23rd European Conference on Information Systems*.

Collins, J., Sainato, V., & Khey, D. (2011). Organizational Data Breaches 2005-2010: Applying SCP to the Healthcare and Education Sectors. *International Journal of Cyber Criminology*, *5*(1), 794–810.

Connolly, L. Y., Lang, M., & Wall, D. S. (2019). Information Security Behavior: A Cross-Cultural Comparison of Irish and US Employees. *Information Systems Management*, *36*(4), 306–322. https://doi.org/10.1080/10580530.2019.1651113

Cooley, M. (2000). Human-Centered Design. In R. . Jacobson & R. Jacobson (Eds.), *Information Design* (pp. 59–81). MIT Press.

Corley, K. G., & Gioia, D. A. (2011). Building Theory about Theory Building: What Constitutes a Theoretical Contribution? *Academy of Management Review*, *36*(1), 12–32. https://doi.org/10.5465/amr.2009.0486

Czaja, S. J., Charness, N., Fisk, A. D., Hertzog, C., Nair, S. N., Rogers, W. A., & Sharit, J. (2006). Factors predicting the use of technology: Findings from the center for research and education on aging and technology enhancement (create). *Psychology and Aging*, *21*(2), 333–352. https://doi.org/10.1037/0882-7974.21.2.333

Dadgar, M., & Joshi, K. D. (2018). The Role of Information and Communication Technology in Self-Management of Chronic Diseases: An Empirical Investigation through Value Sensitive Design. *Journal of the Association for Information Systems*, *19*(2), 86–112. https://doi.org/10.17705/1jais.00485

Daft, R. L., & Lengel, R. H. (1986). Organizational Information Requirements, Media Richness and Structural Design. *Management Science*, *32*(5), 554–571. https://doi.org/10.1287/mnsc.32.5.554

David, N., Kah, M., Tyndall, J., & Longe, O. (2020). Contextual Contradictions to the scaling-up of mobile health in armed-conflict settings of north-eastern nigeria: a case study of ALMANACH. In *Proceedings of the 13th IADIS International Conference Information Systems 2020* (pp. 99–106). IADIS Press. https://doi.org/10.33965/is2020_202006L012

Davidson, E., Baird, A., & Prince, K. (2018). Opening the envelope of health care information systems research. *Information and Organization*, *28*(3), 140–151. https://doi.org/10.1016/j.infoandorg.2018.07.001

Davis, F. D. (1989). Perceived Usefulness, Perceived Ease of Use, and User Acceptance of Information Technology. *MIS Quarterly*, *13*(3), 319. https://doi.org/10.2307/249008

Davison, R., Martinsons, M. G., & Kock, N. (2004). Principles of canonical action research. *Information Systems Journal*, *14*(1), 65–86. https://doi.org/10.1111/j.1365-2575.2004.00162.x

de Carvalho, G., Schmid, A., & Fischer, J. (2021). Classifications of health care systems: Do existing typologies reflect the particularities of the Global South? *Global Social Policy*, *21*(2), 278–300. https://doi.org/10.1177/1468018120969315

De Neve, J. W., Garrison-Desany, H., Andrews, K. G., Sharara, N., Boudreaux, C., Gill, R., Geldsetzer, P., Vaikath, M., Bärnighausen, T., & Bossert, T. J. (2017). Harmonization of community health worker programs for HIV: A four-country qualitative study in Southern Africa. *PLoS Medicine*, *14*(8), e1002374. https://doi.org/10.1371/journal.pmed.1002374

del Río-Lanza, A. B., Vázquez-Casielles, R., & Díaz-Martín, A. M. (2009). Satisfaction with service recovery: Perceived justice and emotional responses. *Journal of Business Research*, *62*(8), 775–781. https://doi.org/10.1016/j.jbusres.2008.09.015

DeLone, W. H., & McLean, E. R. (1992). Information Systems Success: The Quest for the Dependent Variable. *Information Systems Research*, *3*(1), 60–95. https://doi.org/10.1287/isre.3.1.60

DeLone, W. H., & McLean, E. R. (2002). Information systems success revisited. *Proceedings of the Annual Hawaii International Conference on System Sciences*. https://doi.org/10.1109/HICSS.2002.994345

DeLone, W. H., & McLean, E. R. (2003). The DeLone and McLean Model of Information Systems Success: A Ten-Year Update. *Journal of Management Information Systems*, *19*(4), 9–30. https://doi.org/10.1080/07421222.2003.11045748

Demirezen, E. M., Kumar, S., & Sen, A. (2016). Sustainability of Healthcare Information Exchanges: A Game-Theoretic Approach. *Information Systems Research*, *27*(2), 240–258. https://doi.org/10.1287/isre.2016.0626

Dennis, A. R. (2019). An unhealthy obsession with theory. *Journal of the Association for*

Information Systems, *20*(9), 1404–1409. https://doi.org/10.17705/1jais.00572

Dennis, A. R., & Valacich, J. S. (2001). Conducting Experimental Research in Information Systems. *Communications of the Association for Information Systems*, *7*(5), 1–41. https://doi.org/10.17705/1cais.00705

Dery, K., & MacCormick, J. (2012). Managing mobile technology: The shift from mobility to connectivity. *MIS Quarterly Executive*, *11*(4), 159–173.

Dewan, S., Ganley, D., & Kraemer, K. L. (2004). Across the Digital Divide: A Cross-Country Analysis of the Determinants of IT Penetration. *Personal Computing Industry Center, Graduate School of Management, University of California, USA*, *6*(November), 409–432.

Dharmayat, K. I. (2019). Sustainability of 'mHealth' interventions in sub-Saharan Africa: a stakeholder analysis of an electronic community case management project in Malawi. *Malawi Medical Journal*, *31*(3), 177–183. https://doi.org/10.4314/mmj.v31i3.3

Díaz Andrade, A., Techatassanasoontorn, A. A., & Ou, C. (2019). Making the developing world a better place with high-impact IS research. *Information Systems Journal*, *29*(4), isj.12252. https://doi.org/10.1111/isj.12252

Digital Development Principles Working Group. (2021). *Principles for Digital Development*. https://digitalprinciples.org/

Dinev, T., Goo, J., Hu, Q., & Nam, K. (2009). User behaviour towards protective information technologies: The role of national cultural differences. *Information Systems Journal*, *19*(4), 391–412. https://doi.org/10.1111/j.1365-2575.2007.00289.x

Dissanayake, I., Nerur, S., Singh, R., & Lee, Y. (2019). Medical crowdsourcing: Harnessing the "wisdom of the crowd" to solve medical mysteries. *Journal of the Association for Information Systems*, *20*(11), 1589–1610. https://doi.org/10.17705/1jais.00579

Ditsa, G. E. M., & Ojo, S. O. (2011). E-Health technologies in attainment of the millennium development goals for africa healthcare system. *ACIS 2011 Proceedings - 22nd Australasian Conference on Information Systems*.

DLA Piper. (2020). *Data Protection Laws of the World | Bolivia*.

Döringer, S. (2021). 'The problem-centred expert interview'. Combining qualitative interviewing approaches for investigating implicit expert knowledge. *International Journal of Social Research Methodology*, *24*(3), 265–278. https://doi.org/10.1080/13645579.2020.1766777

Duxbury, L., Higgins, C., Smart, R., & Stevenson, M. (2014). Mobile Technology and Boundary Permeability. *British Journal of Management*, *25*(3), 570–588. https://doi.org/10.1111/1467-8551.12027

Early, J., Gonzalez, C., Gordon-Dseagu, V., & Robles-Calderon, L. (2019). Use of Mobile Health (mHealth) Technologies and Interventions Among Community Health Workers Globally: A Scoping Review. *Health Promotion Practice*, *20*(6), 805–817. https://doi.org/10.1177/1524839919855391

Emmanuel, G., Hungilo, G. G., & Emmanuel, A. W. R. (2019). A Mobile Application System for Community Health Workers-A Review. In Unknown (Ed.), *ICCAI 2019. 2019 5th International Conference on Computing and Artificial Intelligence : April 19-22, 2019, Bali, Indonesia* (pp. 106–110). The Association for Computing Machinery.

https://doi.org/10.1145/3330482.3330485

Essén, A., & Värlander, S. W. (2019). How technology-afforded practices at the micro-level can generate change at the field level: Theorizing the recursive mechanism actualized in Swedish rheumatology 2000-2014. *MIS Quarterly*, *43*(4), 1155–1176. https://doi.org/10.25300/MISQ/2019/12164

European Commission. (2009). The Socio-Economic Impact of Interoperable Electronic Health Record (EHR) and ePrescribing Systems in Europe and Beyond. *EHR Impact*, *October*, 44.

Eze, E., Gleasure, R., & Heavin, C. (2020). Mobile health solutions in developing countries: a stakeholder perspective. *Health Systems*, *9*(3), 179–201. https://doi.org/10.1080/20476965.2018.1457134

Fanta, G. B., & Pretorius, L. (2018). A conceptual framework for sustainable ehealth implementation in resource-constrained settings. *South African Journal of Industrial Engineering*, *29*(3 Special Edition), 132–147. https://doi.org/10.7166/29-3-2055

Fanta, G. B., Pretorius, L., & Erasmus, L. (2019, August 1). Hospitals' readiness to implement sustainable smartcare systems in Addis Ababa, Ethiopia. *PICMET 2019 - Portland International Conference on Management of Engineering and Technology: Technology Management in the World of Intelligent Systems, Proceedings*. https://doi.org/10.23919/PICMET.2019.8893824

Fichman, R. G., Kohli, R., & Krishnan, R. (2011). Editorial Overview —The Role of Information Systems in Healthcare: Current Research and Future Trends. *Information Systems Research*, *22*(3), 419–428. https://doi.org/10.1287/isre.1110.0382

Findikoglu, M., & Watson-Manheim, M. B. (2016). Linking macro-level goals to micro-level routines: EHR-enabled transformation of primary care services. *Journal of Information Technology*, *31*(4), 382–400. https://doi.org/10.1057/s41265-016-0023-5

Fjeldsoe, B. S., Marshall, A. L., & Miller, Y. D. (2009). Behavior Change Interventions Delivered by Mobile Telephone Short-Message Service. *American Journal of Preventive Medicine*, *36*(2), 165–173. https://doi.org/10.1016/j.amepre.2008.09.040

Flavián, C., Guinalíu, M., & Gurrea, R. (2006). The role played by perceived usability, satisfaction and consumer trust on website loyalty. *Information and Management*, *43*(1), 1–14. https://doi.org/10.1016/j.im.2005.01.002

Folaranmi, T. (2014). mHealth in Africa: challenges and opportunities. *Perspectives in Public Health*, *134*(1), 14–15. https://doi.org/10.1177/1757913913514703

Fornell, C., & Larcker, D. F. (1981). Evaluating Structural Equation Models with Unobservable Variables and Measurement Error: A Comment. *Journal of Marketing Research*, *18*(1), 39–50.

Fortagne, M. A., Reith, R., Diel, S., Buck, C., Eymann, T., & Lis, B. (2021). Covid-19 Infection Tracing with Mobile Apps: Acceptance and Privacy Concerns. *Forty-Second International Conference on Information Systems, Austin*.

Fox, G., & Connolly, R. (2018). Mobile health technology adoption across generations: Narrowing the digital divide. *Information Systems Journal*, *28*(6), 995–1019. https://doi.org/10.1111/isj.12179

Freeman, R. E. (2010). *Strategic Management: A Stakeholder Approach*.

Gagnon, M.-P., Ngangue, P., Payne-Gagnon, J., & Desmartis, M. (2016). m-Health adoption by healthcare professionals: a systematic review. *Journal of the American Medical Informatics Association*, *23*(1), 212–220. https://doi.org/10.1093/jamia/ocv052

Gale, E. A. M. (2006). Dying of diabetes. *Lancet*, *368*(11), 1626–1628. https://doi.org/10.1016/S0140-6736(07)60226-8

Gallupe, R. B. (2007). The tyranny of methodologies in information systems research. *ACM SIGMIS Database: The DATABASE for Advances in Information Systems*, *38*(3), 20–28. https://doi.org/10.1145/1278253.1278258

Ganju, K. K., Pavlou, P. A., & Banker, R. D. (2016). Does Information and Communication Technology Lead to the Well-Being of Nations? A Country-Level Empirical Investigation. *MIS Quarterly*, *40*(2), 417–430. https://doi.org/10.25300/MISQ/2016/40.2.07

Gaskin, J., Berente, N., Lyytinen, K., & Yoo, Y. (2014). Toward Generalizable Sociomaterial Inquiry: A Computational Approach for Zooming In and Out of Sociomaterial Routines. *MIS Quarterly*, *38*(3), 849–871. https://doi.org/10.25300/MISQ/2014/38.3.10

Gasson, S. (2003). Human-Centered Vs. User-Centered Approaches to Information System Design. *The Journal of Information Technology Theory and Application (JITTA)*, *5*(2), 29–46.

Gastaldi, L., & Corso, M. (2012). Smart Healthcare Digitalization: Using ICT to Effectively Balance Exploration and Exploitation within Hospitals. *International Journal of Engineering Business Management*, *4*, 9. https://doi.org/10.5772/51643

Gefen, D., & Straub, D. (2005). A Practical Guide To Factorial Validity Using PLS-Graph: Tutorial And Annotated Example. *Communications of the Association for Information Systems*, *16*, 91–109. https://doi.org/10.17705/1cais.01605

Gehman, J., Glaser, V. L., Eisenhardt, K. M., Gioia, D., Langley, A., & Corley, K. G. (2018). Finding Theory–Method Fit: A Comparison of Three Qualitative Approaches to Theory Building. *Journal of Management Inquiry*, *27*(3), 284–300. https://doi.org/10.1177/1056492617706029

Gelbrich, K., & Roschk, H. (2011). A meta-analysis of organizational complaint handling and customer responses. *Journal of Service Research*, *14*(1), 24–43.

Geldsetzer, P., De Neve, J. W., Boudreaux, C., Bärnighausen, T., & Bossert, T. J. (2017). Improving the performance of community health workers in Swaziland: Findings from a qualitative study. *Human Resources for Health*, *15*(1), 1–9. https://doi.org/10.1186/s12960-017-0236-x

George, A., Mikhaei, C. A., & Boodraj, M. (2018). Does Internet create Healthier Societies ? A spatial analysis of health outcomes and internet adoption . *ICIS 2018 Proceedings*.

Giansanti, D. (2021). The Role of the mHealth in the Fight against the Covid-19: Successes and Failures. *Healthcare*, *9*(1), 58. https://doi.org/10.3390/healthcare9010058

Ginsburg, A. S., Delarosa, J., Brunette, W., Levari, S., Sundt, M., Larson, C., Tawiah Agyemang, C., Newton, S., Borriello, G., & Anderson, R. (2015). mPneumonia: Development of an Innovative mHealth Application for Diagnosing and Treating

Childhood Pneumonia and Other Childhood Illnesses in Low-Resource Settings. *PLOS ONE*, *10*(10), e0139625. https://doi.org/10.1371/journal.pone.0139625

Gioia, D. A., Corley, K. G., & Hamilton, A. L. (2013). Seeking Qualitative Rigor in Inductive Research: Notes on the Gioia Methodology. *Organizational Research Methods*, *16*(1), 15–31. https://doi.org/10.1177/1094428112452151

Glaser, B. G., & Strauss, A. L. (1999). *The discovery of grounded theory* (3rd ed.). Aldine Transaction.

Globe. (2020). *GLOBE 2020*. https://globeproject.com/

Goel, S., & Shawky, H. A. (2009). Estimating the market impact of security breach announcements on firm values. *Information and Management*, *46*(7), 404–410. https://doi.org/10.1016/j.im.2009.06.005

Goh, J. M., Gao, G. G., & Agarwal, R. (2016). The creation of social value: Can an online health community reduce rural-urban health disparities? *MIS Quarterly*, *40*(1), 247–263. https://doi.org/10.25300/MISQ/2016/40.1.11

Goldkuhl, G. (2012). Pragmatism vs interpretivism in qualitative information systems research. *European Journal of Information Systems*, *21*(2), 135–146. https://doi.org/10.1057/ejis.2011.54

Goode, S., Hoehle, H., Venkatesh, V., & Brown, S. A. (2017). User Compensation as a Data Breach Recovery Action: An Investigation of the Sony PlayStation Network Breach. *MIS Quarterly*, *41*(3), 703–727. https://doi.org/10.25300/misq/2017/41.3.03

Greenhalgh, T., Wherton, J., Papoutsi, C., Lynch, J., Hughes, G., A'Court, C., Hinder, S., Fahy, N., Procter, R., & Shaw, S. (2017). Beyond adoption: A new framework for theorizing and evaluating nonadoption, abandonment, and challenges to the scale-up, spread, and sustainability of health and care technologies. *Journal of Medical Internet Research*, *19*(11). https://doi.org/10.2196/jmir.8775

Gregor, S. (2006). The nature of theory in Information Systems. *MIS Quarterly: Management Information Systems*, *30*(3), 611–642.

Gregor, S., Chandra Kruse, L., Seidel, S., Kruse, L., & Seidel, S. (2020). Research perspectives: The anatomy of a design principle. *Journal of the Association for Information Systems*, *21*(6), 1622–1652. https://doi.org/10.17705/1jais.00649

Gregor, S., & Hevner, A. R. (2013). Positioning and Presenting Design Science Research for Maximum Impact. *MIS Quarterly*, *37*(2), 337–355. https://doi.org/10.25300/MISQ/2013/37.2.01

Gregory, R. L. (1970). The Intelligent Eye. In *Weidenfeld & Nicolson*.

Gregory, R. W., & Muntermann, J. (2014). Research Note —Heuristic Theorizing: Proactively Generating Design Theories. *Information Systems Research*, *25*(3), 639–653. https://doi.org/10.1287/isre.2014.0533

Greve, M., Brendel, A. B., van Osten, N., & Kolbe, L. M. (2021). Overcoming the barriers of mobile health that hamper sustainability in low-resource environments. *Journal of Public Health*. https://doi.org/10.1007/s10389-021-01536-8

Greve, M., Diederich, S., Lembcke, T. B., Brendel, A. B., & Kolbe, L. M. (2020). Healthy by app - Towards a taxonomy of mobile health applications. *Proceedings of the 24th Pacific Asia Conference on Information Systems: Information Systems (IS) for the Future, PACIS 2020*.

Greve, M., Lichtenberg, S., Diederich, S., & Brendel, A. B. (2020). Supporting Non-Communicable Disease Prevention through a mHealth Application in Decentralized Healthcare Systems: Action Design Research in Eswatini. *Proceedings of the European Conference on Information Systems (ECIS)*, 1–17.

Greve, M., Masuch, K., & Trang, S. (2020). The More, the Better? Compensation and Remorse as Data Breach Recovery Actions – An Experimental Scenario-based Investigation. *15th International Conference on Wirtschaftsinformatik.*

Guillamont, A., & Vijil, J. (2019, July 23). *An overview of cyber legislation in Latin America.* Insurance Professionals Miami (Latin America & Caribbean). https://insuranceprofessionalsmiami.com/2019/07/23/an-overview-of-cyber-legislation-in-latin-america/

Gupta, A. (2013). Environment & PEST analysis: an approach to the external business environment. *International Journal of Modern Social Sciences*, *2*(1), 34–43.

Gurman, T. A., Rubin, S. E., & Roess, A. A. (2012). Effectiveness of mHealth Behavior Change Communication Interventions in Developing Countries: A Systematic Review of the Literature. *Journal of Health Communication*, *17*(sup1), 82–104. https://doi.org/10.1080/10810730.2011.649160

Gwebu, K. L., Wang, J., & Wang, L. (2018). The Role of Corporate Reputation and Crisis Response Strategies in Data Breach Management. *Journal of Management Information Systems*, *35*(2), 683–714. https://doi.org/10.1080/07421222.2018.1451962

Hadwick, R. (2011). Should I Use GLOBE or Hofstede? Some Insights That Can Assist Cross-Cultural Scholars, and Others, Choose the Right Study to Support Their Work. *Anzam 2011*, 1–16.

Hailemariam, G., Negash, S., & Musa, P. F. (2010). In search of insights from community of practice and use of telemedicine in low income countries: The case of ethiopia. *16th Americas Conference on Information Systems 2010*, *3*.

Hair, J. F., Hult, G. T. M., Ringle, C. M., & Sarstedt, M. (2014). *A Primer on Partial Least Squares Structural Equation Modeling*. SAGE.

Haj-Bolouri, A., Purao, S., Rossi, M., & Bernhardsson, L. (2018). Action design research in practice: Lessons and concerns. *26th European Conference on Information Systems: Beyond , ECIS 2018.*

Hansen, S. W., & Baroody, A. J. (2020). Electronic Health Records and the Logics of Care: Complementarity and Conflict in the U.S. Healthcare System. *Information Systems Research*, *31*(1), 57–75. https://doi.org/10.1287/isre.2019.0875

Hansen, S. W., Gogan, J. L., Baxter, R. J., & Garfield, M. J. (2019). Informed collaboration in health care: An embedded-cases study in geriatric telepsychiatry. *Information Systems Journal*, *29*(2), 514–547. https://doi.org/10.1111/isj.12218

Hao, H., Padman, R., Sun, B., & Telang, R. (2018). Quantifying the Impact of Social Influence on the Information Technology Implementation Process by Physicians: A Hierarchical Bayesian Learning Approach. *Information Systems Research*, *29*(1), 25–41. https://doi.org/10.1287/isre.2017.0746

Hao, W.-R., Hsu, Y.-H., Chen, K.-C., Li, H.-C., Iqbal, U., Nguyen, P.-A., Huang, C.-W., Yang, H.-C., Lee, P., Li, M.-H., Hlatshwayo, S. L., Li, Y.-C. (Jack), & Jian, W.-S. (2015). LabPush: A pilot study of providing remote clinics with laboratory results via short message service (SMS) in Swaziland, Africa – A qualitative study. *Computer Methods and Programs in Biomedicine*, *118*(1), 77–83. https://doi.org/10.1016/j.cmpb.2014.10.005

Hatakka, M., Thapa, D., & Sæbø, Ø. (2020). Understanding the role of ICT and study circles in enabling economic opportunities: Lessons learned from an educational project in Kenya. *Information Systems Journal*, *30*(4), 664–698. https://doi.org/10.1111/isj.12277

Heeks, R. (2002). Information Systems and Developing Countries: Failure, Success, and Local Improvisations. *The Information Society*, *18*(2), 101–112. https://doi.org/10.1080/01972240290075039

Heeks, R. (2012). Deriving an ICT4D research agenda: A commentary on "Information and communication technologies for development (ICT4D): solutions seeking problems?" *Journal of Information Technology*, *27*(4), 339–341. https://doi.org/10.1057/jit.2012.31

Heeks, R. (2014). *Development Informatics Working Paper Series ICT4D 2016: New Priorities for ICT4D Policy, Practice and WSIS in a Post-2015 World*.

Heeks, R. (2017). *Information and Communication Technology for Development (ICT4D)*. Routledge. https://doi.org/10.4324/9781315652603

Heeks, R. (2020). ICT4D 3.0? Part 1—The components of an emerging "digital-for-development" paradigm. *The Electronic Journal of Information Systems in Developing Countries*, *86*(3), 1–15. https://doi.org/10.1002/isd2.12124

Heeks, R., & Ospina, A. V. (2019). Conceptualising the link between information systems and resilience: A developing country field study. *Information Systems Journal*, *29*(1), 70–96. https://doi.org/10.1111/isj.12177

Heeks, R., & Wall, P. J. (2018). Critical realism and ICT4D research. *The Electronic Journal of Information Systems in Developing Countries*, *84*(6), e12051. https://doi.org/10.1002/isd2.12051

Hellström, J. (2010). Mobile Technology as a means to fight corruption in East Africa. In *SPIDER ICT4D Series* (Vol. 3, pp. 47-69 TS-EndNote Tagged Import Format Y3-02.). https://spider1.blogs.dsv.su.se/wp-content/blogs.dir/362/files/2016/11/Spider-ICT4D-series-3-Increasing-transparency-and-fighting-corruption-through-ICT.pdf#page=53

Henseler, J. (2012). PLS-MGA : A Non-Parametric Approach to Partial Least Squares-based Multi-Group. In *Challenges at the Interface of Data Analysis, Computer Science, and Optimization* (pp. 495–501). https://doi.org/10.1007/978-3-642-24466-7

Hevner, A. R. (2007). A Three Cycle View of Design Science Research. *Scandinavian Journal of Information Systems*, *19*(2), 87–92.

Hevner, March, Park, & Ram. (2004). Design Science in Information Systems Research. *MIS Quarterly*, *28*(1), 75. https://doi.org/10.2307/25148625

Hoehle, H., & Venkatesh, V. (2015). Mobile Application Usability: Conceptualization and Instrument Development. *MIS Quarterly*, *39*(2), 435–472. https://doi.org/10.25300/MISQ/2015/39.2.08

Hofstede, G. (2001). Culture's Consequences: Comparing Values, Behaviors, Institutions and ... - Geert Hofstede - Google Books. In *SAGE Publications*.

Holeman, I., & Barrett, M. (2017). Insights from an ICT4D Initiative in Kenya's Immunization Program: Designing for the Emergence of Sociomaterial Practices. *Journal of the Association for Information Systems*, *18*(12), 900–930. https://doi.org/10.17705/1jais.00476

Holeman, I., Johnson, A., Kayentao, K., Keita, Y., Odindo, S., & Whidden, C. (2018). The case for community health innovation networks. *Proceedings of the 1st ACM SIGCAS Conference on Computing and Sustainable Societies, COMPASS 2018, June*. https://doi.org/10.1145/3209811.3212705

Holeman, I., & Kane, D. (2020). Human-centered design for global health equity. *Information Technology for Development*, *26*(3), 477–505. https://doi.org/10.1080/02681102.2019.1667289

Hong, J., & Lee, A. Y. (2010). Feeling Mixed but Not Torn: The Moderating Role of Construal Level in Mixed Emotions Appeals. *Journal of Consumer Research*, *37*(3), 456–472. https://doi.org/10.1086/653492

Hoque, M. R. (2016). An empirical study of mHealth adoption in a developing country: The moderating effect of gender concern. *BMC Medical Informatics and Decision Making*, *16*(1). https://doi.org/10.1186/s12911-016-0289-0

Hosman, L. (2011). Making the transition from pilot to scale: examining sustainability and scalability issues in a public–private telecenter partnership in Sri Lanka. *Information Technology for Development*, *17*(3), 232–248. https://doi.org/10.1080/02681102.2011.568225

Hossain, M. A. (2016). Assessing m-Health success in Bangladesh. *Journal of Enterprise Information Management*, *29*(5), 774–796. https://doi.org/10.1108/JEIM-02-2014-0013

House, R. J., Hanges, P. J., Javidan, M., Dorfman, P. W., & Gupta, V. (Eds.). (2004). *Culture, leadership, and organizations_ the GLOBE study of 62 societies*. SAGE Publications.

Houts, P. S., Doak, C. C., Doak, L. G., & Loscalzo, M. J. (2006). The role of pictures in improving health communication: A review of research on attention, comprehension, recall, and adherence. *Patient Education and Counseling*, *61*(2), 173–190. https://doi.org/10.1016/j.pec.2005.05.004

Howard-Grenville, J., Davis, G. F., Dyllick, T., Miller, C. C., Thau, S., & Tsui, A. S. (2019). Sustainable Development for a Better World: Contributions of Leadership, Management, and Organizations. *Academy of Management Discoveries*, *5*(4), 355–366. https://doi.org/10.5465/amd.2019.0275

Huang, F., Blaschke, S., & Lucas, H. (2017). Beyond pilotitis: Taking digital health interventions to the national level in China and Uganda. *Globalization and Health*, *13*(1), 1–11. https://doi.org/10.1186/s12992-017-0275-z

Huang, K. Y., Chengalur-Smith, I. S., & Pinsonneault, A. (2019). Sharing is caring: Social support provision and companionship activities in healthcare virtual support communities1. *MIS Quarterly*, *43*(2), 395–423. https://doi.org/10.25300/MISQ/2019/13225

Hui, M. K., & Au, K. (2001). Justice perceptions of complaint-handling: A cross-cultural comparison between PRC and Canadian customers. *Journal of Business Research*, *52*(2), 161–173. https://doi.org/10.1016/S0148-2963(99)00068-5

Hur, I., Cousins, K. C., & Stahl, B. C. (2019). A critical perspective of engagement in online health communities. *European Journal of Information Systems*, *28*(5), 523–548. https://doi.org/10.1080/0960085X.2019.1620477

Hur, I., Schmidt, J. ., & Lee, R. M. (2015). How Healthcare Technology Shapes Health Literacy ? A Systematic Review. *Americas Conference on Information Systems*.

Iivari, J. (2010). *Twelve Theses on Design Science Research in Information Systems. 2004*, 43–62. https://doi.org/10.1007/978-1-4419-5653-8_5

Iivari, J. (2015). Distinguishing and contrasting two strategies for design science research. *European Journal of Information Systems*, *24*(1), 107–115. https://doi.org/10.1057/ejis.2013.35

Iivari, J. (2017). Information system artefact or information system application: that is the question. *Information Systems Journal*, *27*(6), 753–774. https://doi.org/10.1111/isj.12121

Ilavarasan, P. V. (2017). Bridging ICTD research and policy-making: notes from a systematic review on MSMEs in the low- and middle-income countries. *Information Technology for Development*, *23*(4), 723–733. https://doi.org/10.1080/02681102.2017.1315355

International Institute for Management Development. (2018). *The IMD World Digital Competitiveness Ranking 2018 Results* (Vol. 5, Issue 3).

International Telecommunication Union. (2020). Measuring digital development. Facts and figures 2020. In *ITU Publications*. https://www.itu.int/en/mediacentre/Documents/MediaRelations/ITU Facts and Figures 2019 - Embargoed 5 November 1200 CET.pdf

IQVIA Institute. (2021). *Digital Health Trends 2021*.

Iribarren, S. J., Cato, K., Falzon, L., & Stone, P. W. (2017). What is the economic evidence for mHealth? A systematic review of economic evaluations of mHealth solutions. *PLOS ONE*, *12*(2), e0170581. https://doi.org/10.1371/journal.pone.0170581

Iribarren, S. J., Sward, K. A., Beck, S. L., Pearce, P. F., Thurston, D., & Chirico, C. (2015). Qualitative Evaluation of a Text Messaging Intervention to Support Patients With Active Tuberculosis: Implementation Considerations. *JMIR MHealth and UHealth*, *3*(1), e21. https://doi.org/10.2196/mhealth.3971

Islam, S. M. S., Purnat, T. D., Phuong, N. T. A., Mwingira, U., Schacht, K., & Fröschl, G. (2014). Non-Communicable Diseases (NCDs) in developing countries: a symposium report. *Globalization and Health*, *10*(1), 81. https://doi.org/10.1186/s12992-014-0081-9

Istepanian, R. S. H., & AlAnzi, T. (2020). Mobile health (m-health). In D. D. Feng (Ed.), *Biomedical Information Technology* (pp. 717–733). Elsevier. https://doi.org/10.1016/B978-0-12-816034-3.00022-5

Iyawa, G. E., Herselman, M., & Botha, A. (2016). Digital Health Innovation Ecosystems: From Systematic Literature Review to Conceptual Framework. *Procedia Computer Science*, *100*, 244–252. https://doi.org/10.1016/j.procs.2016.09.149

James, T. L., Deane, J. K., & Wallace, L. (2019). An application of goal content theory to examine how desired exercise outcomes impact fitness technology feature set selection. *Information Systems Journal*, *29*(5), 1010–1039. https://doi.org/10.1111/isj.12233

Jawahar, I. M., & McLaughlin, G. L. (2001). Toward a descriptive stakeholder theory: An organizational life cycle approach. *Academy of Management Review*, *26*(3), 397–414. https://doi.org/10.5465/AMR.2001.4845803

Jiang, J. J., Klein, G., & Carr, C. L. (2002). Measuring Information System Service Quality: SERVQUAL from the Other Side. *MIS Quarterly*, *26*(2), 145. https://doi.org/10.2307/4132324

Jobe, W. (2013). Native Apps Vs. Mobile Web Apps. *International Journal of Interactive Mobile Technologies (IJIM)*, *7*(4), 27. https://doi.org/10.3991/ijim.v7i4.3226

Johnston, A. C., Warkentin, M., & Siponen, M. (2015). An Enhanced Fear Appeal Rhetorical Framework: Leveraging Threats to the Human Asset Through Sanctioning Rhetoric. *MIS Quarterly*, *39*(1), 113–134. https://doi.org/10.25300/MISQ/2015/39.1.06

Jones, D., & Gregor, S. (2007). The Anatomy of a Design Theory. *Journal of the Association for Information Systems*, *8*(5), 312–335. https://doi.org/10.17705/1jais.00129

Källander, K., Tibenderana, J. K., Akpogheneta, O. J., Strachan, D. L., Hill, Z., ten Asbroek, A. H. A., Conteh, L., Kirkwood, B. R., & Meek, S. R. (2013). Mobile Health (mHealth) Approaches and Lessons for Increased Performance and Retention of Community Health Workers in Low- and Middle-Income Countries: A Review. *Journal of Medical Internet Research*, *15*(1), e17. https://doi.org/10.2196/jmir.2130

Kantsperger, R., & Kunz, W. H. (2010). Consumer trust in service companies: a multiple mediating analysis. *Managing Service Quality: An International Journal*, *20*(1), 4–25. https://doi.org/10.1108/09604521011011603

Karatepe, O. M. (2006). Customer complaints and organizational responses: The effects of complainants' perceptions of justice on satisfaction and loyalty. *International Journal of Hospitality Management*, *25*(1), 69–90. https://doi.org/10.1016/j.ijhm.2004.12.008

Kau, A. K., & Loh, E. W. Y. (2006). The effects of service recovery on consumer satisfaction: A comparison between complainants and non-complainants. *Journal of Services Marketing*, *20*(2), 101–111. https://doi.org/10.1108/08876040610657039

Kaur, R., & Ahmed, A. (2019). Unpacking actor interactions in ICT4D ecosystem. *Proceedings of the 23rd Pacific Asia Conference on Information Systems: Secure ICT Platform for the 4th Industrial Revolution, PACIS 2019*.

Kelley, H., Chiasson, M., Downey, A., & Pacaud, D. (2011). The Clinical Impact of eHealth on the Self-Management of Diabetes: A Double Adoption Perspective. *Journal of the Association for Information Systems*, *12*(3), 208–234. https://doi.org/10.17705/1jais.00263

Kenny, G., & Connolly, R. (2015). Citizens' Health Information Privacy Concerns: A Multifaceted Approach. *ECIS 2015 Proceedings*.

Khurana, S., Qiu, L., & Kumar, S. (2019). When a Doctor Knows, It Shows: An Empirical Analysis of Doctors' Responses in a Q&A Forum of an Online Healthcare Portal. *Information Systems Research*, *30*(3), 872–891. https://doi.org/10.1287/isre.2019.0836

Kiberu, V. M., Mars, M., & Scott, R. E. (2017). Barriers and opportunities to implementation of sustainable e-Health programmes in Uganda: A literature review.

African Journal of Primary Health Care & Family Medicine, *9*(1), 1–10. https://doi.org/10.4102/phcfm.v9i1.1277

Kim, H.-W., Xu, Y., & Koh, J. (2004). A Comparison of Online Trust Building Factors between Potential Customers and Repeat Customers. *Journal of the Association for Information Systems*, *5*(10), 392–420. https://doi.org/10.17705/1jais.00056

Kim, S. S., & Son, J.-Y. (2009). Out of Dedication or Constraint? A Dual Model of Post-Adoption Phenomena and Its Empirical Test in the Context of Online Services. *MIS Quarterly*, *33*(1), 49–70.

Klecun, E., Zhou, Y., Kankanhalli, A., Wee, Y. H., & Hibberd, R. (2019). The dynamics of institutional pressures and stakeholder behavior in national electronic health record implementations: A tale of two countries. *Journal of Information Technology*, *34*(4), 292–332. https://doi.org/10.1177/0268396218822478

Klein, H. K., & Myers, M. D. (1999). A Set of Principles for Conducting and Evaluating Interpretive Field Studies in Information Systems. *MIS Quarterly*, *23*(1), 67. https://doi.org/10.2307/249410

Kliner, M., Knight, A., Mamvura, C., Wright, J., & Walley, J. (2013). Using no-cost mobile phone reminders to improve attendance for HIV test results: A pilot study in rural Swaziland. *Infectious Diseases of Poverty*, *2*(1), 1. https://doi.org/10.1186/2049-9957-2-12

Koffi, B. J. B., Yazdanmehr, A., & Mahapatra, R. K. (2018). Mobile health privacy concerns - A systematic review. *Americas Conference on Information Systems 2018*, 1–10.

Koh, D., & Naing, L. (2006). Health, Workers: a global profile. In *The World Health Report 2006*. John Wiley & Sons, Ltd. https://doi.org/10.1002/9781118410868.wbehibs168

Kohli, R., & Tan, S. S. (2016). Electronic Health Records: How can IS Researchers contribute to transforming Healthcare? *MIS Quarterly*, *40*(3), 553–573.

Kordzadeh, N., & Warren, J. (2017). Communicating Personal Health Information in Virtual Health Communities: An Integration of Privacy Calculus Model and Affective Commitment. *Journal of the Association for Information Systems*, *18*(1), 45–81. https://doi.org/10.17705/1jais.00446

Krah, E. F., & de Kruijf, J. G. (2016). Exploring the ambivalent evidence base of mobile health (mHealth): A systematic literature review on the use of mobile phones for the improvement of community health in Africa. *DIGITAL HEALTH*, *2*, 205520761667926. https://doi.org/10.1177/2055207616679264

Krishna, A., Dangayach, G. S., & Sharma, S. (2014). Service Recovery Paradox: The Success Parameters. *Global Business Review*, *15*(2), 263–277. https://doi.org/10.1177/0972150914523567

Kruk, M. E., Porignon, D., Rockers, P. C., & Van Lerberghe, W. (2010). The contribution of primary care to health and health systems in low- and middle-income countries: A critical review of major primary care initiatives. *Social Science & Medicine*, *70*(6), 904–911. https://doi.org/10.1016/j.socscimed.2009.11.025

Kruse, C., Betancourt, J., Ortiz, S., Valdes Luna, S. M., Bamrah, I. K., & Segovia, N. (2019). Barriers to the Use of Mobile Health in Improving Health Outcomes in Developing Countries: Systematic Review. *Journal of Medical Internet Research*, *21*(10), e13263. https://doi.org/10.2196/13263

Kruse, C. S., Frederick, B., Jacobson, T., & Monticone, D. K. (2017). Cybersecurity in healthcare: A systematic review of modern threats and trends. *Technology and Health Care*, *25*(1), 1–10. https://doi.org/10.3233/THC-161263

Kupfer, A., Tiefenbeck, V., & Staake, T. (2018). The ambiguious boundary between professional and private use of information systems: A bibliometric analysis. *26th European Conference on Information Systems*.

Lansing, J., Benlian, A., & Sunyaev, A. (2018). "Unblackboxing" Decision Makers' Interpretations of IS Certifications in the Context of Cloud Service Certifications. *Journal of the Association for Information Systems*, *19*(11), 1064–1096. https://doi.org/10.17705/1jais.00520

Latif, S., Rana, R., Qadir, J., Ali, A., Imran, M. A., & Younis, M. S. (2017). Mobile Health in the Developing World: Review of Literature and Lessons from a Case Study. *IEEE Access*, *5*(June), 11540–11556. https://doi.org/10.1109/ACCESS.2017.2710800

Lee, A. S., Thomas, M., & Baskerville, R. L. (2015). Going back to basics in design science: From the information technology artifact to the information systems artifact. *Information Systems Journal*, *25*(1), 5–21. https://doi.org/10.1111/isj.12054

Lee, E., Asiimwe, C., Sundaram, L., Amor, Y. Ben, Quinto, E., Gelvin, D., Bell, D., Berg, M., & Katureebe, C. (2011). Use of an Innovative, Affordable, and Open-Source Short Message Service–Based Tool to Monitor Malaria in Remote Areas of Uganda. *The American Journal of Tropical Medicine and Hygiene*, *85*(1), 26–33. https://doi.org/10.4269/ajtmh.2011.10-0528

Lee, H. Y., Huang, C. W., Li, C. C., Wu, W. C., Liu, T. C., Wu, C. C., Tsai, Y. F., & Juan, Y. S. (2012). Malignant renal epithelioid angiomyolipoma with an inferior vena cava and right atrium thrombus. *Urological Science*, *23*(4), 133–136.

Lee, M., Lee, K., Shim, J., Cho, S. J., & Choi, J. (2016, January 3). Security threat on wearable services: Empirical study using a commercial smartband. *2016 IEEE International Conference on Consumer Electronics-Asia*. https://doi.org/10.1109/ICCE-Asia.2016.7804766

Lee, S., Cho, Y.-M., & Kim, S.-Y. (2017). Mapping mHealth (mobile health) and mobile penetrations in sub-Saharan Africa for strategic regional collaboration in mHealth scale-up: an application of exploratory spatial data analysis. *Globalization and Health*, *13*(1), 63. https://doi.org/10.1186/s12992-017-0286-9

Lehoux, P., Roncarolo, F., Rocha Oliveira, R., & Pacifico Silva, H. (2016). Medical innovation and the sustainability of health systems: A historical perspective on technological change in health. *Health Services Management Research*, *29*(4), 115–123. https://doi.org/10.1177/0951484816670192

Leidner, D. E. (2020). What's in a contribution. *Journal of the Association for Information Systems*, *21*(1), 238–245. https://doi.org/10.17705/1jais.00598

Leidner, & Kayworth. (2006). Review: A Review of Culture in Information Systems Research: Toward a Theory of Information Technology Culture Conflict. *MIS Quarterly*, *30*(2), 357. https://doi.org/10.2307/25148735

Lemay, N. V., Sullivan, T., Jumbe, B., & Perry, C. P. (2012). Reaching Remote Health Workers in Malawi: Baseline Assessment of a Pilot mHealth Intervention. *Journal of Health Communication*, *17*(sup1), 105–117. https://doi.org/10.1080/10810730.2011.649106

Leon, N., Schneider, H., & Daviaud, E. (2012). Applying a framework for assessing the health system challenges to scaling up mHealth in South Africa. *BMC Medical Informatics and Decision Making*, *12*(123). https://doi.org/10.1186/1472-6947-12-123

Leon, N., Surender, R., Bobrow, K., Muller, J., & Farmer, A. (2015). Improving treatment adherence for blood pressure lowering via mobile phone SMS-messages in South Africa: a qualitative evaluation of the SMS-text Adherence SuppoRt (StAR) trial. *BMC Family Practice*, *16*(1), 80. https://doi.org/10.1186/s12875-015-0289-7

Lester, R. T., Ritvo, P., Mills, E. J., Kariri, A., Karanja, S., Chung, M. H., Jack, W., Habyarimana, J., Sadatsafavi, M., Najafzadeh, M., Marra, C. A., Estambale, B., Ngugi, E., Ball, T. B., Thabane, L., Gelmon, L. J., Kimani, J., Ackers, M., & Plummer, F. A. (2010). Effects of a mobile phone short message service on antiretroviral treatment adherence in Kenya (WelTel Kenya1): a randomised trial. *The Lancet*, *376*(9755), 1838–1845. https://doi.org/10.1016/S0140-6736(10)61997-6

Levy, Y., & Ellis, T. J. (2006). A systems approach to conduct an effective literature review in support of information systems research. *Informing Science*, *9*, 181–211.

Lewin, S., Dick, J., Pond, P., Zwarenstein, M., Aja, G. N., van Wyk, B. E., Bosch-Capblanch, X., & Patrick, M. (2005). Lay health workers in primary and community health care. In S. Lewin (Ed.), *Cochrane Database of Systematic Reviews*. John Wiley & Sons, Ltd. https://doi.org/10.1002/14651858.CD004015.pub2

Lewis, T., Synowiec, C., Lagomarsino, G., & Schweitzer, J. (2012). E-health in low- and middle-income countries: findings from the Center for Health Market Innovations. *Bulletin of the World Health Organization*, *90*(5), 332–340. https://doi.org/10.2471/BLT.11.099820

Liang, H., & Xue, Y. (2013). Online Health Information Use by Disabled People: the Moderating Role of Disability. *ICIS 2013 Proceedings*, 1–16.

Liang, H., Xue, Y., & Zhang, Z. (2017). Understanding Online Health Information Use: The Case of People with Physical Disabilities. *Journal of the Association for Information Systems*, *18*(6), 433–460. https://doi.org/10.17705/1jais.00461

Lichtenberg, S., Greve, M., Brendel, A. B., & Kolbe, L. M. (2019). Towards the Design of a Mobile Application to Support Decentralized Healthcare in Developing Countries – The Case of Diabetes Care in eSwatini Completed Research Full Paper. *Proceedings of the 25th Americas Conference of Information Systems*.

Lii, Y. shuh, & Lee, M. (2012). The joint effects of compensation frames and price levels on service recovery of online pricing error. *Managing Service Quality*, *22*(1), 4–20. https://doi.org/10.1108/09604521211198083

Lim, M. S. C., Hocking, J. S., Hellard, M. E., & Aitken, C. K. (2008). SMS STI: A review of the uses of mobile phone text messaging in sexual health. *International Journal of STD and AIDS*, *19*(5), 287–290. https://doi.org/10.1258/ijsa.2007.007264

Lin, Y.-K., Chen, H., Brown, R. A., Li, S. H., & Yang, H. J. (2017). Healthcare predictive analytics for risk profiling in chronic care: A Bayesian multitask learning approach. *MIS Quarterly*, *41*(2), 473–495. https://doi.org/10.25300/MISQ/2017/41.2.07

Lin, Y.-K., Lin, M., & Chen, H. (2019). Do Electronic Health Records Affect Quality of Care? Evidence from the HITECH Act. *Information Systems Research*, *30*(1), 306–318. https://doi.org/10.1287/isre.2018.0813

Littman-Quinn, R., Mibenge, C., Antwi, C., Chandra, A., & Kovarik, C. L. (2013). Implementation of m-health applications in Botswana: Telemedicine and education on mobile devices in a low resource setting. *Journal of Telemedicine and Telecare*, *19*(2), 120–125. https://doi.org/10.1177/1357633X12474746

Liu, Q. Ben, Liu, X., & Guo, X. (2020). The Effects of Participating in a Physician-Driven Online Health Community in Managing Chronic Disease: Evidence from Two Natural Experiments. *MIS Quarterly*, *44*(1), 391–419. https://doi.org/10.25300/misq/2020/15102

Liu, Fei, Guo, X., & Ju, X. (2018). Routine Use of Mobile Health Services : Promotion or Prevention. *AMCIS 2018 Proceedings*, 1–10.

Liu, Franklin, & Myers, M. D. (2011). An analysis of the AIS basket of top journals. *Journal of Systems and Information Technology*, *13*(1), 5–24. https://doi.org/10.1108/13287261111118322

Liu, J., & Sun, W. (2016). Smart Attacks against Intelligent Wearables in People-Centric Internet of Things. *IEEE Communications Magazine*, *54*(12), 44–49.

Liu, Xiao, Zhang, B., Susarlia, A., & Padman, R. (2020). Go to You Tube and Call Me in the Morning: Use of Social Media for Chronic Conditions. *MIS Quarterly*, *44*(1), 257–283. https://doi.org/10.25300/misq/2020/15107

Liu, Xinying, & Varshney, U. (2020). Mobile health: A carrot and stick intervention to improve medication adherence. *Decision Support Systems*, *128*(October 2019), 113165. https://doi.org/10.1016/j.dss.2019.113165

Lowry, P. B., Moody, G. D., Gaskin, J., Galletta, D. F., Humpherys, S. L., Barlow, J. B., & Wilson, D. W. (2013). Evaluating Journal Quality and the Association for Information Systems Senior Scholars' Journal Basket Via Bibliometric Measures: Do Expert Journal Assessments Add Value? *MIS Quarterly*, *37*(4), 993–1012.

Lozano, R., Fullman, N., Abate, D., & Abay, S. M. (2018). Measuring progress from 1990 to 2017 and projecting attainment to 2030 of the health-related Sustainable Development Goals for 195 countries and territories: a systematic analysis for the Global Burden of Disease Study 2017. *The Lancet*, *November*, 2091–2138. https://doi.org/10.1016/S0140-6736(18)32281-5

Lülfs, R., & Hahn, R. (2013). Corporate Greening beyond Formal Programs, Initiatives, and Systems: A Conceptual Model for Voluntary Pro-environmental Behavior of Employees. *European Management Review*, *10*(2), 83–98. https://doi.org/10.1111/emre.12008

Mahmud, N., Rodriguez, J., & Nesbit, J. (2010). A text message - Based intervention to bridge the healthcare communication gap in the rural developing world. *Technology and Health Care*, *18*(2), 137–144. https://doi.org/10.3233/THC-2010-0576

Majchrzak, A., Lynne Markus, M., & Wareham, J. (2016). Designing for digital transformation: Lessons for information systems research from the study of ICT and societal challenges. *MIS Quarterly: Management Information Systems*, *40*(2), 267–277. https://doi.org/10.25300/MISQ/2016/40

Manne-Goehler, J., Atun, R., Stokes, A., Goehler, A., Houinato, D., Houehanou, C., Hambou, M. M. S., Mbenza, B. L., Sobngwi, E., Balde, N., Mwangi, J. K., Gathecha, G., Ngugi, P. W., Wesseh, C. S., Damasceno, A., Lunet, N., Bovet, P., Labadarios, D., Zuma, K., ... Bärnighausen, T. (2016). Diabetes diagnosis and care in sub-Saharan Africa: pooled analysis of individual data from 12 countries. *The Lancet*

Diabetes & Endocrinology, *4*(11), 903–912. https://doi.org/10.1016/S2213-8587(16)30181-4

Mansell, G. (1991). Action research in information systems development. *Information Systems Journal*, *1*(1), 29–40. https://doi.org/10.1111/j.1365-2575.1991.tb00025.x

Marcolino, M. S., Oliveira, J. A. Q., D'Agostino, M., Ribeiro, A. L., Alkmim, M. B. M., & Novillo-Ortiz, D. (2018). The Impact of mHealth Interventions: Systematic Review of Systematic Reviews. *JMIR MHealth and UHealth*, *6*(1), e23. https://doi.org/10.2196/mhealth.8873

Martínez-Pérez, B., de la Torre-Díez, I., & López-Coronado, M. (2015). Privacy and Security in Mobile Health Apps: A Review and Recommendations. *Journal of Medical Systems*, *39*(1), 181. https://doi.org/10.1007/s10916-014-0181-3

Martínez-Pérez, B., De La Torre-Díez, I., & López-Coronado, M. (2013). Mobile health applications for the most prevalent conditions by the world health organization: Review and analysis. *Journal of Medical Internet Research*, *15*(6), 1–22. https://doi.org/10.2196/jmir.2600

Martinsons, M. G., & Ma, D. (2009). Sub-cultural differences in information ethics across China: Focus on Chinese management generation gaps. *Journal of the Association for Information Systems*, *10*(11), 816–833. https://doi.org/10.17705/1jais.00213

Masuch, K., Greve, M., & Trang, S. (2021). What to do after a data breach? Examining apology and compensation as response strategies for health service providers. *Electronic Markets*, *forthcomin*.

Matavire, R., & Manda, T. D. (2014). Intervention Breakdowns as Occasions for Articulating Mobile Health Information Infrastructures. *The Electronic Journal of Information Systems in Developing Countries*, *62*(1), 1–17. https://doi.org/10.1002/j.1681-4835.2014.tb00441.x

Mattila, A. S. (2009). How to handle PR disasters? An examination of the impact of communication response type and failure attributions on consumer perceptions. *Journal of Services Marketing*, *23*(4), 211–218. https://doi.org/10.1108/08876040910965548

Mattila, A. S., & Patterson, P. G. (2004a). Service Recovery and Fairness Perceptions in Collectivist and Individualist Contexts. *Journal of Service Research*, *6*(4), 336–346. https://doi.org/10.1177/1094670503262947

Mattila, A. S., & Patterson, P. G. (2004b). The impact of culture on consumers' perceptions of service recovery efforts. *Journal of Retailing*, *80*(3), 196–206. https://doi.org/10.1016/j.jretai.2004.08.001

Maxham, J. G., & Netemeyer, R. G. (2002). Modeling customer perceptions of complaint handlich over time: the effects of perceived justice on satisfaction and intent. *Journal of Retailing*, *78*, 239–252.

Maxham, J. G., & Netemeyer, R. G. (2003). Firms Reap what they Sow: The Effects of Shared Values and Perceived Organizational Justice on Customers' Evaluations of Complaint Handling. *Journal of Marketing*, *67*(1), 46–62. https://doi.org/10.1509/jmkg.67.1.46.18591

Mayring, P. (2002). Einführung in die qualitative Sozialforschung. In *Studium Paedagogik*.

McCollough, M. A., Berry, L. L., & Yadav, M. S. (2000). An Empirical Investigation of Customer Satisfaction after Service Failure and Recovery. *Journal of Service*

Research, *3*(2), 121–137. https://doi.org/10.1177/109467050032002

McCurdie, T., Taneva, S., Casselman, M., Yeung, M., McDaniel, C., Ho, W., & Cafazzo, J. (2012). mHealth Consumer Apps: The Case for User-Centered Design. *Biomedical Instrumentation & Technology*, *46*, 49–56. https://doi.org/10.2345/0899-8205-46.s2.49

McLeod, A., & Dolezel, D. (2018). Cyber-analytics: Modeling factors associated with healthcare data breaches. *Decision Support Systems*, *108*(April), 57–68. https://doi.org/10.1016/j.dss.2018.02.007

Mechael, P. N. (2008). Towards the Development of an mHealth Strategy : A Literature Review. In *The Millennium Villages Project*.

Mechael, P. N. (2009). The Case for mHealth in Developing Countries. *Innovations: Technology, Governance, Globalization*, *4*(1), 103–118. https://doi.org/10.1162/itgg.2009.4.1.103

Mechael, P. N., Batavia, H., Kaonga, N., Searle, S., Kwan, A., Goldberger, A., Fu, L., & Ossman, J. (2010). *Barriers and gaps affecting mHealth in low and middle income countries: Policy white paper.*

Medhanyie, A. A., Little, A., Yebyo, H., Spigt, M., Tadesse, K., Blanco, R., & Dinant, G.-J. (2015). Health workers' experiences, barriers, preferences and motivating factors in using mHealth forms in Ethiopia. *Human Resources for Health*, *13*(1), 2. https://doi.org/10.1186/1478-4491-13-2

Melville, N. P. (2010). Information Systems Innovation for Environmental Sustainability. *MIS Quarterly*, *34*(1), 1. https://doi.org/10.2307/20721412

Meskó, B., Drobni, Z., Bényei, É., Gergely, B., & Győrffy, Z. (2017). Digital health is a cultural transformation of traditional healthcare. *MHealth*, *3*, 38–38. https://doi.org/10.21037/mhealth.2017.08.07

Metfula, A. S., & Chigona, W. (2014). In search of development in a national ICT policy: The case of Swaziland. *ACM International Conference Proceeding Series*, *28-Septemb*, 183–191. https://doi.org/10.1145/2664591.2664598

Mettler, T. (2018). Contextualizing a professional social network for health care: Experiences from an action design research study. *Information Systems Journal*, *28*(4), 684–707. https://doi.org/10.1111/isj.12154

Miah, S. J., Gammack, J., & Hasan, N. (2017). Extending the framework for mobile health information systems Research: A content analysis. *Information Systems*, *69*, 1–24. https://doi.org/10.1016/j.is.2017.04.001

Middleton, C., Scheepers, R., & Tuunainen, V. K. (2014). When mobile is the norm: Researching mobile information systems and mobility as post-adoption phenomena. *European Journal of Information Systems*, *23*(5), 503–512. https://doi.org/10.1057/ejis.2014.21

Milat, A. J., King, L., Bauman, A. E., & Redman, S. (2013). The concept of scalability: Increasing the scale and potential adoption of health promotion interventions into policy and practice. *Health Promotion International*, *28*(3), 285–298. https://doi.org/10.1093/heapro/dar097

Miles, M. B., Huberman, A. M., & Saldana, J. (2014). *Qualitative Data Analysis: A Methods Sourcebook* (3rd TS-). Sage Publications Ltd.

Mills, A. J., Watson, R. T., Pitt, L., & Kietzmann, J. (2016). Wearing safe: Physical and informational security in the age of the wearable device. *Business Horizons*, *59*(6), 615–622. https://doi.org/10.1016/j.bushor.2016.08.003

Mintzberg, H. (1989). The Structuring of Organizations. In *Readings in Strategic Management* (pp. 322–352). Macmillan Education UK. https://doi.org/10.1007/978-1-349-20317-8_23

Miscione, G., & Sahay, S. (2007). Scalability as Institutionalization - Practicing District Health Information System in an Indian State Health Organization. *Taking Stock of E-Development Conference, International Federation for Information Processing - Working Group 9.4*, 1–15.

Molnár-Gábor, F. (2018). Germany: a fair balance between scientific freedom and data subjects' rights? *Human Genetics*, *137*(8), 619–626. https://doi.org/10.1007/s00439-018-1912-1

Mori, C. K., & Assumpcao, R. O. (2007). Brazilian digital inclusion public policy: Achievements and challenges. *Journal of Community Informatics*, *3*(3), 1–7.

Morrisson, O., & Huppertz, J. W. (2010). External equity, loyalty program membership, and service recovery. *Journal of Services Marketing*, *24*(3), 244–254. https://doi.org/10.1108/08876041011040640

Morse, E. A., Raval, V., & Wingender, J. R. (2011). Market Price Effects of Data Security Breaches. *Information Security Journal*, *20*(6), 263–273. https://doi.org/10.1080/19393555.2011.611860

Motamarri, S., Akter, S., Ray, P., & Tseng, C.-L. (2014). Distinguishing "mHealth" from Other Healthcare Services in a Developing Country: A Study from the Service Quality Perspective. *Communications of the Association for Information Systems*, *34*(1), 669–692. https://doi.org/10.17705/1CAIS.03434

Mthoko, H., & Khene, C. (2018). Building theory in ICT4D evaluation: a comprehensive approach to assessing outcome and impact. *Information Technology for Development*, *24*(1), 138–164. https://doi.org/10.1080/02681102.2017.1315359

Murungi, D., Wiener, M., & Marabelli, M. (2019). Control and emotions: Understanding the dynamics of controllee behaviours in a health care information systems project. *Information Systems Journal*, *29*(5), 1058–1082. https://doi.org/10.1111/isj.12235

Myers, M. D., & Newman, M. (2007). The qualitative interview in IS research: Examining the craft. *Information and Organization*, *17*(1), 2–26. https://doi.org/10.1016/j.infoandorg.2006.11.001

Nacinovich, M. (2011). Defining mHealth. *Journal of Communication in Healthcare*, *4*(1), 1–3. https://doi.org/10.1179/175380611X12950033990296

Nambisan, S., Lyytinen, K., Majchrzak, A., & Song, M. (2017). Digital Innovation Management: Reinventing Innovation Management Research in a Digital World. *MIS Quarterly*, *41*(1), 223–238. https://doi.org/10.25300/MISQ/2017/41:1.03

Ndlovu, K., Littman-Quinn, R., Park, E., Dikai, Z., & Kovarik, C. L. (2014). Scaling up a mobile telemedicine solution in Botswana: Keys to sustainability. *Frontiers in Public Health*, *2*(DEC), 1–6. https://doi.org/10.3389/fpubh.2014.00275

Ngabo, F., Nguimfack, J., Nwaigwe, F., Mugeni, C., Muhoza, D., Wilson, D. R., Kalach, J., Gakuba, R., Karema, C., & Binagwaho, A. (2012). Designing and Implementing an Innovative SMS-based alert system (RapidSMS-MCH) to monitor pregnancy and reduce maternal and child deaths in Rwanda. *The Pan African Medical Journal*. https://doi.org/10.11604/pamj.2012.13.31.1864

Nhamo, G., Chikodzi, D., Kunene, H. P., & Mashula, N. (2021). COVID-19 vaccines and treatments nationalism: Challenges for low-income countries and the attainment of the SDGs. *Global Public Health*, *16*(3), 319–339. https://doi.org/10.1080/17441692.2020.1860249

Nhavoto, J. A., Grönlund, Å., & Klein, G. O. (2017). Mobile health treatment support intervention for HIV and tuberculosis in Mozambique: Perspectives of patients and healthcare workers. *PLOS ONE*, *12*(4), e0176051. https://doi.org/10.1371/journal.pone.0176051

Nickerson, R. C., Varshney, U., & Muntermann, J. (2013). A method for taxonomy development and its application in information systems. *European Journal of Information Systems*, *22*(3), 336–359. https://doi.org/10.1057/ejis.2012.26

Nickerson, R. C., Varshney, U., Muntermann, J., & Isaac, H. (2009). Taxonomy development in information systems: developing a taxonomy of mobile applications. *17th European Conference on Information Systems*, *January*, 1–13.

Niemöller, C., Metzger, D., Berkemeier, L., Zobel, B., Thomas, O., & Thomas, V. (2016). Designing mhealth applications for developing countries. *24th European Conference on Information Systems, ECIS 2016*, *January 2018*.

O' Connor, Y., & O' Donoghue, J. (2015). Contextual Barriers to Mobile Health Technology in African Countries: A Perspective Piece. *Journal of Mobile Technology in Medicine*, *4*(1), 31–34. https://doi.org/10.7309/jmtm.4.1.7

Olaniran, A., Smith, H., Unkels, R., Bar-Zeev, S., & van den Broek, N. (2017). Who is a community health worker? – a systematic review of definitions. *Global Health Action*, *10*(1), 1272223. https://doi.org/10.1080/16549716.2017.1272223

Oliver, R. L. (1980). A Cognitive Model of the Antecedents and Consequences of Satisfaction Decisions. *Journal of Marketing Research*, *17*(4), 460.

Olla, P., & Shimskey, C. (2015). mHealth taxonomy: a literature survey of mobile health applications. *Health and Technology*, *4*(4), 299–308. https://doi.org/10.1007/s12553-014-0093-8

Orlikowski, W. J., & Baroudi, J. J. (1991). Studying Information Technology in Organizations: Research Approaches and Assumptions. *Information Systems Research*, *2*(1), 1–28. https://doi.org/10.1287/isre.2.1.1

Ostern, N., Perscheid, G., Reelitz, C., & Moormann, J. (2021). Keeping pace with the healthcare transformation: a literature review and research agenda for a new decade of health information systems research. *Electronic Markets*, *July*. https://doi.org/10.1007/s12525-021-00484-1

Otto, L., Harst, L., Schlieter, H., Wollschlaeger, B., Richter, P., & Timpel, P. (2018). Towards a Unified Understanding of eHealth and Related Terms – Proposal of a Consolidated Terminological Basis. *Proceedings of the 11th International Joint Conference on Biomedical Engineering Systems and Technologies*, *5*(Biostec), 533–539. https://doi.org/10.5220/0006651005330539

Ouma, P. O., Maina, J., Thuranira, P. N., Macharia, P. M., Alegana, V. A., English, M., Okiro, E. A., & Snow, R. W. (2018). Access to emergency hospital care provided by the public sector in sub-Saharan Africa in 2015: a geocoded inventory and spatial analysis. *The Lancet Global Health*, *6*(3), e342–e350. https://doi.org/10.1016/S2214-109X(17)30488-6

Palma, A. M., Rabkin, M., Simelane, S., Gachuhi, A. B., McNairy, M. L., Nuwagaba-Biribonwoha, H., Bongomin, P., Okello, V. N., Bitchong, R. A., & El-Sadr, W. M. (2018). A time-motion study of cardiovascular disease risk factor screening integrated into HIV clinic visits in Swaziland. *Journal of the International AIDS Society*, *21*(3). https://doi.org/10.1002/jia2.25099

Parasuraman, A., Zeithaml, V. A., & Malhotra, A. (2005). E-S-QUAL a multiple-item scale for assessing electronic service quality. *Journal of Service Research*, *7*(3), 213–233. https://doi.org/10.1177/1094670504271156

Parmar, V., Keyson, D., & De Bont, C. (2009). Persuasive technology to shape social beliefs: A case of persuasive health information systems for rural women in India. *Communications of the Association for Information Systems*, *24*(1), 427–454. https://doi.org/10.17705/1CAIS.02425

Patterson, P. G., Cowley, E., & Prasongsukarn, K. (2006). Service failure recovery: The moderating impact of individual-level cultural value orientation on perceptions of justice. *International Journal of Research in Marketing*, *23*(3), 263–277. https://doi.org/10.1016/j.ijresmar.2006.02.004

Peffers, K., Tuunanen, T., & Niehaves, B. (2018). Design science research genres: introduction to the special issue on exemplars and criteria for applicable design science research. *European Journal of Information Systems*, *27*(2), 129–139. https://doi.org/10.1080/0960085X.2018.1458066

Peffers, K., Tuunanen, T., Rothenberger, M. A., & Chatterjee, S. (2007). A Design Science Research Methodology for Information Systems Research. *Journal of Management Information Systems*, *24*(3), 45–77. https://doi.org/10.2753/MIS0742-1222240302

Peiris, D., Praveen, D., Johnson, C., & Mogulluru, K. (2014). Use of mHealth Systems and Tools for Non-Communicable Diseases in Low- and Middle-Income Countries: a Systematic Review. *Journal of Cardiovascular Translational Research*, *7*(8), 677–691. https://doi.org/10.1007/s12265-014-9581-5

Peng, G. C., & Nunes, M. B. (2007). *Using PEST Analysis as a Tool for Refining and Focusing Contexts for Information Systems Research*.

Pentland, B. T., Recker, J., Wolf, J., & Wyner, G. (2020). Bringing Context Inside Process Research with Digital Trace Data. *Journal of the Association for Information Systems*, *21*(5), 1214–1236. https://doi.org/10.17705/1jais.00635

Peters, C., Blohm, I., & Leimeister, J. M. (2015). Anatomy of Successful Business Models for Complex Services: Insights from the Telemedicine Field. *Journal of Management Information Systems*, *32*(3), 75–104. https://doi.org/10.1080/07421222.2015.1095034

Pinsonneault, A., Addas, S., Qian, C., Dakshinamoorthy, V., & Tamblyn, R. (2017). Integrated Health Information Technology and the Quality of Patient Care: A Natural Experiment. *Journal of Management Information Systems*, *34*(2), 457–486. https://doi.org/10.1080/07421222.2017.1334477

Plachkinova, M., Andres, S., & Chatterjee, S. (2015). A Taxonomy of mHealth Apps -- Security and Privacy Concerns. *2015 48th Hawaii International Conference on System Sciences*, *2015-March*, 3187–3196.

https://doi.org/10.1109/HICSS.2015.385

Podsakoff, P. M., MacKenzie, S. B., Lee, J. Y., & Podsakoff, N. P. (2003). Common Method Biases in Behavioral Research: A Critical Review of the Literature and Recommended Remedies. *Journal of Applied Psychology*, *88*(5), 879–903.

Ponemon Institute. (2019). Cost of a data breach report. In *IBM Security*.

Pouloudi, N., Currie, W., & Whitley, E. (2016). Entangled Stakeholder Roles and Perceptions in Health Information Systems: A Longitudinal Study of the U.K. NHS N3 Network. *Journal of the Association for Information Systems*, *17*(2), 107–161. https://doi.org/10.17705/1jais.00421

Prasongsukarn, K., & Patterson, P. G. (2012). An extended service recovery model: The moderating impact of temporal sequence of events. *Journal of Services Marketing*, *26*(7), 510–520. https://doi.org/10.1108/08876041211266477

Praveen, D., Patel, A., Raghu, A., Clifford, G. D., Maulik, P. K., Mohammad Abdul, A., Mogulluru, K., Tarassenko, L., MacMahon, S., & Peiris, D. (2014). SMARTHealth India: Development and Field Evaluation of a Mobile Clinical Decision Support System for Cardiovascular Diseases in Rural India. *JMIR MHealth and UHealth*, *2*(4), e54. https://doi.org/10.2196/mhealth.3568

Preston, L. E., & Sapienza, H. J. (1990). Stakeholder management and corporate performance. *The Journal of Behavioral Economics*, *19*(4), 361–375. https://doi.org/10.1016/0090-5720(90)90023-Z

Purao, S., Henfridsson, O., Rossi, M., & Sein, M. (2013). Ensemble artifacts : from viewing to designing in action design research. *Systems, Signs & Actions*, *7*(1), 73–81.

Qureshi, S. (2015). Are we making a Better World with Information and Communication Technology for Development (ICT4D) Research? Findings from the Field and Theory Building. *Information Technology for Development*, *21*(4), 511–522. https://doi.org/10.1080/02681102.2015.1080428

Rabkin, M., Melaku, Z., Bruce, K., Reja, A., Koler, A., Tadesse, Y., Kamiru, H. N., Sibanyoni, L. T., & El-Sadr, W. (2012). Strengthening Health Systems for Chronic Care: Leveraging HIV Programs to Support Diabetes Services in Ethiopia and Swaziland. *Journal of Tropical Medicine*, *2012*, 1–6. https://doi.org/10.1155/2012/137460

Rana, Y., Haberer, J., Huang, H., Kambugu, A., Mukasa, B., Thirumurthy, H., Wabukala, P., Wagner, G. J., & Linnemayr, S. (2015). Short Message Service (SMS)-Based Intervention to Improve Treatment Adherence among HIV-Positive Youth in Uganda: Focus Group Findings. *PLOS ONE*, *10*(4), e0125187. https://doi.org/10.1371/journal.pone.0125187

Rawls, J. (1971). A theory of justice. In *The Beknap Press of Harvard University Press*.

Recker, J. (2021). *Scientific Research in Information Systems*. Springer International Publishing. https://doi.org/10.1007/978-3-030-85436-2

Reinecke, K., & Bernstein, A. (2013). Knowing What a User Likes: A Design Science Approach to Interfaces that Automatically Adapt to Culture. *MIS Quarterly Management Information Systems*, *37*(2), 427–453.

Riemer, K., & Johnston, R. B. (2014). Rethinking the place of the artefact in IS using Heidegger's analysis of equipment. *European Journal of Information Systems*, *23*(3),

273–288. https://doi.org/10.1057/ejis.2013.5

Riggins, F., & Dewan, S. (2005). The Digital Divide: Current and Future Research Directions. *Journal of the Association for Information Systems*, *6*(12), 298–337. https://doi.org/10.17705/1jais.00074

Robey, D., Anderson, C., & Raymond, B. (2013). Information Technology, Materiality, and Organizational Change: A Professional Odyssey. *Undefined*, *14*(7), 379–398. https://doi.org/10.17705/1JAIS.00337

Romanow, Cho, & Straub. (2018). Riding the Wave: Past Trends and Future Directions for Health IT Research. *MIS Quarterly*, *36*(3), iii.

Romanow, D., Cho, S., & Straub, D. (2012). Editor ' s Comments Riding the Wave : Past Trends and Future Directions for Health IT Research. *MIS Quarterly*, *36*(3), iii–x.

Romanow, D., Rai, A., & Keil, M. (2018). Cpoe-enabled coordination: Appropriation for deep structure use and impacts on patient outcomes. *MIS Quarterly*, *42*(1), 189–212. https://doi.org/10.25300/MISQ/2018/13275

Rothe, F.-F. (2020). Rethinking positive and negative impacts of 'ICT for development' through the holistic lens of the sustainable development goals. *Information Technology for Development*, *26*(4), 653–669. https://doi.org/10.1080/02681102.2020.1756728

Rowland, S. P., Fitzgerald, J. E., Holme, T., Powell, J., & McGregor, A. (2020). What is the clinical value of mHealth for patients? *Npj Digital Medicine*, *3*(1), 4. https://doi.org/10.1038/s41746-019-0206-x

Sæbø, Ø., & Thapa, D. (2012). Towards scalability of ICT4D projects : a salience stakeholder perspective. *GlobDev*, 1–13.

Sahay, S. (2001). Special Issue on "IT and Health Care in Developing Countries." *The Electronic Journal of Information Systems in Developing Countries*, *5*(1), 1–6. https://doi.org/10.1002/j.1681-4835.2001.tb00029.x

Sahay, S., Sæbø, J., & Braa, J. (2013). Scaling of HIS in a global context: Same, same, but different. *Information and Organization*, *23*(4), 294–323. https://doi.org/10.1016/j.infoandorg.2013.08.002

Sahay, S., Sein, M. K., & Urquhart, C. (2017). Flipping the Context: ICT4D, the Next Grand Challenge for IS Research and Practice. *Journal of the Association for Information Systems*, *18*(12), 837–847.

Saifee, D. H., Bardhan, I. R., Lahiri, A., & Zheng, Z. (2019). Adherence to Clinical Guidelines, Electronic Health Record Use, and Online Reviews. *Journal of Management Information Systems*, *36*(4), 1071–1104. https://doi.org/10.1080/07421222.2019.1661093

San Nicolas-Rocca, T., Schooley, B., & Joo, S.-J. (2014). Design and Development of a Patient-Centered E-Health System to Improve Patient Understanding at Discharge. *Communications of the Association for Information Systems*, *34*(1), 453–476. https://doi.org/10.17705/1CAIS.03424

Sanner, T. A., Roland, L. K., & Braa, K. (2012). From pilot to scale: Towards an mHealth typology for low-resource contexts. *Health Policy and Technology*, *1*(3), 155–164. https://doi.org/10.1016/j.hlpt.2012.07.009

Sarker, S., Chatterjee, S., Xiao, X., & Elbanna, A. (2019). The Sociotechnical Axis of

Cohesion for the IS Discipline: Its Historical Legacy and its Continued Relevance. *MIS Quarterly*, *43*(3), 695–719. https://doi.org/10.25300/MISQ/2019/13747

Sarstedt, M., Henseler, J., & Ringle, C. M. (2011). Multigroup analysis in partial least squares (PLS) path modeling: Alternative methods and empirical results. *Advances in International Marketing*, *22*(January), 195–218. https://doi.org/10.1108/S1474-7979(2011)0000022012

Scheepers, R., Scheepers, H., & Ngwenyama, O. K. (2006). Contextual influences on user satisfaction with mobile computing: findings from two healthcare organizations. *European Journal of Information Systems*, *15*(3), 261–268. https://doi.org/10.1057/palgrave.ejis.3000615

Schelenz, L., & Pawelec, M. (2021). Information and Communication Technologies for Development (ICT4D) critique. *Information Technology for Development*, 1–24. https://doi.org/10.1080/02681102.2021.1937473

Sein, Henfridsson, Purao, Rossi, & Lindgren. (2011). Action Design Research. *MIS Quarterly*, *35*(1), 37. https://doi.org/10.2307/23043488

Sein, M. K., Thapa, D., Hatakka, M., & Sæbø, Ø. (2019). A holistic perspective on the theoretical foundations for ICT4D research. *Information Technology for Development*, *25*(1), 7–25. https://doi.org/10.1080/02681102.2018.1503589

Senkubuge, F., Modisenyane, M., & Bishaw, T. (2014). Strengthening health systems by health sector reforms. *Global Health Action*, *7*(1), 23568. https://doi.org/10.3402/gha.v7.23568

Sernac. (2018). *Luego de demanda del SERNAC: Consumidores recibirán compensaciones por 30 millones de dólares tras doble cobro de comisiones por Banco de Chile - SERNAC: Noticias*. https://www.sernac.cl/portal/604/w3-article-13268.html

Sezgin, E., Özkan-Yildirim, S., & Yildirim, S. (2018). Understanding the perception towards using mHealth applications in practice: Physicians' perspective. *Information Development*, *34*(2), 182–200. https://doi.org/10.1177/0266666916684180

Sharp, A., Riches, N., Mims, A., Ntshalintshali, S., McConalogue, D., Southworth, P., Pierce, C., Daniels, P., Kalungero, M., Ndzinisa, F., Elston, E., Okello, V., & Walley, J. (2020). Decentralising NCD management in rural southern Africa: evaluation of a pilot implementation study. *BMC Public Health*, *20*(1), 44. https://doi.org/10.1186/s12889-019-7994-4

Shaw, M., & Stahl, B. (2011). On Quality and Communication: The Relevance of Critical Theory to Health Informatics. *Journal of the Association for Information Systems*, *12*(3), 255–273. https://doi.org/10.17705/1jais.00261

Shediac-Rizkallah, M. C., & Bone, L. R. (1998). Planning for the sustainability of community-based health programs: conceptual frameworks and future directions for research, practice and policy. *Health Education Research*, *13*(1), 87–108. https://doi.org/10.1093/her/13.1.87 PM

Sherer, S. A. (2014a). Patients Are Not Simply Health IT Users or Consumers: The Case for "e Healthicant" Applications. *Communications of the Association for Information Systems*, *34*. https://doi.org/10.17705/1CAIS.03417

Sherer, S. A. (2014b). Advocating for Action Design Research on IT Value Creation in Healthcare. *Journal of the Association for Information Systems*, *15*(12), 860–878.

https://doi.org/10.17705/1jais.00384

Shinar, D., Dewar, R. E., Summala, H., & Zakowska, L. (2003). Traffic sign symbol comprehension: A cross-cultural study. *Ergonomics*, *46*(15), 1549–1565. https://doi.org/10.1080/00140130310001594451

Silva, B. M. C., Rodrigues, J. J. P. C., de la Torre Díez, I., López-Coronado, M., & Saleem, K. (2015). Mobile-health: A review of current state in 2015. *Journal of Biomedical Informatics*, *56*, 265–272. https://doi.org/10.1016/j.jbi.2015.06.003

Sim, I. (2019). Mobile Devices and Health. *N Engl J Med*, *381*, 956–968. https://doi.org/10.1056/NEJMra1806949

Singh, P., & Sachs, J. D. (2013). 1 million community health workers in sub-Saharan Africa by 2015. *The Lancet*, *382*(9889), 363–365. https://doi.org/10.1016/S0140-6736(12)62002-9

Singhal, S., Latko, B., & Martin, C. P. (2018). *The future of healthcare : Finding the opportunities that lie beneath the uncertainty* (Issue January). https://www.mckinsey.com/industries/healthcare-systems-and-services/our-insights/the-future-of-healthcare-finding-the-opportunities-that-lie-beneath-the-uncertainty#

Smith, A. K., Bolton, R. N., & Wagner, J. (1999). A Model of Customer Satisfaction with Service Encounters Involving Failure and Recovery. *Journal of Marketing Research*, *36*(3), 356–372. https://doi.org/10.2307/3152082

Solanas, A., Patsakis, C., Conti, M., Vlachos, I., Ramos, V., Falcone, F., Postolache, O., Perez-martinez, P., Pietro, R., Perrea, D., & Martinez-Balleste, A. (2014). Smart health: A context-aware health paradigm within smart cities. *IEEE Communications Magazine*, *52*(8), 74–81. https://doi.org/10.1109/MCOM.2014.6871673

Sommer, C., Zuccolin, D., Arnera, V., Schmitz, N., Adolfsson, P., Colombo, N., Gilg, R., & McDowell, B. (2018). Building clinical trials around patients: Evaluation and comparison of decentralized and conventional site models in patients with low back pain. *Contemporary Clinical Trials Communications*, *11*(June), 120–126. https://doi.org/10.1016/j.conctc.2018.06.008

Son, J., Flatley Brennan, P., & Zhou, S. (2020). A Data Analytics Framework for Smart Asthma Management Based on Remote Health Information Systems with Bluetooth-Enabled Personal Inhalers. *MIS Quarterly*, *44*(1), 285–303. https://doi.org/10.25300/misq/2020/15092

Sondaal, S. F. V., Browne, J. L., Amoakoh-Coleman, M., Borgstein, A., Miltenburg, A. S., Verwijs, M., & Klipstein-Grobusch, K. (2016). Assessing the Effect of mHealth Interventions in Improving Maternal and Neonatal Care in Low- and Middle-Income Countries: A Systematic Review. *PLOS ONE*, *11*(5), e0154664. https://doi.org/10.1371/journal.pone.0154664

Spohrer, K., Fallon, M., Hoehle, H., & Heinzl, A. (2021). Designing Effective Mobile Health Apps: Does Combining Behavior Change Techniques Really Create Synergies? *Journal of Management Information Systems*, *38*(2), 517–545. https://doi.org/10.1080/07421222.2021.1912936

Srite, & Karahanna. (2006). The Role of Espoused National Cultural Values in Technology Acceptance. *MIS Quarterly*, *30*(3), 679. https://doi.org/10.2307/25148745

Steelman, Z. R., Hammer, B. I., & Limayem, M. (2014). Data Collection in the Digital Age: Innovative Alternatives to Student Samples. *MIS Quarterly*, *38*(2), 355–378. https://doi.org/10.25300/MISQ/2014/38.2.02

Steg, L., Dreijerink, L., & Abrahamse, W. (2005). Factors influencing the acceptability of energy policies: A test of VBN theory. *Journal of Environmental Psychology*, *25*(4), 415–425. https://doi.org/10.1016/j.jenvp.2005.08.003

Steinhubl, S. R., Muse, E. D., & Topol, E. J. (2015). The emerging field of mobile health. *Science Translational Medicine*, *7*(283). https://doi.org/10.1126/scitranslmed.aaa3487

Stephani, V. (2019). Effective and needed, but not used: why do mobile phone-based health interventions in Africa not move beyond the project status? In *Working papers in health policy and management* (Vol. 13). Universitätsverlag der TU Berlin. http://www.worldcat.org/oclc/1104932176

Stroetmann, K. F. M. for E. C. and D. S. P. D. A. (2018). Digital Health Ecosystem for African countries A Guide for Public and Private Actors for establishing holistic Digital Health Ecosystems in Africa. *Federal Ministry for Economic Cooperation and Development*, *November*, 46. https://www.bmz.de/en/publications/topics/health/Materilie345_digital_health_africa.pdf

Sundin, P., Callan, J., & Mehta, K. (2016). Why do entrepreneurial mHealth ventures in the developing world fail to scale? *Journal of Medical Engineering & Technology*, *40*(7–8), 444–457. https://doi.org/10.1080/03091902.2016.1213901

Sweetney, S. (2015). *Boom or Bust? Cyber Security and Data Breach Loss in Latin America | Wilson Elser - JDSupra*. JD Supra. https://www.jdsupra.com/legalnews/boom-or-bust-cyber-security-and-data-br-50568/

Tamrat, T., & Kachnowski, S. (2012). Special Delivery: An Analysis of mHealth in Maternal and Newborn Health Programs and Their Outcomes Around the World. *Maternal and Child Health Journal*, *16*(5), 1092–1101. https://doi.org/10.1007/s10995-011-0836-3

Tan, F. T. C., & Vasa, R. (2011). Toward a Social Media Usage Policy. *ACIS 2011 Proceedings*.

Taringa. (2017). *Un mensaje importante sobre la seguridad de tu cuenta -... en Taringa!* https://www.taringa.net/+taringa/un-mensaje-importante-sobre-la-seguridad-de-tu-cuenta_wlscx

Tariq, A., & Akter, S. (2011). An assessment of m-Health in developing countries using task technology fit model. *Proceedings of the Seventeenth Americas Conference on Information Systems*, 1–12.

Terranova Security. (2015). *Risk of data breaches, cybercrime growing in Latin America*. https://terranovasecurity.com/risk-of-data-breaches-cybercrime-growing-in-latin-america/

Thompson, S., Whitaker, J., Kohli, R., & Jones, C. (2020). Chronic Disease Management: How IT and Analytics Create Healthcare Value Through the Temporal Displacement of Care. *MIS Quarterly*, *44*(1), 227–256. https://doi.org/10.25300/misq/2020/15085

Thondoo, M., Strachan, D. L., Nakirunda, M., Ndima, S., Muiambo, A., Källander, K., &

Hill, Z. (2015). Potential Roles of Mhealth for Community Health Workers: Formative Research With End Users in Uganda and Mozambique. *JMIR MHealth and UHealth*, *3*(3), e76. https://doi.org/10.2196/mhealth.4208

Tibben, W. J. (2015). Theory Building for ICT4D: Systemizing Case Study Research Using Theory Triangulation. *Information Technology for Development*, *21*(4), 628–652. https://doi.org/10.1080/02681102.2014.910635

Tomlinson, M., Rotheram-Borus, M. J., Swartz, L., & Tsai, A. C. (2013). Scaling Up mHealth: Where Is the Evidence? *PLoS Medicine*, *10*(2), 1–5. https://doi.org/10.1371/journal.pmed.1001382

Trang, S., Trenz, M., Weiger, W. H., Tarafdar, M., & Cheung, C. M. K. (2020). One app to trace them all? Examining app specifications for mass acceptance of contact-tracing apps. *European Journal of Information Systems*, *29*(4), 415–428. https://doi.org/10.1080/0960085X.2020.1784046

Traxler, J. (2012). Ethics and ICTD Research. In A. Chib & R. Harris (Eds.), *Linking Research to Practice: Strengthening ICT for Development Research Capacity in Asia* (pp. 68–81).

TWT Digital Health. (2020). *Der Weg zur erstattungsfährigen App.*

UN. (2015). Transforming Our World: The 2030 Agenda for Sustainable Development. In *A New Era in Global Health*. https://doi.org/10.1891/9780826190123.ap02

UNDP. (2015). *Sustainable Developmend Goals.* http://www.undp.org/content/dam/undp/library/corporate/brochure/SDGs_Booklet_Web_En.pdf

Urbach, N., & Ahlemann, F. (2010). Structural Equation Modeling in Information Systems Research Using Partial Least Squares. *Journal of Information Technology Theory and Application (JITTA)*, *11*(2), 5–40.

Vaidya, R., & Myers, M. D. (2020). Symbolic practices and power asymmetries in ICT4D projects: The case of an Indian Agricultural Marketing Board. *Journal of Information Technology*, 026839622096481. https://doi.org/10.1177/0268396220964813

van Dam, J., Omondi Onyango, K., Midamba, B., Groosman, N., Hooper, N., Spector, J., Pillai, G. C., & Ogutu, B. (2017). Open-source mobile digital platform for clinical trial data collection in low-resource settings. *BMJ Innovations*, *3*(1), 26–31. https://doi.org/10.1136/bmjinnov-2016-000164

van der Heijden, H., & Junglas, I. (2006). Introduction to the special issue on mobile user behaviour. *European Journal of Information Systems*, *15*(3), 249–251. https://doi.org/10.1057/palgrave.ejis.3000613

van Dyk, L. (2014). A review of telehealth service implementation frameworks. *International Journal of Environmental Research and Public Health*, *11*(2), 1279–1298. https://doi.org/10.3390/ijerph110201279 PM - 24464237

van Laere, J., & Aggestam, L. (2016). Understanding champion behaviour in a health-care information system development project – how multiple champions and champion behaviours build a coherent whole. *European Journal of Information Systems*, *25*(1), 47–63. https://doi.org/10.1057/ejis.2015.5

van Olmen, J., Erwin, E., García-Ulloa, A. C., Meessen, B., Miranda, J. J., Bobrow, K., Iwelunmore, J., Nwaozuru, U., Obiezu Umeh, C., Smith, C., Harding, C., Kumar, P., Gonzales, C., Hernández-Jiménez, S., & Yeates, K. (2020). Implementation barriers for mHealth for non-communicable diseases management in low and middle income countries: a scoping review and field-based views from implementers. *Wellcome Open Research*, *5*, 7. https://doi.org/10.12688/wellcomeopenres.15581.2

Varshney, U. (2003). Mobile and Wireless Information Systems: Applications, Networks, and Research Problems. *Communications of the Association for Information Systems*, *12*(July). https://doi.org/10.17705/1cais.01211

Varshney, U. (2014). Mobile health: Four emerging themes of research. *Decision Support Systems*, *66*, 20–35. https://doi.org/10.1016/j.dss.2014.06.001

Venkatesh, V., Bala, H., & Sambamurthy, V. (2016). Implementation of an Information and Communication Technology in a Developing Country: A Multimethod Longitudinal Study in a Bank in India. *Information Systems Research*, *27*(3), 558–579. https://doi.org/10.1287/isre.2016.0638

Venkatesh, V., Rai, A., Sykes, T. A., & Aljafari, R. (2016). Combating infant mortality in Rural India: Evidence from a field study of Ehealth Kiosk implementations. *MIS Quarterly*, *40*(2), 353–380. https://doi.org/10.25300/MISQ/2016/40.2.04

Venkatesh, V., Sykes, T. A., & Zhang, X. (2020). ICT for Development in Rural India: A Longitudinal Study of Women's Health Outcomes. *MIS Quarterly*, *44*, 605–629. https://doi.org/10.25300/MISQ/2020/12342

Venkatesh, V., Thong, J., & Xu, X. (2012). Consumer Acceptance and User of Information Technology: Extending the Unified Theory of Acceptance and Use of Technology. *MIS Quarterly*.

Vesel, L., Hipgrave, D., Dowden, J., & Kariuki, W. (2015). Application of mHealth to improve service delivery and health outcomes: Opportunities and challenges. *African Population Studies*, *29*(1), 1683. https://doi.org/10.11564/29-1-718

Vessey, I. (1991). Cognitive Fit: A Theory-Based Analysis of the Graphs Versus Tables Literature. *Decision Sciences*, *22*(2), 219–240. https://doi.org/10.1111/j.1540-5915.1991.tb00344.x

Vogel, D., Viehland, D., Wickramasinghe, N., & Mula, J. M. (2013). Mobile health. *Electronic Markets*, *23*(1), 3–4. https://doi.org/10.1007/s12525-013-0121-y

vom Brocke, J., Simons, A., Niehaves, B., Niehaves, B., Reimer, K., Plattfaut, R., & Cleven, A. (2009). Reconstructing the Giant: On the Importance of Rigour in Documenting the Literature Search Process. *European Conference on Information Systems (ECIS 2009)*. https://doi.org/10.1108/09600031211269721

vom Brocke, J., Simons, A., Riemer, K., Niehaves, B., Plattfaut, R., & Cleven, A. (2015). Standing on the shoulders of giants: Challenges and recommendations of literature search in information systems research. *Communications of the Association for Information Systems*, *37*, 205–224.

Wahle, F., & Kowatsch, T. (2014). Towards the design of evidence-based mental health information systems: A preliminary literature review. *35th International Conference on Information Systems*, 1–12.

Wallis, L., Blessing, P., Dalwai, M., & Shin, S. Do. (2017). Integrating mHealth at point of care in low- and middle-income settings: the system perspective. *Global Health Action*, *10*(sup3), 1327686. https://doi.org/10.1080/16549716.2017.1327686

Walsham, G. (2012). Are we making a better world with ICTs? Reflections on a future agenda for the IS field. *Journal of Information Technology*, *27*(2), 87–93.

https://doi.org/10.1057/jit.2012.4

Walsham, G. (2017). ICT4D research: reflections on history and future agenda. *Information Technology for Development*, *23*(1), 18–41. https://doi.org/10.1080/02681102.2016.1246406

Walsham, G. (2020). Health information systems in developing countries: some reflections on information for action. *Information Technology for Development*, *26*(1), 194–200. https://doi.org/10.1080/02681102.2019.1586632

Walsham, G., & Sahay, S. (2006). Research on information systems in developing countries: Current landscape and future prospects. *Information Technology for Development*, *12*(1), 7–24. https://doi.org/10.1002/itdj.20020

Walsham, Robey, & Sahay. (2007). Foreword: Special Issue on Information Systems in Developing Countries. *MIS Quarterly*, *31*(2), 317. https://doi.org/10.2307/25148793

Walster, E., Berscheid, E., & Walster, G. W. (1973). New directions in equity research. *Journal of Personality and Social Psychology*, *25*(2), 151–176.

Wan, L., & Zhang, C. (2014). Responses to trust repair after privacy breach incidents. *Journal of Service Science Research*, *6*(2), 193–224.

Wang, C. ya, & Mattila, A. S. (2011). A cross-cultural comparison of perceived informational fairness with service failure explanations. *Journal of Services Marketing*, *25*(6), 429–439. https://doi.org/10.1108/08876041111161023

Waruingi, M., & Underdahl, L. (2009). Opportunity in delivery of health care over mobile devices in developing countries. *African Journal of Food Agriculture Nutrition and Development*, *9*(5), 1–11.

Waugaman, A. (2016). *Implementing the Principles for Digital Development*.

Webster, J., & Watson, R. T. (2002). Analyzing the Past tp Prepare for the Future: Writing a Literature Review. *Management Information Systems Quarterly*, *26*(2), xiii–xxiii.

Wesolowski, A., Eagle, N., Noor, A. M., Snow, R. W., & Buckee, C. O. (2012). Heterogeneous mobile phone ownership and usage patterns in Kenya. *PloS ONE*, *7*(4), e35319. https://doi.org/10.1371/journal.pone.0035319

Whidden, C. E., Kayentao, K., Liu, J. X., Lee, S., Keita, Y., Diakité, D., Keita, A., Diarra, S., Edwards, J., Yembrick, A., Holeman, I., Samaké, S., Plea, B., Coumaré, M., & Johnson, A. D. (2018). Improving Community Health Worker performance by using a personalised feedback dashboard for supervision: A randomised controlled trial. *Journal of Global Health*, *8*(2). https://doi.org/10.7189/jogh.08.020418

Whiting, D. R., Hayes, L., & Unwin, N. C. (2003). Challenges to health care for diabetes in Africa. *Journal of Cardiovascular Risk*, *10*(2), 103–110. https://doi.org/10.1097/00043798-200304000-00005

WHO. (2011). mHealth: New horizons for health through mobile technologies. In *Observatory* (Vol. 3). http://www.who.int/goe/publications/goe_mhealth_web.pdf%5Cnhttp://www.who.int/goe/publications/ehealth_series_vol3/en/index.html

WHO. (2018). *Noncommunicable diseases*. World Health Organisation. https://www.who.int/news-room/fact-sheets/detail/noncommunicable-diseases

WHO. (2019). *WHO Guideline: Recommendation in digital interventions for health systems strengthening.*

WHO. (2021). *World Health Statistics 2021: monitoring health for the SDGs*.

WHO (World Health Organization). (2013). *Global Action Plan for the Prevention and Control of Noncommunicable Diseases*.

WHO (World Health Organization). (2019). *WHO Country Cooperation Strategy 2014-2019*.

Wilson, E. V., Wang, W., & Sheetz, S. D. (2014). Underpinning a guiding theory of patient-centered e-health. *Communications of the Association for Information Systems*, *34*(1), 337–350. https://doi.org/10.17705/1cais.03416

Wilson, K., Gertz, B., Arenth, B., & Salisbury, N. (2014). *The journey to scale: Moving together past digital health pilots*. https://path.azureedge.net/media/documents/PATH_Journey_to_Scale_R2.pdf

Wirtz, J., & Mattila, A. S. (2004). Consumer responses to compensation, speed of recovery and apology after a service failure. *International Journal of Service Industry Management*, *15*(2), 150–166.

Wong, N. Y. (2004). The role of culture in the perception of service recovery. *Journal of Business Research*, *57*(9), 957–963. https://doi.org/10.1016/S0148-2963(03)00002-X

Wong, R. C.-W., Fu, A. W.-C., Wang, K., Yu, P. S., & Pei, J. (2011). Can the Utility of Anonymized Data be Used for Privacy Breaches? *ACM Transactions on Knowledge Discovery from Data*, *5*(3), 1–24. https://doi.org/10.1145/1993077.1993080

World Health Organization. (2020). *Digital Health*.

WorldBank. (2008). ICT: Connecting People and Making Markets Work. In *World Bank*. http://documents.worldbank.org/curated/en/878971468316431008/ICT-connecting-people-and-making-markets-work

Wu, J. H., & Wang, S. C. (2005). What drives mobile commerce? An empirical evaluation of the revised technology acceptance model. *Information and Management*, *42*(5), 719–729. https://doi.org/10.1016/j.im.2004.07.001

Yan, L., & Tan, Y. (2017). The Consensus Effect in Online Health-Care Communities. *Journal of Management Information Systems*, *34*(1), 11–39. https://doi.org/10.1080/07421222.2017.1296742

Yang, A., & Varshney, U. (2016). A Taxonomy for Mobile Health Implementation and Evaluation. *Proceedings of the International Conference on Information Systems (ICIS)*, 1–10.

Yaraghi, N., Gopal, R. D., & Ramesh, R. (2019). Doctors' orders or patients' preferences? Examining the role of physicians in patients' privacy decisions on health information exchange platforms. *Journal of the Association for Information Systems*, *20*(7), 928–952. https://doi.org/10.17705/1jais.00557

Yin, R. K. (2016). *Qualitative research from start to finish* (Second edi). The Guilford Press.

Yusof, M. M., Paul, R. J., & Stergioulas, L. K. (2006). Towards a Framework for Health Information Systems Evaluation. *Proceedings of the 39the Hawaii International Conference on System Sciences*.

Zhang, P., & Li, N. (2004). An assessment of human–computer interaction research in management information systems: topics and methods. *Computers in Human*

Behavior, *20*(2), 125–147. https://doi.org/10.1016/j.chb.2003.10.011

Zhang, W., & Ram, S. (2020). A Comprehensive Analysis of Triggers and Risk Factors for Asthma Based on Machine Learning and Large Heterogeneous Data Sources. *MIS Quarterly*, *44*(1), 305–349. https://doi.org/10.25300/misq/2020/15106

Zhang, X., Guo, X., Lai, K. hung, & Yi, W. (2019). How does online interactional unfairness matter for patient–doctor relationship quality in online health consultation? The contingencies of professional seniority and disease severity. *European Journal of Information Systems*, *28*(3), 336–354. https://doi.org/10.1080/0960085X.2018.1547354

Zhao, X., Lynch, J. G., & Chen, Q. (2010). Reconsidering Baron and Kenny: Myths and Truths about Mediation Analysis. *Journal of Consumer Research*, *37*(2), 197–206. https://doi.org/10.1086/651257

Appendix

The appendix of this thesis contains three parts. First, the individual contribution of the authors of the papers presented in this thesis is depicted. Second, other published papers (only VHB ranking A and B) are presented. Third, the curriculum vitae is provided.

Appendix A. Overview of the Contributions in the Studies of this Thesis

No.	Section	Title	Authors	Authors' contribution [%]
1	B.I.1	Framing Research Questions Intersecting Information Systems and Health: A New Research Perspective at Micro- and Macro-Level	**Greve, M.**	**45**
			Gantner, M.	20
			Harnischmacher, C.	20
			Brendel, A.B.	10
			Kolbe, L.M.	5
2	B.II.1	Fostering Non-Communicable Disease Prevention in The Global South: An Action De-sign Research Project of a Mobile Health Intervention in eSwatini	Brendel, A.B.	40
			Greve, M.	**40**
			Lichtenberg, S.	15
			Kolbe, L.M.	5
3	B.II.2	Overcoming the Divide of Digital Challenges: A Cross-Cultural Experimental Investigation of Recovering from Data Breaches	**Greve, M.**	**50**
			Masuch, K.	30
			Hengstler, S.	10
			Trang, S.	10
4	B.III.1	Healing the 'Pilotitis' in Mobile Health – A Holistic Stakeholder Perspective on Making Interventions Scalable and Sustainable in Low-Resource Environments	**Greve, M.**	**50**
			Brendel, A.B.	35
			Mirbabaie, M.	10
			Kolbe, L.M.	5

Appendix B. Overview of Further Published Studies (VHB A and B Only)

Title	Year	Authors	Outlet	Ranking[15]
"Even the Wisest Machine Makes Errors" – An Experimental Investigation of Human-like Designed and Flawed Conversational Agents	2021	Riquel, J. Brendel, A. B. Hildebrandt, F. **Greve, M.** Kolbe, L	Proceedings of the 42nd International Conference on Information Systems (ICIS)	A
"F*** You!" – An Investigation of Humanness, Frustration, and Aggression in Conversational Agent Communication	2021	Riquel, J. Brendel, A. B. Hildebrandt, F. **Greve, M.** Dennis, A. R.	Proceedings of the 42nd International Conference on Information Systems (ICIS)	A
What to do after a data breach? Examining apology and compensation as response strategies for health service providers	2021	Masuch, K. **Greve, M.** Trang, S	Electronic Markets	B
Openness always pays off – Investigation of Diverse Actions in Response Strategies to Data Breaches	2021	Masuch, K. Diesterhöft, T. O. **Greve, M.** Massaneck, S. Nguyen, D. K. Trang, S. Kolbe, L. M	European Conference on Information Systems (ECIS)	B
Please be Silent? Examining the Impact of Data Breach Response Strategies on the Stock Value	2020	Masuch, K. **Greve, M.** Trang, S.	Proceedings of the International Conference on Information Systems (ICIS)	A
Supporting Non-Communicable Disease Prevention through an mHealth Application in Decentralized Healthcare Systems: Action Design Research in Eswatini	2020	**Greve, M.** Lichtenberg, S. Diederich, S. Brendel, A.B.	Proceedings of European Conference on Information Systems (ECIS)	B
Do I get what I expect? An experimental Investigation of different Data Breach Recovery Actions	2020	Masuch, K. **Greve, M.** Cyrenius, J. Wimmel, B. Trang, S.	Proceedings of European Conference on Information Systems (ECIS)	B
Why Electrify? – A Qualitative-Empirical Study on Electrification of Fleet Transportation Systems, Research in Progress	2020	Masuch, K. Harnischmacher, C. **Greve, M.** Trang, S.	Proceedings of European Conference on Information Systems (ECIS)	B
Investigating end-user acceptance of autonomous electric buses to accelerate diffusion	2019	Herrenkind, B. Brendel, A.B. Nastjuk, I. **Greve, M.** Kolbe, L.M.	Transportation Research Part D: Transport and Environment	B

[15] According to VHB-JOURQUAL 3. Only A and B ranked Outlets included.

Appendix C. Curriculum Vitae

Personal Details

Name	Maike Greve
Date of Birth	10.05.1992
Place of Birth	Göttingen, Germany
Nationality	German

Academic Experience

2018-2021	Doctorate in Information Systems, Chair of Information Management, University of Goettingen
2015 – 2018	Master of Science in Applied Statistics, University of Goettingen
2012 – 2015	Bachelor of Arts in Business and Human Resource Education, University of Goettingen
2009 – 2011	International Baccalaureate, Felix-Klein-Gymnasium Goettingen

Work Experience

Since 06/2020	Head of Research Group, Digital Health Research Group (DHRG), Chair of Information Management, University of Goettingen
Since 10/2018	Research Associate, Chair of Information Management, University of Goettingen
04/2017 - 08/2017	Intern, Data Science, eoda GmbH, Kassel
06/2015 - 10/2015	Intern, Monitoring, Evaluation & Studies, Deutscher Akademischer Austauschdienst (DAAD), Bonn
10/2012 - 10/2017	Teaching Associate for Mathematics; Statistics; Further Mathematics: Optimization; Introduction to LaTex, Chairs of Statistics and Econometrics, University of Goettingen

International Experience

08/2011 – 01/2012	Voluntary Service at the Entoto Freedom School and Hope for Children in Ethiopia in Addis Abeba, Ethiopia
08/2008 – 06/2009	Exchange Student, Junior Year, The Harker School, San Jose, USA

Social Engagement

Since 2009	Basketballcoach for Kids and Youth Teams at ASC Göttingen von 1846 e.V.
2017	„Social Talent 2017“ awarded by the Stadtsportbund Göttingen

Göttinger Wirtschaftsinformatik

Herausgeber: Prof. Dr. J. Biethahn† • Prof. Dr. L. M. Kolbe • Prof. Dr. M. Schumann

Band 31: Christian Stummeyer
Integration von Simulationsmethoden und hochintegrierter betriebswirtschaftlicher PPS-Standardsoftware im Rahmen eines ganzheitlichen Entwicklungsansatzes
ISBN 3-89712-874-8

Band 32: Stefan Wegert
Gestaltungsansätze zur IV-Integration von elektronischen und konventionellen Vertriebsstrukturen bei Kreditinstituten
ISBN 3-89712-924-8

Band 33: Ernst von Stegmann und Stein
Ansätze zur Risikosteuerung einer Kreditversicherung unter Berücksichtigung von Unternehmensverflechtungen
ISBN 3-89873-003-4

Band 34: Gerald Wissel
Konzeption eines Managementsystems für die Nutzung von internen sowie externen Wissen zur Generierung von Innovationen
ISBN 3-89873-194-4

Band 35: Wolfgang Greve-Kramer
Konzeption internetbasierter Informationssysteme in Konzernen
Inhaltliche, organisatorische und technische Überlegungen zur internetbasierten Informationsverarbeitung in Konzernen
ISBN 3-89873-207-X

Band 36: Tim Veil
Internes Rechnungswesen zur Unterstützung der Führung in Unternehmensnetzwerken
ISBN 3-89873-237-1

Band 37: Mark Althans
Konzeption eines Vertriebscontrolling-Informationssystems für Unternehmen der liberalisierten Elektrizitätswirtschaft
ISBN 3-89873-326-2

Band 38: Jörn Propach
Methoden zur Spielplangestaltung öffentlicher Theater
Konzeption eines Entscheidungsunterstützungssystems auf der Basis Evolutionärer Algorithmen
ISBN 3-89873-496-X

Göttinger Wirtschaftsinformatik

Herausgeber: Prof. Dr. J. Biethahn† • Prof. Dr. L. M. Kolbe • Prof. Dr. M. Schumann

Band 39: Jochen Heimann
DV-gestützte Jahresabschlußanalyse
Möglichkeiten und Grenzen beim Einsatz computergeschützter Verfahren zur Analyse und Bewertung von Jahresabschlüssen
ISBN 3-89873-499-4

Band 40: Patricia Böning Spohr
Controlling für Medienunternehmen im Online-Markt
Gestaltung ausgewählter Controllinginstrumente
ISBN 3-89873-677-6

Band 41: Jörg Koschate
Methoden und Vorgehensmodelle zur strategischen Planung von Electronic-Business-Anwendungen
ISBN 3-89873-808-6

Band 42: Yang Liu
A theoretical and empirical study on the data mining process for credit scoring
ISBN 3-89873-823-X

Band 43: Antonios Tzouvaras
Referenzmodellierung für Buchverlage
Prozess- und Klassenmodelle für den Leistungsprozess
ISBN 3-89873-844-2

Band 44: Marina Nomikos
Hemmnisse der Nutzung Elektronischer Marktplätze aus der Sicht von kleinen und mittleren Unternehmen eine theoriegeleitete Untersuchung
ISBN 3-89873-847-7

Band 45: Boris Fredrich
Wissensmanagement und Weiterbildungsmanagement
Gestaltungs- und Kombinationsansätze im Rahmen einer lernenden Organisation
ISBN 3-89873-870-1

Band 46: Thomas Arens
Methodische Auswahl von CRM Software
Ein Referenz-Vorgehensmodell zur methodengestützten Beurteilung und Auswahl von Customer Relationship Management Informationssystemen
ISBN 3-86537-054-3

Göttinger Wirtschaftsinformatik

Herausgeber: Prof. Dr. J. Biethahn† • Prof. Dr. L. M. Kolbe • Prof. Dr. M. Schumann

Band 47: Andreas Lackner
Dynamische Tourenplanung mit ausgewählten Mataheuristiken
Eine Untersuchung am Beispiel des kapazitätsrestriktiven dynamischen Tourenplanungsproblems mit Zeitfenstern
ISBN 3-86537-084-5

Band 48: Tobias Behrensdorf
Service Engineering in Versicherungsunternehmen
unter besonderer Berücksichtigung eines Vorgehensmodells zur Unterstützung durch Informations- und Kommunikationstechnologien
ISBN 3-86537-110-8

Band 49: Michael Range
Aufbau und Betrieb konsumentenorientierter Websites im Internet
Vorgehen und Methoden unter besonderer Berücksichtigung der Anforderungen von kleinen und mittleren Online-Angeboten
ISBN 3-86537-490-5

Band 50: Gerit Grübler
Ganzheitliches Multiprojektmanagement
Mit einer Fallstudie in einem Konzern der Automobilzulieferindustrie
ISBN 3-86537-544-8

Band 51: Birte Pochert
Konzeption einer unscharfen Balanced Scorecard
Möglichkeiten der Fuzzyfizierung einer Balanced Scorecard zur Unterstützung des Strategischen Managements
ISBN 3-86537-671-1

Band 52: Manfred Peter Zilling
Effizienztreiber innovativer Prozesse für den Automotive Aftermarket
Implikationen aus der Anwendung von kollaborativen und integrativen Methoden des Supply Chain Managements
ISBN 3-86537-790-4

Band 53: Mike Hieronimus
Strategisches Controlling von Supply Chains
Entwicklung eines ganzheitlichen Ansatzes unter Einbeziehung der Wertschöpfungspartner
ISBN 3-86537-799-8

Band 54: Dijana Bergmann
Datenschutz und Datensicherheit unter besonderer Berücksichtigung des elektronischen Geschäftsverkehrs zwischen öffentlicher Verwaltung und privaten Unternehmen
ISBN 3-86537-894-3

Göttinger Wirtschaftsinformatik

Herausgeber: Prof. Dr. J. Biethahn† • Prof. Dr. L. M. Kolbe • Prof. Dr. M. Schumann

Band 63: Thorsten Caus
Anwendungen im mobilen Internet
Herausforderungen und Lösungsansätze für die Entwicklung und Gestaltung mobiler Anwendungen
ISBN 978-3-86955-399-3

Band 64: Nils-Holger-Schmidt
Environmentally Sustainable Information Management
Theories and concepts for Sustainability, Green IS, and Green IT
ISBN 978-3-86955-825-7

Band 65: Lars Thoroe
RFID in Reverse-Logistics-Systemen
ISBN 978-3-86955-902-5

Band 66: Stefan Bitzer
Integration von Web 2.0-Technologien in das betriebliche Wissensmanagement
ISBN 978-3-86955-918-6

Band 67: Matthias Kießling
IT-Innovationsmanagement
Gestaltungs- und Steuerungsmöglichkeiten
ISBN 978-3-95404-104-6

Band 68: Marco Klein
HR Social Software
Unternehmensinterne Weblogs, Wikis und Social Networking
Services für Prozesse des Personalmanagements
ISBN 978-3-95404-247-0

Band 69: Malte Schmidt
Migration vom Barcode zur passiven RFID-Technologie in der automobilen Logistik
Exemplarische Untersuchung am Beispiel eines Automobilherstellers
ISBN 978-3-95404-441-2

Band 70: Janis Kossahl
Konzeptuelle Grundlagen zur Etablierung einer Informationsplattform in der Energiewirtschaft
Ein Beitrag zur Energiewende aus der Perspektive der Wirtschaftsinformatik
ISBN 978-3-95404-524-2

Cuvillier Verlag Göttingen

Nonnenstieg 8 • 37075 Göttingen

Göttinger Wirtschaftsinformatik

Herausgeber: Prof. Dr. J. Biethahn† • Prof. Dr. L. M. Kolbe • Prof. Dr. M. Schumann

Band 71: Stefan Friedemann
IT-gestützte Produktionsplanung mit nachwachsenden Rohstoffen unter Berücksichtigung von Unsicherheiten
ISBN 978-3-95404-606-5

Band 72: Arne Frerichs
Unternehmensfinanzierung mit Peer-to-Peer-gestützter Mittelvergabe
ISBN 978-3-95404-624-9

Band 73: Ullrich C. C. Jagstaidt
Smart Metering Information Management
Gestaltungsansätze für das Informationsmanagement und für Geschäftsmodelle der Marktakteure in der Energiewirtschaft
ISBN 978-3-95404-696-6

Band 74: Sebastian Busse
Exploring the Role of Information Systems in the Development of Electric Mobility
Understanding the Domain and Designing the Path
ISBN 978-3-95404-727-7

Band 75: Christoph Beckers
Management von Wasserinformationen in der Fleischindustrie
Analyse von Sytemanforderungen zur produktspezifischen Ausweisung von Water Footprints
ISBN 978-3-95404-809-0

Band 76: Hendrik Hilpert
Informationssysteme für die Nachhaltigkeitsberichterstattung in Unternehmen
Empirische Erkenntnisse und Gestaltungsansätze zur Datengrundlage, Erfassung und Berichterstattung von Treibhausgasemissionen
ISBN 978-3-95404-908-0

Band 77: Simon Thanh-Nam Trang
Adoption, Value Co-Creation, and Governance of Inter-Organizational Information Technology in Wood Networks
ISBN 978-3-7369-9031-9

Band 78: Stefan Gröger
IT-Unterstützung zur Verbesserung der Drittmittel-Projekt-Bewirtschaftung an Hochschulen - Referenzprozessgestaltung, Artefakt-Design und Nutzenpotenziale
ISBN 978-3-7369-9077-7

Cuvillier Verlag Göttingen
Nonnenstieg 8 • 37075 Göttingen

Göttinger Wirtschaftsinformatik

Herausgeber: Prof. Dr. J. Biethahn† • Prof. Dr. L. M. Kolbe • Prof. Dr. M. Schumann

Band 79: Johannes Schmidt
Demand-Side Integration Programs for Electric Transport Vehicles unter Berücksichtigung von Unsicherheiten
ISBN 978-3-7369-9123-1

Band 80: Christian Tornack
IT-gestütztes Nachfolgemanagement in Großunternehmen
ISBN 978-3-7369-9161-3

Band 81: Shanna Appelhanz
Tracking & Tracing-Systeme in Wertschöpfungsnetzwerken für die industrielle stoffliche Nutzung nachwachsender Rohstoffe
ISBN 978-3-7369-9207-8

Band 82: Henning Krüp
IT Corporate Entrepreneurship – Identifying Factors for IT Innovations in Non-IT Companies
ISBN 978-3-7369-9253-5

Band 83: Andre Hanelt
Managing the Digital Transformation of Business Models – An Incumbent Firm Perspective
ISBN 978-3-7369-9254-2

Band 84: Björn Pilarski
Mobile Personalinformationssysteme
Empirische Erkenntnisse und Gestaltungsansätze zum Einsatz mobiler Anwendungen im Personalmanagement
ISBN 978-3-7369-9291-7

Band 85: Everlin Piccinini
Digital Transformation of Business - Understanding this Phenomenon in the Context of the Automotive Industry
ISBN 978-3-7369-9323-5

Band 86: Matthias Eisel
Analyzing the Range Barrier to Electric Vehicle Adoption - The Case of Range Anxiety
ISBN 978-3-7369-9379-2

Cuvillier Verlag Göttingen

Nonnenstieg 8 • 37075 Göttingen

Göttinger Wirtschaftsinformatik

Herausgeber: Prof. Dr. J. Biethahn† • Prof. Dr. L. M. Kolbe • Prof. Dr. M. Schumann

Band 87: Gerrit Remané
Digital Business Models in the Mobility Sector: Using Components and Types to Understand Existing and Design New Business Models
ISBN 978-3-7369-9544-4

Band 88: Thierry Jean Ruch
Consumerization of IT –
Studies to Explore the Phenomenon and Implications for IT Management, Information Security, and Organizational Security
ISBN 978-3-7369-9558-1

Band 89: Carolin Ebermann
Die Förderung von nachhaltigem Mobilitätsverhalten durch erhöhte User-Experience und den Einsatz von Informationssystemen
ISBN 978-3-7369-9568-0

Band 90: Sebastian Zander
Interorganizational Information Systems for the Efficient Utilization of Renewable Resources - Insights from Networks in the Wood Industry
ISBN 978-3-7369-9584-0

Band 91: Ilja Nastjuk
The Dark and the Bright Side of Digitalization -
The Case of Sustainable Mobility
ISBN 978-3-7369-9586-4

Band 92: Aaron Mengelkamp
Informationen zur Bonitätsprüfung auf Basis von Daten aus sozialen Medien
ISBN 978-3-7369-9628-1

Band 93: Alfred Benedikt Brendel
Applied Design Science Research in the Context of Smart and Sustainable Mobility
The Case of Vehicle Supply and Demand Management in Shared Vehicle Services
ISBN 978-3-7369-9685-4

Band 94: Markus Mandrella
IT-Based Value Co-Creation in Inter-Organizational Networks
Theory Integration, Extension, and Adaptation to the Wood Industry
ISBN 978-3-7369-9695-3

Cuvillier Verlag Göttingen
Nonnenstieg 8 • 37075 Göttingen

Göttinger Wirtschaftsinformatik

Herausgeber: Prof. Dr. J. Biethahn† • Prof. Dr. L. M. Kolbe • Prof. Dr. M. Schumann

Band 95: Benjamin Brauer
Persuasive User-Centric Green IS
Exploring the Role and Paving the Way of Information Systems to Induce Pro-Environmental Behavior Change
ISBN 978-3-7369-9764-6

Band 96: Sebastian Hobert
Empirische Erkenntnisse und Gestaltungsansätze zum Einsatz von Wearable Computern im Industriesektor
ISBN 978-3-7369-9794-3

Band 97: Björn Hildebrandt
Digitalization of Mobility - Understanding the Transformational Impacts of Pervasive Digital Technologies on Business Models in the Mobility Sector
ISBN 978-3-7369-9827-8

Band 98: Jasmin Decker
Micro Learning und Mobile Learning in Unternehmen – Empirische Erkenntnisse und Gestaltungsempfehlungen zum Einsatz mobiler Lernanwendungen
ISBN 978-3-7369-9835-3

Band 99: Jan Moritz Anke
IT-gestützte Lern- und Assessmentmodule für nachhaltiges Wirtschaften
Empirische Erkenntnisse und Gestaltungsansätze zum Einsatz IT-gestützter Lern- und Assessmentmodule
ISBN 978-3-7369-9986-2

Band 100: Daniel Leonhardt
Organizing for Digital Innovation – The Role of the IT Function
ISBN 978-3-7369-7060-1

Band 101: Schahin Tofangchi
Towards a Theory for Designing Machine Learning Systems for Complex Decision Making Problems
ISBN 978-3-7369-7200-1

Band 102: Stephan Diederich
Designing Anthropomorphic Conservational Agents in Enterprises: A Nascent Theory and Conceptual Framework for Fostering a Human-Like Interaction
ISBN 978-3-7369-7216-2

Cuvillier Verlag Göttingen
Nonnenstieg 8 • 37075 Göttingen

Göttinger Wirtschaftsinformatik

Herausgeber: Prof. Dr. J. Biethahn† • Prof. Dr. L. M. Kolbe • Prof. Dr. M. Schumann

Band 103: Bernd Herrenkind
Driving the Future Diffusion of Mobility
Investigating User Acceptance of Autonomous Driving in Shared Mobility Services
ISBN 978-3-7369-7214-8

Band 104: Sromona Chatterjee
Computer Vision and Machine Learning in Sustainable Mobility:
The Case of Road Surface Defects
ISBN 978-3-7369-7258-2

Band 105: Fabian Nischak
Ecosystems in the Era of Digital Innovation:
Exploring the Transformational Impact of Pervasive Digital Technologies on Industrial-Age Business Contexts and Incumbent Firms
ISBN 978-3-7369-7328-2

Band 106: Pascal Freier
Empirische Erkenntnisse und Gestaltungsansätze für Entscheidungsunterstützungs-systeme in der Ablaufplanung im Kontext von Cyber-Physischen Systemen
ISBN 978-3-7369-7349-7

Band 107: Daniel Hodapp
How Incumbent Firms Navigate Nascent Digital Platform Ecosystems in the Internet of Thing: A Contextualized Perspective on Value Co-Creation in Platform Ecosystems
ISBN 978-3-7369-7362-6

Band 108: David Marz
Technology Acceptance in the Context of Digital Transformation
Studies on How and Why People Use Connected Objects
ISBN 978-3-7369-7370-1

Band 109: Hannes Kurtz
Digital Business Strategy: An Investigation of Generic Types,
Performance Implications, an Path Dependence
ISBN 978-3-7369-7402-9

Band 110: Patryk Zapadka
Digital Innovation in incumbent Firm Contexts:
A Knowledge Integration Perspektive
ISBN 978-3-7369-7463-0

Cuvillier Verlag Göttingen

Nonnenstieg 8 • 37075 Göttingen

Göttinger Wirtschaftsinformatik

Herausgeber: Prof. Dr. J. Biethahn† • Prof. Dr. L. M. Kolbe • Prof. Dr. M. Schumann

Band 111: Henrik Wesseloh
Einsatz von Gamification zum Fördern intrinsischer Motivation
Empirische Erkenntnisse und Gestaltungsempfehlungen
ISBN 978-3-7369-7487-6

Band 112: Kevin Koch
IT-gestützte Früherkennung digitaler unternehmensbezogener
Empörungswellen in sozialen Medien
ISBN 978-3-7369-7568-2

Cuvillier Verlag Göttingen

Nonnenstieg 8 • 37075 Göttingen

www.ingramcontent.com/pod-product-compliance
Ingram Content Group UK Ltd.
Pitfield, Milton Keynes, MK11 3LW, UK
UKHW021652190726
13853UKWH00001B/214

9 783736 975705